The struggle for the Eastern Cape 1800 - 1854:
Subjugation and the roots of South African democracy

The struggle for the Eastern Cape 1800 - 1854:
Subjugation and the roots of South African democracy

Martin Legassick
University of the Western Cape

Johannesburg

First published in 2010

KMM Review Publishing Company
PO Box 782114
Sandton 2147
© Martin Legassick

ISBN 978-0-620-36610-9

All rights reserved.
No part of this publication may be reproduced, stored in a retrieval system, or transmitted in any form or by any means, electronic, mechanical, photocopying, recording or otherwise, without the prior written permission of the copyright holder.

Democracy in Africa Series
Volume 1
The Struggle for the Eastern Cape 1800-1854:
Subjucation and the roots of South African democracy

Acknowledgements:
Book Design & Layout: Mizpah Marketing Concepts
Cover Design: Culture Publishing Industry
Printing: Colors

Pictures courtesy of:
National Library of South Africa:
Johannes van der Kemp, James Read, Lord Charles Somerset, John Philip, John Fairbairn, Maqoma and his wife, Robert Godlonton, Sandile, Fighting in the Waterkloof 1851, Xhosa's attacking wagon train, in 1850-1853 war, Blinkwater and Waterkloof, Andries Botha
Museum Africa:
View of a Xhosa homestead, Ndlambe in 1820's, Sir Benjamin D'Urban, Hintsa, Sir Andries Stockenstrom, Battle in war of the Axe 1846, Sir Harry Smith, Kat River settlement, Attack on Fort Armstrong.
Albany Museum:
Nxele (Makana), Grahamstown in 1823

Dedication

To the memory of
Mazisi "Raymond" Kunene, (1930-2006),
poet and philosopher, from whom I learned much
about many things.

Preface

This text is an interpretation of the struggle between the British-ruled Cape Colony and the Xhosa over land and over independence in the first half of the nineteenth century. South Africa – possibly the original home of humankind – had been colonised first by the Dutch East India Company (DEIC) in the mid 17th century. As a result, during the 18th century the indigenous San were virtually exterminated and the indigenous Khoi subjugated. But the Xhosa were encountered by colonists only in the second half of the 18th century, and the main battles for their land and subjugation took place only after the British conquered the Cape in the early 19th century.

The title of this book is an amalgam of titles proposed for it by the author and by the publisher. Ironically, in view of the history of national oppression in South Africa, it was the (white) author who initially wanted to title it *The struggle for the Eastern Cape: the roots of subjugation* while the (black) publisher wanted to title it *The struggle for the Eastern Cape: the roots of democracy*. The final title chosen embraces both the ideas of the subjugation of the Xhosa, and of the roots of democracy in the non-racial franchise introduced into the Cape Colony in 1854 which by the end of the 19th century had nurtured generations of African voters among whom were founders of 20th century African nationalism and of the struggle for democracy against white minority rule. The book therefore covers a period that was a vital turning point in the history of South Africa.

The author would like to thank Moeletsi Mbeki for his interest in this text and taking on the task of publishing it, and Ipuseng Kotsokoane for organising the editing of the manuscript. He also would like to thank Sindamani Bridglal for debating with him many important issues dealt with in the book. Finally he would like to thank his partner Margie Struthers for her assistance in many ways in the course of writing and editing the book.

Contents

	Introduction	VIII
Chapter 1	Historiography	1
Chapter 2	The 1799-1803 Xhosa-Khoi revolt and Bethelsdorp	5
Chapter 3	The expulsion of the Xhosa from the Zuurveld, 1812	13
Chapter 4	From 1812 to the 'agreement' with Ngqika in 1819	17
Chapter 5	British settlers and the 1820's revolution in government	22
Chapter 6	The expulsion of Maqoma and the Kat River settlement: 1829	30
Chapter 7	Maqoma's war: or the war of Hintsa; 1834-1836	42
Chapter 8	The treaty period: 1836-1844	51
Chapter 9	The road to war: 1844-1846	60
Chapter 10	The War of the Axe: 1846-1847	69
Chapter 11	Smith's governorship: the first years: 1848-1850	78
Chapter 12	The struggle for representative government and the war and rebellion of 1850-1853	85
Chapter 13	The establishment of representative government	99
Chapter 14	Conclusion	105
	Footnotes	111
	Glossary	151

Introduction

In the first half of the 19th century the Cape Colony became not merely a colony of European settlement based on coerced black labour, but one capable of expelling the agricultural Xhosa from their land, annexing it, and driving them into the colony for work.

In 1795 the colony, characterised by slavery and near-slavery (of the indigenous pastoral Khoi) as well as racial hierarchy (a legal status order) was ruled by the senescent mercantilist Dutch East India Company (DEIC), its veeboer frontier having recently encountered resistance from San and Xhosa in the east. DEIC rule was replaced by the rising industrial power of Britain. Britain initially occupied the Cape in 1795 as a strategic wartime naval base in the Napoleonic wars. In 1803 the Cape reverted temporarily to the Batavian Republic, but was retaken by the British in 1806 and permanently ceded to them in 1814.

The Napoleonic wars flowed from political revolutions in France and America - which also triggered a successful slave revolt in Haiti. This 'age of democratic revolution' gave rise to new universalist ideas about freedom. The same era saw industrial capitalism emerge from a brand new factory system, chiefly in Britain. The new British empire constructed in this period – "autocratically ruled yet uncentralised"[1] - had as its premise the central role of overseas markets to sustain industrial development. India was the central market, and China the huge untapped market to be aspired to. "Free trade" was projected as the way for the British to dominate the world. Within this, the Cape was taken over above all as a way-station on the route to the East. Some of these new influences touched the Cape Colony from the 1770s (the Cape Patriots). What were the effects of this new world-situation on the peoples that were already in or became embraced within the colony? This is the main issue this book tries to address.

●●●

Chapter 1
Historiography

For much of this century, the standard history of the 19th century Cape Colony and of its wars with the Xhosa was provided by the works of George McCall Theal and sir George Cory, regarded as the founders of SA historiography.[2] Recently, however, Andrew Bank has argued that *Researches in South Africa* (1828), by the Enlightenment-influenced humanitarian, the Reverend John Philip, was the first history of the Colony, sparking off a polemic - the 'great debate' - that has continued, more or less, ever since.[3]

Philip arrived at the Cape in 1819 as resident director of the London Missionary Society and remained until his death in 1851. His *Researches* described the violent colonial dispossession of the Khoisan, their reduction to slavery, and the lack of improvement in their condition under British rule, and was specifically directed against "unjust insinuations, caricatures, and calumnies invented to disparage the natives'. It contained a denunciation of the autocratic colonial system and of Boer master-servant relations and combated the prevailing conception of the "Hottentots" as a dying savage race. Philip's interpretation was challenged by Cape Dutch historians as well as those of 1820 British settlers (such as Donald Moodie).[4]

Philip's *Researches* was almost exclusively concerned with the Khoisan, but humanitarian history was extended to the Xhosa through the well-known *Report of the Select Committee on Aborigines* (as well as in works by Saxe Bannister, Thomas Pringle and 'Justus' [A. Campbell].)[5] Against these were set the settler histories of Robert Godlonton, who painted a picture of a benevolent extension of British civilisation shattered by 'thievish and land-hungry Xhosa', and claimed that the Xhosa had no more prior land rights in the Eastern Cape than British settlers.[6] Bank does not deal with the pro-settler missionary histories by, for example, the Wesleyan William Boyce, which laid the ground for a whole later genre of missionary writings.[7]

Theal and Cory's histories were constructed out of pro-settler historiography and perpetuated its opposition to humanitarianism. They presented a history of benevolent conquest and rule over the black barbarian ("the Other") in which the settlers sought to be free of the influence of the imperial power. This viewpoint shaped the mind of white South Africa for a century, fixing "the predatory barbarian image of the Xhosa in the schoolbooks" - and, it might be added, the image of "the idle and dissolute" and even "comical" coloured.[8]

White settler historiography was first challenged by W.M.Macmillan, whose main concern was to rehabilitate the reputation of Philip.[9] Macmillan turned land-hungry Boers into the villains, said little to nothing about British settlers, and dealt with policies towards the Khoi (a subject taken further by J.S. Marais)[10] and the Xhosa. For Macmillan and his followers the Cape Colony in the first half of the 19th century was the seed-bed of Cape liberalism, nurtured initially by the missionaries.[11] Where for settler historians the Khoi and Xhosa "savages" were "irreclaimable", for the liberals they were, at least, "reclaimable."[12] Where Afrikaner historians celebrated the Great Trek away from the colony in the 1830s, for the liberals it was a tragedy which created the racism of the twentieth century.[13]

The first standard history reflecting this liberal viewpoint was the South African volume of the 1938 *Cambridge History of the British Empire*, which also contained no less than nine chapters (228 pages) dealing in whole or part with the early 19th century Cape Colony and the Xhosa.[14] Other writings in this tradition reassessed missionary activity. All were silent on the racial attitudes of British settlers.[15] At the end of the 1970s Elphick and Giliomee's *The Shaping of South African Society*, represented the marrying of the liberal tradition with a 'verligte' (enlightened) or 'oorbeligte' (over-enlightened) Afrikaner tradition: focusing on the 17th and 18th centuries, its first and even more its second edition spilled over into the 19th century.[16] The liberalism of the Cape Colony and the conquest of the Xhosa remained essentially separate, however, in all these writings. Liberalism was first seriously challenged in the 1950s by Nosipho Majeke's examination of the 'role of the missionaries in conquest'.[17]

From the 1960s there was the beginnings of a less hagiographical appraisal than Theal's and Cory's of the role of British settlers in the Eastern Cape, associated particularly with Basil Le Cordeur, and pioneered also by Tony Kirk.[18] By 1974 Saunders was encouraging investigation into *Beyond the Frontier*.[19] Jeff Peires, the first white to use vernacular sources, began to integrate the Xhosa historical tradition more directly into the mainstream.[20] Peires first book had an important appendix, tracing Xhosa historiography from oral tradition to historians such as Walter Rubusana, S.E.K. Mqhayi, J.H. Soga, and S.M. Burns-Ncamashe ('Sogwali kaNtaba').[21] Peires could also have mentioned A. C. Jordan as a notable Xhosa historian.[22]

It is worth remembering that, for the Xhosa, history has passed down to this day mainly through oral tradition. As Nelson Mandela relates: "It was at Mqhekezweni that I developed my interest in African history. Until then I had heard only of Xhosa heroes but at the Great Place I learned of other African heroes ... from the chiefs and headmen who came ... to settle disputes and try cases... They spoke in an idiom that I'd never heard before. Their speech was formal and lofty, their manner slow and unhurried, and the traditional clicks of our language were long and dramatic."

"The most ancient of the chiefs ... was Zwelibhangile Joyi, a son from the Great House of King Ngubengcuka... But as grizzled as Chief Joyi often seemed, the decades fell off him when he spoke of the *impi*, or warriors, in the army of King Ngangelizwe. In pantomime, Chief Joyi would fling his spear and creep along the veld as he narrated the victories and defeats. He spoke of Ngangelizwe's heroism, generosity and humility."

"Chief Joyi railed against the white man, whom he believed had deliberately sundered the Xhosa tribe, dividing brother from brother. The white man had told the Thembus that their true chief was the great white queen across the ocean and that they were her subjects. But the white queen brought nothing but misery and perfidy to the black people; if she was a chief, she was an evil chief... The white man shattered the *abantu*, the fellowship, of the various tribes. The white man was hungry and greedy for land, and the black man shared the land with him as they shared the air and water; land was not for man to possess. But the white man took the land as you might seize another man's horse."[23]

In the 1980s and early 1990s an emphasis on social history resulted in a series of more specialised studies on slavery and its abolition, on the Khoi and on farm workers. Much of this is synthesised in *Breaking the Chains*.[24] An initial landmark here was Suzie Newton-King's economic reinterpretation of Ordinance 50 of 1828 which legislated Khoi equality.[25] Other work which contributed to significant reinterpretation included Maclennan on Colonel Graham's clearing of the Zuurveld in 1812,[26] Lewis's class analysis of the colonial penetration of Xhosa society[27], Meltzer's investigation of the politics of John Fairbairn[28] and Trapido's work on 'Hottentot nationalism'.[29] Together with this Julian Cobbing initiated a re-examination of the M*fecane*, claiming that it was a settler myth that the emergence of the Zulu kingdom in the early years of the nineteenth century set in motion a chain of dislocating and disrupting effects throughout Southern Africa. For the purposes of this book, this re-examination has effects particularly on the characterisation of the Mfengu which have had subsequent reverberations.[30]

The 1990s saw a series of important syntheses, by Clifford Crais and Tim Keegan, as well the mammoth one of more than 1300 pages by non-academic historian Noel Mostert. The main significance of these has been their attempt to integrate the story of the (partial and ambivalent) liberation of the slaves and Khoi with that of the conquest of the Xhosa.[31] Crais and Keegan in particular have insisted that the racism of the 19th century highlighted the role of British settler leaders in the Eastern Cape in promoting a new discourse of racism, differing from that of the 18th century.[32] They have exposed the paradox of 'Janus-faced Cape liberalism', a paradox identified more generally by Cooper and Stoler: that, from the late 18th century, conquest, exploitation and subjugation by European powers coexisted and coincided with increasingly powerful claims in political discourse to universal principles as the basis for organising a polity.[33] Together with this, Crais and Keegan have emphasised the incipiently capitalist land-grabbing activities of the British settlers, and pointed to the model provided by the early 19th century Cape for other colonial societies in Africa, from the Rhodesias to Kenya.[34] In addition Crais charts the early phases in the formation of a rural working class moulded from former slaves, Khoisan and Xhosa: the unfree within the colony and those becoming unfree outside of it, even while they were being pulled 'within'.[35] This book is indebted to the narrative strength of Mostert's account, the theoretical insights of Keegan, and the more pointillist approach of Crais.

In the 1990s Elizabeth Elbourne pioneered a re-examination of missionary-Khoi relations with important new insights.[36] Recently both Pat van der Spuy and Helen Bradford have submitted slavery and Xhosa society to a rigorous analysis drawing out the significance of gendering.[37] Ross and McKenzie (the latter with a particular focus on gender) have traced the development of an ethos of 'respectability' among middle-class whites which also drew in Christianised coloureds - the creation of a rational public sphere out of which a distinctive middle class identity could be formed.[38] Historiography has spilled over into literary enquiry, and into examination of the controversy surrounding the head of Hintsa.[39]

Keegan and Crais's concern is with the impact of the Cape Colony on the wider formation of South Africa. This book while not oblivious to this, tries to take further the integration of Xhosa history into that of the rest of the Colony by focusing on the factors which determined Khoi (slave, Baster) and Xhosa consciousness and the relations between them (or, as they became, 'coloured'-black relations.) In a UWC history tutorial early in the 1990s a Xhosa-speaking student asked, "How is it that if we were independent and the coloureds were originally slaves, that they are now above us?" The answer is complicated and still requires much research, but is of continued relevance.

• • •

Chapter 2

The 1799-1803 Xhosa-Khoi revolt and Bethelsdorp

The period with which this book is concerned commenced and ended, significantly, with revolts by both Xhosa and Khoisan together against the colonial order (1799-1803 and 1851-1853) and was punctuated by four further wars with the Xhosa (1812, 1819, 1834-1835, 1846-1847).

The state established initially by the British as a state of occupation as a result remained essentially military, ruled by masculinist white male governors with military backgrounds, until mid-century - a "Horse Guards dynasty", in Walker's phrase.[40] Marx in *Capital* wrote of the role of the colonial state as "to hasten, hothouse fashion" the transformation of social relations to those of capitalism.[41] To facilitate primitive accumulation, and to generate markets, however, it also had to function as an instrument of conquest and the crushing of resistance. Until after the Napoleonic wars this was the main function of British rule. At the core of the state were British troops, some 4000-5000 until the end of the Napoleonic wars, declining thereafter to 1500 in 1834, but increasing again to some 6200 after the 1846-1847 war. In 1850, after Governor Sir Harry Smith had reduced the garrison, there were 4068, but this had doubled to 8660 by the end of 1851.[42] (These were supplemented by Boer, and Khoisan levies, and, later, British settlers). Rather than transforming the social order, British rule based itself politically, moreover, on the old Dutch order of "ancient corruptions and monopolies"[43], with local government by notables rooted in the Dutch landed slave-owning class.[44] Masculine militarism at the top consolidated and reinforced the tendencies to patriarchy among Boer settlers, coloureds and Xhosa. At the same time the British sought to consolidate the rule of law around a rhetoric of equality before the law.[45]

The colony's population in 1806 was estimated at 26,768 white 'free burghers (14,074 men to 12,694 women), some 1200 free blacks, 29,861 slaves (with 19,346 men against 10,313 women), and 20, 426 Khoi (9,781 men and 10,642 women).'[46] Wine was by far the most important export commodity, produced by slaves - 80% them living in Cape Town and the arable southwest - who constituted a big capital investment. In 1808 and 1825 there were abortive and localised slave revolts. Urban slavery began to crumble *inter alia* as slaves were redeployed to vineyards.⁴⁷ Mainly in Cape Town, from the early 19th century slaves began to convert to Islam.⁴⁸

The revolt by the Xhosa and Khoi in 1799 was precipitated by the arrest by British troops of the leaders of a renewed Boer frontier rebellion in Graaff-Reinet, which was taken as a sign of colonial weakness. Frontier Khoi, facing a hardening of labour relations with their land-owning Boer masters and the growth of violence in those relations, seized the opportunity to break from them.⁴⁹ Equally the Gqunukhwebe under Chunga were resisting attempts by the British to push them out of the Zuurveld across the Fish river. San hunting bands in the mountains were also struggling to maintain independence. The resulting combined revolt forced the colonists to evacuate much of the eastern frontier, and even led to a British defeat in one battle.⁵⁰ A temporary peace concluded at the end of the year broke down and the revolt continued until the takeover of the Cape by the Batavian regime in 1803.⁵¹ Colonial order was seriously threatened.

The Batavian regime made peace by leaving the Xhosa in occupation of the Zuurveld. It also established a new magistracy at Uitenhage, to the south and west of Graaff-Reinet, and closer to the Zuurveld.⁵² And it confirmed the allocation of land by the British to the Khoi at Bethelsdorp, under the supervision of missionaries of the London Missionary Society (LMS), Dr Johannes van der Kemp and James Read.⁵³ Van der Kemp, arriving in 1799, had initially established a mission with the Rharabe chief Ngqika, but retired from it at the end of 1800. Having taken up the cause of the Khoi rebels, he persuaded the British to establish Bethelsdorp, which they agreed to in an attempt to reconcile with the rebellious Khoi and divide them from the Xhosa. ⁵⁴ The struggle between the Bethelsdorp missionaries and the government was the most significant development in shaping social relations in the Colony in the first decade of British rule, and resonated thereafter.

The missionary societies in Europe resulted from a renewed proselytizing Protestant movement, reacting against secularisation of Christian beliefs and relaxation of moral norms, which some have linked to the insecurities associated with industrial transformation and others to the results of political and religious conflict. From reviving religion among the domestic working class there grew the idea of converting the 'heathen' around the world. The London Missionary Society founded in 1795 was a part of this re-invigoration of dissenting denominations in Britain with roots in 17th century Puritanism.⁵⁵ Many missionaries added the concerns of the Enlightenment to these roots, and the evangelical movement came to take the form of humanitarianism, and, in particular, in the late 18th century, of anti-slavery. By 1783 the Quakers had established a committee to work for abolition, and others followed. However the dissenting societies were viewed with extreme suspicion in Britain by the Anglican establishment prior at least to 1810, suspected of being in league with French revolutionaries.[56]

If this book dwells on the various forms of mission activities and ideas it is because missionaries were the main mediators of colonial politics and culture among the Khoisan and Xhosa. Correspondingly, most voices of the Khoisan and the Xhosa are heard through their mediation. There has been considerable debate as to whether and in what sense missionaries were agents of colonial conquest. Undoubtedly, as we shall see, many were. As Xhosa oral tradition has it to this day, "when the missionaries came, they carried a Bible in front, but behind their backs a musket."[57] At the same time the important point made by Elbourne should not be ignored: that religious ideas - like all ideas -- were elastic, and that they were "a tool which could be used in a number of ways, both for and against domination", and by the oppressed as well as the oppressor.[58]

Van der Kemp laid down an exceptional tradition, especially when viewed against the other main missionary society then present in the Cape Colony - from 1737 to 1743 and again after 1792 - the conservative, quasi-Anglican, and deferential Moravians.[59] Newton King writes of van der Kemp's "shining example of ... liberatory theology".[60] He was Dutch, from a well-off family and well-educated. Profligate as a young man, he turned to missionary life perhaps to expiate a sense of guilt.[61] His religiosity was strongly millenarian: his belief in the imminent intervention of God on the side of the oppressed resonated closely with rebelliousness among the indigenous people. This millenarianism echoed that of the dissenters of the 17th century English revolution, and even peasants in medieval Europe - and it would be passed down to the Khoi as well as the Xhosa.[62] He was both non-racial and an abolitionist. He purchased the freedom of and then married a slave girl 14 years old from Madagascar. He stressed the inwardness of conversion, rather than (as did later missionaries) the 'outward signs' of 'civilisation'. Faith rather than good works.[63] A well-known description describes him in 1803 "without a hat... dressed in a threadbare blackcoat, waistcoat and breeches, without shirt, neckcloth or stockings, and leather sandals bound upon his feet, the same as are worn by the Hottentots."[64] Much later his successor Philip praised him for going amongst the Xhosa, "wearing their clothes and eating their food."[65] In 1814 it was even alleged by another LMS missionary that van der Kemp said "all civilisation is from the Divil [Devil]".[66]

Van der Kemp's ideas first became rooted in Bethelsdorp. The mission started as a refugee camp for Khoi displaced during the revolt or fleeing brutal masters.[67] (On the northern frontier the LMS mission at Griquatown performed a similar function, though with a core of Basters and Kora.)[68] At a minimum Bethelsdorp provided shelter for women, children and the old while Khoi (mainly) men sought work with farmers. It came to reflect the thirst for Christianity among many Khoisan, their indigenous institutions essentially destroyed, and now brutally oppressed by the Boers.[69] Of perhaps 12,000 Khoisan in the Eastern Cape at this time, some 450 came to live at Bethelsdorp by 1812.[70] The mission was by its very existence subversive to the Boer master-servant order. It stood for an egalitarian non-racial Christianity as opposed to the exclusivist version of the Boers, demarcating membership in the moral community and access to the law.[71] Boers tried to prevent Khoi from going to Bethelsdorp, to break up the institution and to kill Van der Kemp and Read. The mission served also, as Elbourne brings out, as a place where remnants of traditional lifestyle, even if not the whole of a herding transhumant economy, could be sustained.[72]

From the start van der Kemp and his close colleague Read constituted Bethelsdorp as an *imperium in imperio* - a place with its own moral code. As early as April 1804 van der Kemp refused to cooperate with government in dispatching labour to farmers, or to compel inhabitants to join the military.[73] The Batavian government accused them of fomenting dissension and revolt, recalled them to the Western Cape, and refused to allow the teaching of literacy at the mission. With the second British takeover in January 1806, however, they were allowed to return.[74] From this time Bethelsdorp was to become a centre of equality and literacy. From it Khoi 'native agents' spread religion far and wide among the Khoi: van der Kemp and Read believed in making the greatest possible use of indigenous people in spreading the gospel.[75] Moreover Bethelsdorp was closely linked from the start to the Xhosa. Not only was the son of the chief of the amaNtinde, Jan Tshatshu, an early resident and convert; also its Gona (part-khoi) residents provided a link to the Gqunukhwebe Xhosa.[76]

When the LMS had sent van der Kemp to South Africa, it was "to make the first serious and effectual inroads upon the territories of the Prince of Darkness, and to open the way for the deliverance of the wretched Caffres from the idolatory and barbarism which overwhelms their extensive country."[77] As Elbourne has remarked, however, van der Kemp found Satan not among the 'wild savages' but among the Boers![78] As early as 1801 he warned the British authorities that "there is no way of saving this country, other than by the government doing justice to the natives. In no other way can the boers escape the hand of Providence than by acknowledging their guilt."[79] From at least the second British occupation, if not earlier, both van der Kemp and Read bombarded government officials with complaints against the treatment of Khoi by the Boers.[80] They clashed repeatedly with the newly appointed landrost of Uitenhage, the American Colonel Cuyler, so that relations degenerated "to the point of vitriolic hatred."[81]

In March 1807 the British government withdrew the country from its major share of the slave trade, and from then slavery became somewhat tempered by the legal paternalism of 'amelioration', particularly as slaves attempted to use the law.[82] For most rural slaves and the Khoi however the abolition of the slave trade may well have worsened their situation, since it reduced the inflow of labour.[83] It was later to be debated in the Cape as to whether the condition of the Khoi was better or worse than that of slavery.[84] Khoi did not wish to live on the farms and wanted to be hired. But farmers were extremely reluctant to pay cash wages to them, and tried by every means to tie them to their farms for a lifetime of service. The abolition of the slave trade also stimulated trans-frontier raiding by colonists for slave-substitutes, mainly across the northern border.[85]

In 1809 Colonel Collins, appointed commissioner to the frontier districts, reported a severe labour shortage, and Boers' unhappiness with Bethelsdorp. He recommended that the mission should be broken up and its inhabitants dispersed among the Boers or sent to the Moravian missions.[86] In an attempt to bring Boer-Khoi relations under regulation, governor Earl Alexander of Caledon issued a code in the same year, hailed at the time as the "Magna Carta of the Hottentots"[87] Elbourne concludes that it "represented a stab at reform, but in fact codified existing coercive labour practices without ensuring that the Code's enshrinement of work contracts and limits on their duration could be enforced."[88] Crais writes that it "represented a deliberate attempt on the part of the colonial state to directly intervene in the patterns of social life to provide the 'order' necessary for sustained economic growth and social stability."[89] It demanded that each Khoisan should have a 'fixed place of abode', whose alteration must be approved by a local official. It provided for mandatory contracts of service, as well as entrenching the oppressive controls of the Boer farmers. It lacked explicit recognition of Khoisan rights to land. Attempting to suppress the violent private oppression of the Boers, it instead submitted Khoisan to the more systematic oppression of the colonial order through the state and the law as a means of social control - and locally it was Boer notables who were the 'state'.[90] Soon the complaints of the missionaries embraced the Code as well - that little attention was paid to verifying contracts, and that the pass laws formalised in the Code were abused to keep the Khoisan in service.[91]

It was also in 1809 that Caledon saw a copy of the *Transactions of the London Missionary Society* in which was published a letter from Read of 30th August 1808.[92] Giliomee, following Cory, makes much of this letter: the missionaries had "totally swung round and sent their complaints directly to London." He questions "why the missionaries suddenly decided to go over the Governor's head and not direct their complaints to him," and explains this as an attempt to evade Cuyler. In fact both before and after this the missionaries continued to address complaints both to Cuyler and the Governor. Moreover publication of letters in London was a normal practice of the LMS. Giliomee then mixes up the publication of **this** letter in the *Transactions* with another letter, eighteen months later, which the LMS indirectly drew to the attention of the Colonial Office: "It goes without saying that a letter of such a nature, which appeared in the official organ of the influential London Missionary Society, would cause a great sensation. It came to the attention of the Colonial Minister who in turn brought it to the attention of Caledon."[93] However, as Elbourne's careful investigation makes clear, the LMS intervened with the British government only in 1811, after van der Kemp and Read had exhausted every avenue in the Colony.[94] Caledon instructed Cuyler to investigate the complaints. Cuyler reported there was little to them, though Read believed witnesses were intimidated.[95] Dissatisfied with this investigation, Read wrote twice to Caledon. After further letters to Caledon, in January 1811 Read wrote another of his customary letters to the LMS, again published by them, accusing Cuyler of partiality, and claiming that there were upwards of 100 uninvestigated murders of Khoi in the magistracy. He asked for an appeal to the abolitionist leader William Wilberforce.[96] Van der Kemp wrote to Caledon, dealing with abuse of the pass laws and labour legislation by local officials and the flawed administration of justice by landrosts. The Dutch, he claimed, continued to "take and keep Hottentots in service by force."[97] As Elbourne writes, "Read and van der Kemp were calling for a more thorough overhaul of the labour system than historians have recognised."[98]

Caledon asked Truter, the Fiscal, to establish a commission to investigate the complaints and prefer criminal charges "in all cases of capital nature which have occurred since last surrender of the Colony, reserving for my successor an ultimate decision upon cases of alleged murder in former times."[99] The Fiscal concluded that Cuyler's investigation had been incomplete. Consequently in March Read and van der Kemp were summoned to Cape Town. Read wrote to the LMS how their "prayers have been incessant that the sufferings of the poor Hottentot nation might come to a termination" and how he and van der Kemp left Bethelsdorp "with many cries and lamentations on both sides and the whole institution led us about a quarter of a mile from the village and with almost broken hearts we parted."[100] In Cape Town they presented 113 cases of injustice to the Fiscal's commission.[101]

At this point, by a proclamation of 16th May, Caledon took the unprecedented step of appointing a circuit court, to travel annually around the districts of the Cape to judge crimes - a first attempt to override local abuse of the law. Elbourne makes a strong case that this was in response to a call from van der Kemp, though other historians disagree.[102] The first circuit court travelled to the eastern frontier late in 1811 but did not investigate the Bethelsdorp complaints because they were still in the hands of the Commission. Instead it investigated a complaint by Cuyler against Bethelsdorp missionaries![103]

Caledon left the Cape in July. Only at that time, in August in fact, did the

LMS, according to Elbourne, feel it had emerged sufficiently from its shadow of war-time revolutionary unrespectability to approach the (Anglican) Wilberforce with James Read's list of atrocities against the Khoisan.[104] Wilberforce compared the 'savage' Dutch farmers with West Indian slave plantation owners, believed that the execution of one or two farmers would stop such 'Systematic... Abominations', and took the matter up with the British government.[105] In the letter of instructions from Lord Liverpool to the new governor Sir John Cradock there apparently appeared for the first time in such a dispatch the word "justice".[106] He was urged to investigate the cases, make an example of the guilty, and "shield injured natives from future oppression." Cradock arrived in September, but his initial preoccupation was with expelling the Xhosa from the Zuurveld.[107] The Fiscal's commission did not pursue its investigations until mid-1812, and then recommended some of the cases to the second circuit court.[108] In August 1812 Read complained to the LMS that no steps had yet been taken to punish any of the reported crimes: "The fact is, as long as the country Magistrates and courts are not cleansed, and misdemeanours taken notice of, and example made of them, all commissions appointed, and proclamations issued will have no effect." Soon after this however, the government summoned Read to meet the second circuit court whose terms of reference, however, according to Elbourne, "removed the issue of the systematic abuse of Khoisan labour from the agenda" - restricting itself to individual cases of violence.[109] In a sign of his lack of interest in the complaints, around the same time Cradock issued supplementary regulations to the Caledon Code, compelling Khoi children to be 'apprenticed' to farmers until the age of 18.[110]

This circuit court became known as the 'Black Circuit'.[111] It was the first result of humanitarian pressure reinforced from Britain. However it "returned few verdicts favourable to Khoi plantiffs"[112] Read told the LMS that "few [cases] have been wholly proved but much less proved to be false, not a Hottentot was permitted to an oath whether baptised or not, not one accused was arrested except he or she confessed his crime viz when 'tis a Christian [white person] that accused. In civil cases however many of the Hottentots got justice done them."[113] "Curiously", writes Elbourne, "historians have repeated the judgements of the court as though they indicated the legal weakness of the Khoi cases."[114] The report of the court, moreover, went much further than rejecting most of the charges. It was also, writes Elbourne, "an implicit defence of frontier labour policy." It went out of its way to make a scathing condemnation of Bethelsdorp for encouraging laziness, idleness and filth, in contrast with the praiseworthy Moravian stations. While adopting the rhetoric of the 'rule of law', it projected the Khoi as an inferior order of beings, enjoying inferior natural rights, with an obligation to serve the colonists.[115] Bethelsdorp, it stated, had "established such an overstrained principle of liberty as the ground work, that the natural state of barbarism appears there to supercede civilisation and social order."[116]

Van der Kemp died on 19th December 1811, without seeing the results of the 'Black Circuit'. But his influence persisted - on his colleague James Read and, in a certain way, on John Philip.[117] His memory continued to be treasured among the Khoi, and he remained for a long time respected among the Xhosa.

●●●

Chapter 3

The expulsion of the Xhosa from the Zuurveld, 1812

Elbourne marks the death of van der Kemp and the results of the 'Black Circuit' (together with the 'synod' of 1817,) as a defeat for Bethelsdorp missionary methods (and hence for Khoi equality).[118] Equally the expulsion of the Xhosa from the Zuurveld in January 1812 by British troops, the first successful dispossession of their land, was a serious setback for them.

The dynamics of Xhosa society militated in favour of constant expansion into new territory.[119] By the late 17th century they had penetrated much of the area between the Kei and Fish rivers, where they had absorbed many Khoi pastoralists. Until the mid 18th century, the inhabitants of the Zuurveld had been the Khoisan Gonaqua, who were subsequently joined by the Gqunukhwebe, the Ntinde, the Gwali, the Dange, and the Mbala.[120] In the 1770s the chief Rharabe crossed the Kei to settle between it and the Keiskamma river, absorbed Khoisan, and tried to assert his dominance over the area.[121] However it was his son Ndlambe, as regent for Ngqika from about 1782, who was the "real architect of Rharabe greatness"[122] in the area, driving other Xhosa westward. In 1795 Ngqika rebelled against Ndlambe and attempted to construct a centralised Xhosa state against centrifugal pressures that were eventually too great. By 1800 Ngqika was at the height of his power.[123]

When the Boers were encountered, the Xhosa assumed they would come to absorb them as they already had the San, Khoi and Thembu.[124] Between the 1700s and the 1790s there was mutual skirmishing and cattle-raiding, including two "frontier wars" in which, as Giliomee puts it, Boers and Xhosa "jostled" each other.[125] In 1800 Ndlambe escaped from virtual captivity with Ngqika across the Fish river to the Zuurveld where he came to dominate along with Chungwa of the Gqunukhwebe - who by September 1807 was settled near the Gamtoos river west of Algoa Bay.[126] In the same year Ngqika, having been unsuccessful in luring the Colony into alliance in crushing Ndlambe, abducted one of his wives, provoking a revenge attack. Though peace between Ngqika and Ndlambe was concluded, this was the start of the decline of Ngqika's power.[127] At this time there were some 38,400-40,000 Xhosa west of the Kei river and there may have been similar numbers to the east of it, as well as Thembu,

Mpondo, etc - as against only some 1500 Boers dispersed across the south-western Cape.[128]

Many of the British troops used in the expulsion of the Xhosa from the Zuurveld were of Khoi origins, in the Cape Regiment commanded by Lieutenant-Colonel Graham. Under the DEIC Khoi and Basters had been enlisted for military service in a separate corps.[129] The British changed its name to the Cape Regiment, which soon enrolled 500-800 Khoi, some from Bethelsdorp.[130] Like those at the mission stations, these adhered readily to Christianity.[131] There were contradictions in all this. Van der Kemp, for example, had established an anti-militarist tradition, objecting to coercive recruitment to the force, and claiming to the British that the Batavians had exempted Bethelsdorp people from serving on commandos against the Xhosa or Khoisan. He also demanded decent conditions and pensions for those Khoi who joined voluntarily.[132] Similar sentiments were expressed at other LMS stations.[133] Now, less than a month after van der Kemp's death, however, the Khoi were used militarily to eject the Xhosa from the Zuurveld.[134] Elbourne points out that in this war, because of recent expulsion of many Xhosa-related people from Bethelsdorp, the "Khoisan were fighting old acquaintances and in some cases relatives."[135]

In the expulsion some 450-500 British troops were involved, together with some 700 from the Cape Regiment and up to 900 Boers.[136] The war lasted only from January to March because the Xhosa offered little resistance. In the course of it, Anders Stockenstrom, landdrost of Graaff-Reinet was killed by the Xhosa during a parley[137], and the elderly and ailing Gqunukhwebe chief Chungwa was shot dead by the British as he lay asleep in hiding in the bushes.[138] The war was fought by the British with "concentrated brutality and total alien viciousness".[139] More Xhosa were killed than wounded - among them many women and children. Up to 20,000 Xhosa were driven out of an area of 4000 square miles.[140] Ndlambe's people were pushed back onto Ngqika's, eventually intensifying the conflict between them. To assuage a reluctant colonial office, Cradock, however, wrote to London that "there has not been shed more Kaffir blood than would seem to be necessary to impress on the minds of these savages a proper degree of terror and respect."[141]

More than this, Cradock had urged on Lieutenant-Colonel Graham 'the expediency of destroying the Kaffer kraals, laying waste their gardens and fields and in fact totally removing any object that could hold out to their chiefs an inducement to revisit the regained territory.'[142] The Xhosa chiefs' request to stay on until the summer crops were fully harvested was hence deliberately turned down. As a result, not only were many huts burned, but their means of subsistence were destroyed. "The only way of getting rid" of the Xhosa, wrote Graham to his father, "is by depriving them of the means of subsistence and continually harassing them, for which purpose the whole force is constantly employed in destroying the prodigious quantities of Indian corn and millet which they have planted... taking from them the few cattle which they conceal in the woods...and shooting every man who can be found... as to fighting it is out of the question; we are forced to hunt them like wild beasts."[143] LMS director John Campbell, visiting the area in 1813, commented on a valley: "Formerly it was strewn over with Kaffir villages, but now not a living soul is to be found. Universal stillness reigns."[144]

The Xhosa were the first firmly agricultural indigenous community encountered by British colonialism. Agriculture, the sphere of women, was one of the solid bases of their lengthy 100-year resistance to conquest. From early on, however, in times of war, the British military attacked that base. The persistent cattle-raiding between colonists and Xhosa involved solely the men, but in the real wars of the 19th century the whole of society was attacked.

Cradock established thirty small forts along the Fish River and attempted to encourage settler villages practicing agriculture, introducing a new (quit-rent) system of land tenure in the process.[145] Graham, on leaving, recommended to Cradock that to stop Xhosa cattle-theft, "the most effectual measure... would be to pursue parties of plundering Kaffirs to the kraal they belong to, and, if possible, burn their huts and destroy every man Kaffir it contains" - thus elaborating the germ of the 'reprisal system' that was in use through the 1820s and early 1830s.[146] Graham's Town, guarding the eastern borders of the Zuurveld, was the first fort founded, and the headquarters of the Cape Regiment were transferred to it, thereby marking out the regiment for defence against the Xhosa.[147] As a reward for military service, land was allocated to Bethelsdorp Khoi at Theopolis, which became an LMS station. However from 1814, a tax amounting to more than half their average yearly income was levelled on the residents of mission stations in an attempt to force them to work for farmers.[148] In the wake of the war, moreover, the colonial government strengthened its relations with Ngqika at the expense of the other bordering Xhosa chiefs.[149]

Read had visited Xhosaland in 1810 and expressed the desire to renew the LMS mission there.[150] Yet the Bethelsdorp missionaries seemed oblivious to the effects of war, and, particularly, the expulsion on the Xhosa and offered no criticism of it - save lamenting that it placed them further from evangelisation. The annual report for 1812 remarked: "The Caffres had, for several years, **been annoying this part of the colony;** ... Government ... at last came to a resolution to bring a considerable body of men into the field, **and endeavour to drive them into King Geika's** country. Accordingly Lieutenant Colonel Graham (a gentleman of singular abilities and much beloved by every person, especially the natives) with the whole of the Cape Regiment and a few European troops marched into the country, and were joined by about fifteen hundred farmers.... in about three months, the Caffres were expelled.... **We were convinced that some such steps were necessary,** yet we were grieved for those Caffres, who had long shewed a desire for instruction, as being now so far separated from us. Brother Read had several interviews with Colonel Graham, who was extremely well disposed towards the Institution, and informed him with joy, of the flourishing state of religion among the soldiers of the Cape Regiment."[151] (my emphasis). Perhaps, as Elbourne speculates, the desire of Bethelsdorp for favourable verdicts on the complaints then being investigated by government encouraged their collaboration and blinded them to its effects.[152]

● ● ●

Chapter 4

From 1812 to the 'agreement' with Ngqika in 1819

There was a change in British colonial policy towards the Xhosa around 1816. It involved "long term cultural transformation" in addition to military exclusion: an attempt "to neutralise the Xhosa 'otherness' which was so threatening to order." This included a change in policy towards the missionaries.[153] Instead of being viewed as potential rivals to government's authority, they became seen as potential allies and even agents. The transition took place under the rule of the aristocratic Lord Charles Somerset, friend of horse-racing and jackal-hunting. He arrived in 1814 and was the longest serving British governor of the Colony ever. His rule was effete and corrupt, riddled with monopoly and patronage, and his departure in 1826 ushered in a revolution in government in the Colony.[154] The rapprochement between government and missionaries took place in the context of a concentrated reconceptualisation of the meaning of the "civilisation" imparted by the missionaries. Over time, the meaning of this word was worked out not in armchairs in Britain, but in practice on the ground, through contestations which included both debate and rebellion. The main aim of the state was to turn from the millenarianism of van der Kemp to a more 'respectable' Christianity.

Late in 1815 Cuyler, landrost of Uitenhage and van der Kemp's old foe, endorsed Read's request to re-establish a mission among the Xhosa, a step which Somerset approved. As a result, Joseph Williams of the LMS settled in 1816 in the territory of Ngqika, near the latter's recently-initiated (circumcised) son Maqoma.[155] Why this change? In 1815 Boers on the frontier had rebelled because of a series of events leading to the shooting of a colonist by a member of the Cape Regiment. Some historians say that the new policy was a counter-measure against the rebels' attempt to enlist Ngqika's assistance against the British. Others present it as an alternative strategy towards the Xhosa necessitated by reduction of the imperial garrison.[156] Somerset's change of attitude may also have had something to do with the reconciliation from about 1815 of the Anglican establishment in Britain with evangelicism, as it began to take on a more nationalist and bourgeois form, combating "continental Catholicism."[157] However, for Somerset, as he explained it in May

1819, missionary "civilising" of the Xhosa could only be "gradual", therefore, "this system is not solely to be trusted to... it is essential that it should be supported by that prudential strength which shall tend to overawe the restlessness of our hostile and wily neighbours."[158]

That Williams settled near Ngqika reinforced the government's attempts to support Ngqika against Ndlambe and others.[159] For the government, he was expected to be a 'means of contact with' and a 'quieting influence upon' the Xhosa, and to co-operate "in putting a stop to that system of plunder which has kept the frontier so long in a state of ferment."[160] He was required to communicate with the government on robberies by Xhosa or on the chief's complaints against the colonists, and the 'intimate knowledge' he could provide was expected to assist government. Williams only reluctantly accepted this role as a mediator and spy.[161] He soon wrote to a government official complaining that a view among the Xhosa was that "Government have given me permission to come here to betray them and give them over to the English and this I hear has been circulated through the land by the Boars [sic] and I am inclined to think that if they know that I keep a constant correspondence with you for the sake of informing you and complaining against them they will very soon be weary of me and take means to get me out of the way."[162] (At the same time Read went north across the Orange to re-establish the LMS mission among the Tlhaping, where he was to remain until 1820.)[163]

In April 1817 Somerset met Ngqika - together with Williams - at the Kat River and offered him sole rights to permit Xhosa access to the colony to trade, and active military assistance against his supposed 'subordinate' chiefs - provided that he consented to allow colonists to track stolen cattle to kraals and seize suspect animals. Ndlambe tried, but failed to make a separate agreement with the colony.[164] Thus the colony firmly committed itself to Ngqika as senior chief west of the Kei. But Somerset was not yet wholly reconciled to missionary activity. In 1817 he forbade four newly-arrived from the LMS from stationing themselves beyond the northern colonial border. The following year he closed LMS missions to the San across the northern border, and the Griquatown mission was threatened with closure through 1819 and 1820.

In addition, in 1817 the government drew the attention of George Thom to sexual improprieties committed by LMS missionaries. Thom, an LMS pastor with a white and slave-owning congregation in Cape Town, allied with the conservative South African Missionary Society, summoned a "synod" in August which laid charges against Read and others. It was an attempt to purge the LMS of pro-van der Kemp views: or, as Stuart puts it, to "reformulate van der Kemp's regulations for the Society and to re-assess the attitude to slavery." Read, who like van der Kemp had in 1803 married a woman of colour, was charged with adultery with another woman, the daughter of a convert (a matter for which he had already confessed and been forgiven by the Bethelsdorp congregation). Others were charged with illegal marriages with persons of colour, and de facto fornication.[165] It was a redefinition of what constituted 'civilised behaviour' for missionaries: it tightened up (racially as well as sexually) the idea of marriage and foreshadowed the emphasis on 'respectability' in the later Cape discussed by Ross and Mackenzie.[166] Thus missionary-government relations were not merely political but involved cultural redefinition. After the 'synod' Thom and two others resigned from the LMS to become Dutch Reformed Church Ministers. Read, dismissed as a missionary, remained as an artisanal and educational mission assistant.[167] Much later in his life Philip was to write of the ""most virulent and intemperate resolutions" of this meeting, and that "in consequence of the representations this made to the government... an order was sent out by Lord Bathurst to the Colonial government authorising it to put down all our Missions and disperse the people among the farmers. This order from the Home government would have been carried into effect if Mr Campbell and I had been three months later in arriving at the Cape [in 1819]."[168]

Williams, not very effectual in his role, died in August 1818.[169] Two months later the young Maqoma led an army on behalf of Ngqika against Ndlambe. But Ndlambe was reinforced by the Gcaleka of Hintsa, and the colony refused Ngqika's request for assistance. At the battle of Amalinde, Ndlambe's and Hintsa's forces were led by the millenarian war prophet Nxele (Makana), with syncretic Christian and Xhosa beliefs - the first to prophesy the rising of the dead and their cattle. A severe defeat was inflicted on Ngqika, killing many of his men, and wounding Maqoma near-fatally.[170] In retaliation, in December 1818 colonial forces responded to Ngqika's pleas and joined him in a counter-attack on Ndlambe, seizing 23,000 cattle of which 11,000 were given to Ngqika. This triggered a new frontier war, with the Xhosa invading the colony and besieging Grahamstown during the early months of 1819. On 22 April, Nxele led 6000 of Ndlambe's forces in a daylight attack on Grahamstown itself. They were repulsed and severely defeated. In late July colonial forces counter-attacked, and in August Nxele surrendered and was exiled to Robben Island, where he drowned while trying to escape.[171] Virtually all Xhosa were driven across the Keiskamma. Against the colony the Xhosa learnt from the experience the dangers of mass frontal attack, and in future resorted to guerrilla methods of fighting, using the dense bush (where British guns and horses were less effective) and the mountains.

In October Somerset and Andries Stockenstrom, now landrost of Graaff Reinet in place of his father, met again with Ngqika, and declared that the colony's boundary would be moved east to the Keiskamma river, and all Xhosa within the colony must move with it. This meant, inter alia, abandoning the fertile Kat River valley, where Maqoma was situated. Historians have since debated what was intended to be done with the land acquired by the colony: was it intended to be colonised, as 'ceded territory', or was it intended to be kept vacant (save for military forts) as 'neutral' territory.[172] Peires is correct, however, to conclude that "one of the hardy myths of South African history is that Somerset intended to create a 'neutral belt' of open territory between colonist and Xhosa.... Somerset's official dispatch on the subject unambiguously refers to the land in question as 'ceded' to Great Britain, describes it as 'as fine a portion of ground as is to be found in any part of the world, and strongly recommends it to the Colonial Secretary as a suitable area for systematic colonisation.'"[173] Somerset, in other words, was specifically promoting the idea of British settlers not merely in the Zuurveld, but in the area between the Fish and the Keiskamma.[174]

The combined effects of the war and this agreement were a blow to the Xhosa and particularly to Ngqika. With colonial support, he had asserted his supremacy over Ndlambe - and in some measure over Hintsa - only to be forced from his land by the British. The 'agreement' with the colony was never set down and signed, but remained verbal. Essentially it was rejected by the Xhosa as invalid and unfair.[175] As Read wrote in 1833, "All the chiefs knew of the transaction was that Gaika [Ngqika] proposed to them that that part of the country should be neutral and that soldiers should be stationed in the neighbourhood till Slambie [Ndlambe] was reconciled and Peace restored - but by no means finally to lose their country."[176] For Maqoma, as Stapleton relates, "the disaster at Amalinde, the collaboration of his father, and the treachery of the whites became the formative experiences of [his] early adult life" - and by 1821 he had defiantly returned to his home in the 'ceded' territory.[177]

From early in 1820 to late in 1821 Somerset took leave in Britain, and was replaced by Acting Governor Sir Rufane Donkin, who became his rival. In mid-year Donkin, influenced by the newly-arrived LMS superintendent John Philip, reversed Somerset's prohibition on further missionaries proceeding beyond the borders of the colony. Donkin also, after meeting with Ngqika, proposed to establish parties of settlers in the 'ceded' territory. As a result on his return Somerset opposed this and, according to Peires, claimed his policy was for vacant space between the Fish and Keiskamma.[178]

Already before the war, John Brownlee had been appointed by the government as missionary to replace Williams among Ngqika's people. He took up his post, on the Tyumie river, initially with an important headman of Maqoma's, in June 1820.[179] His letter of appointment, used for subsequent missionaries too, mandated him to introduce Christianity and civilisation, to try to end cross-border cattle-theft, to convince chiefs that the colony was friendly; and to collect information for frontier officials on the strength and position of border chiefs, their relations with one another, and details of their polities and economies. He was to concentrate on Ngqika and "to form from thence a system of interior control among the Caffers themselves which shall have the effect of keeping them at peace with the colonists."[180] In Britain, however, Somerset and George Thom together recruited a further government missionary, William Ritchie Thomson, from the Glasgow Missionary Society, who established himself at Brownlee's station.[181] Thus the LMS lost its monopoly on evangelising the Xhosa.

Chapter 5
British settlers and the 1820s revolution in government

The 1819 agreement with Ngqika ushered in fifteen years of uncertainty in colony-Xhosa power relations altered only by the 1834-5 war and its aftermath, though the shift began with Maqoma's expulsion from the Kat River area in 1829. In the meantime a revolution took place in the Cape Colony - economically, in the character of government, and in the legal position of the Khoi and the slaves.

The revolution represented the working out in the Colony of the changes flowing from the industrial revolution in Britain. These involved the ideas of 'free trade' and of 'civilisation'. A new sense of British imperial mission developed in the first half of the 19th century, fostered significantly by missionaries, promoting the ideas of 'Christianity, commerce, and civilisation'. The penetration of evangelism into the established (Anglican) church had transformed its character. It led to an "unprecedented surge in support for missions across Britain and across denominational lines. The newly-won approval of church and state made the missionary cause respectable. At the same time it became more nationalist and more closely tied to ideas of imperial mission and commercial enterprise. The empire of conquest and free trade thus also took on an aura of evangelical self-justification."[182] At the Cape in the 1820s, missionary promorion of these ideas was spurred and materially underpinned by the interests of a local merchant class which had grown up under British rule and was oriented to trade with Britain.

The advocacy of these ideas in the Colony was above all associated with Dr John Philip, superintendent of the LMS from 1819, and with John Fairbairn, who arrived in 1823 and, after a struggle with the government to establish a free press, became editor of the humanitarian *South African Commercial Advertiser*. An arch-champion of free trade, Fairbairn became leading spokesman for the (changing) interests of the Cape merchant class in commercial expansion. He also became Philip's son-in-law. Both had polemical skills and enthusiasm in promoting their views.[183]

At the same time some 5000 other British settlers were aided by the government to establish themselves in the Zuurveld. From the point of view of the Colony, this furthered Somerset's plans to establish a rural buffer against the Xhosa - though most, however, moved to the towns within two years.[184] (In the early 1820s it was even argued by colonial officials that British settlement on the frontier would stop the spread of slavery.[185]) Keegan argues however that from the home point of view, frontier defence was not the underlying motivation. Colonial settlement acquired importance in the 19th century to generate expanding demand for British products and in relieving Britain of 'redundant' population. This particular movement, however, for him was stimulated by "a temporary crisis of domestic unrest in Britain."[186] The importance of the arrival of British settlers for recent historiography has been that they came to develop "an ideology of accumulation and dispossession that was a new force in colonial society".[187]

In the 1820s missionary and merchant interests - and even, at first, British settler interests - became closely fused in campaigning for colonial reform. The movement gained sustenance from the appointment by the British government in 1822 of a commission of enquiry into the affairs of the colony with the aim of liberalising and anglicising social relations. At the start settlers, missionaries and merchants together challenged Somerset's autocratic government with demands for freedom of speech and of the press. As time passed, however, the interests of the 'humanitarian alliance' diverged from that of settlers. While all wanted the removal of obstacles to free enterprise and trade, missionaries (and merchants, too, at this time) wanted the Khoi and the slaves freed, and to try to create peasant consumers with new 'wants'. Their vision, in the words of Keegan, was of "free indigenous communities, generating ever-expanding markets for British produce... the colonial economy was fragile, underdeveloped and unpromising. But beyond settlerdom lay a great hinterland of potentially free producers and consumers, innocent of the archaic inhibitions of imported slavery and Khoi servitude."As Fairbairn put it: 'To stimulate Industry, to encourage Civilisation, and convert the hostile Natives into friendly Customers is... a more profitable speculation than to exterminate or reduce them to Slavery."[188]

A material basis for the revolution which transpired consisted in the removal, from 1825, of preferential tariffs in Europe which destroyed the main export of wine, produced by Western Cape Dutch notables: the economy of slavery was thereby undermined.[189] Meanwhile the British settlers pioneered the opening up of trade both in Xhosaland and the hinterland of Port Natal. They broke down the state-regulated 'trade fair' system by penetrating deeper into Xhosa territory, knocking out Xhosa middlemen. (In parallel Griqua and Boers traded northwards.) Ivory and arms and ammunition (illegally) were central items. "Out of this new enterprise", writes Keegan, "a new accumulating British settler elite in the eastern Cape was born."[190]

Central to the humanitarian standpoint was Philip. When he arrived in the

Cape he had tended to support the views of Thom and to disparage Read. But on a trip to Bethelsdorp in 1821, he discovered documents which vindicated Read and began a crusade against the entire labour system and its underpinnings in government. "The Hottentots are acknowledged to be a free people" he wrote in October 1822, "but labour is every day becoming scarcer and the colonists are resolved to indemnify themselves for the loss of the slave trade by reducing the Hottentots to a condition of slavery the most shocking and oppressive."[191] The philosophy which underpinned his crusade, however, differed from van der Kemp's. Its full statement is in his *Researches*, written in Britain and published in April 1828, already mentioned as a founding history of the colony. The philosophy was important not only in reshaping the concept of civilisation to suit the combined purposes of merchants, missionaries, and government. It was also to have lasting effects on the consciousness of the evolving 'coloured' community.

Its strong side was its universalist conception of human nature; of the capacity of each individual given freedom from confining regulations, to progress spiritually and materially, thus contributing to the greater good of society.[192] But the prescriptions were spelled out in a particular way. Van der Kemp and Read, as Elbourne puts it, had been "in favour of economic progress as a pragmatic means to minimise poverty and hunger", but they "did not believe in a systematic way in the transformatory function of economic development, or in a necessary relationship between Christianity and 'civilisation'". Philip, however, presented "a case for the convergence of colonial interest and the 'civilisation' of the Khoisan as well as weaving a complicated ideology of economic progress intimately related to spiritual enlightenment."[193] For Keegan, *Researches* "asserted the beneficial effects civil equality and liberty would have on good order and mercantile profit in the British empire" and Philip was "unashamedly pro-imperialist in his conviction of the ultimate beneficence of British rule."[194] While condemning settler stereotypes of the indigenous people, at the same time Philip believed that they had to be saved from their own culture because it was inferior and barbarous.[195] This was a contradiction.

As Alan Lester puts it, missionaries "benevolence and their will to control were indissoluble": their charges, whether slaves or British workers, "would be free to pursue their own self-interest but not free to reject the cultural conditioning that defined what that self-interest should be. They would have opportunities for social mobility, but only after they learned their proper place." "What happened in the 1820s and 30s", concludes Elbourne, was that the "economic and social assumptions of leading LMS personnel moved closer to those of the governing elite even as evangelical tenets in general exercised a greater hold upon a broader spectrum of British society." For Keegan, Philip represented "the domestication of missionary humanitarianism in respectable metropolitan society."[196] Philip believed in the salvatory function of self-knowledge.[197] He wrote: "One of the first steps in attempting the elevation of a savage people, in connection with religious and moral instruction, is to endeavour to impart to them a relish for the decencies and comforts of life. Little can be done towards their general improvement, till you can get them to exchange their straw cabins for decent houses. Their miserable reed-huts are unfavourable to health and morals... These huts are as unfavourable to industry as they are to health... While they live in these huts, habits of cleanliness can never be acquired... These habitations are also unfavourable to decency."[198] Likewise in an early memorandum to Governor Donkin in 1820 he wrote, concerning the Griqua, "Every house they build, every garden which they inclose, and every acre of corn-land which they cultivate, are so many securities for their peaceable conduct towards the colony... by increasing their artificial wants, you increase the dependence of the Griquas on the colony, and you make for the preservation of peace."[199]

On this basis in October 1821 he presented an improvement plan to the Khoi at Bethelsdorp and Theopolis, involving the replacement of wattle-and-daub houses by stone houses built in a rectangular pattern along straight streets.[200] The emphasis, in contrast to van der Kemp, was thus on outward signs of 'civilisation' rather than on inner faith. In a sense, it married the methods of the Moravians to the campaigning of the Bethelsdorp missionaries. Crehan in her insightful thesis, has argued that such promotion of square houses "enshrined capitalist values, as it permitted family privacy, fostered individualism, provided evidence for the industriousness, or otherwise, of the inhabitants, allowed possessions to be shown off, and embodied 'a clear sense of social order and hierarchy'"[201]

Unlike van der Kemp, Philip had no qualms about the British state. From the start, Philip promoted as a virtue the role of the inhabitants of the LMS missions as military defenders of the colony, and encouraged the colonial government to support this role on the eastern and the northern frontiers (the Griqua).[202] The Cape Regiment and Khoi recruited from the mission stations had already been involved in the 1812 and 1819 wars against the Xhosa. In 1822 Philip noted with pride that "the greater part of the able-bodied men" from Bethelsdorp, Theopolis and Zuurbraak were "serving the Government".[203] He promoted Christianity, in other words, in part as an ideology which would make the indigenous people loyal militarily to the British crown.

In sum, Philip aimed for the missionaries "To raise uncivilised and wandering hordes, which formerly subsisted by the chase or by plunder, to the condition of settled labourers and cultivators of the soil, to lead them to increase the sum of productive labour and to become consumers of the commodities of other countries, to convert such as were a terror to the inhabitants of an extended frontier into defenders of that frontier against the inroads of remoter barbarians."²⁰⁴ Read endorsed these ideas.

The philosophy as a whole created an ideology of 'respectability' for coloured artisanal and peasant classes, and formed a basis on which there emerged a Khoi elite.²⁰⁵ The ideas were spread between Bethelsdorp and Griquatown and far wider, by 'native agents' and others.²⁰⁶ As Ross writes, by the 1840s, "a significant minority of the mission stations' inhabitants had given heed to the missionaries call for an outward reformation of manners as well as an inner realignment of their beliefs. In their housing, clothing, sexual mores and attitudes and schooling, they were behaving as their mentors wished."²⁰⁷ For the Khoi all this provided a new order of society when their old was already crumbled - whereas for the still unconquered Xhosa they would appear as an assault on their core social institutions.

Philip left South Africa early in 1826 to tie the issue of Khoi rights to a once-again rising tide of sentiment and petitioning for the abolition of slavery in Britian.²⁰⁸ While making recommendations on other issues, the commissioners had not yet reported on the Khoi (and did not in fact publish a report until 1830). ²⁰⁹ In Britian Philip began to forge relations with Sir Thomas. F. Buxton, Wilberforce's heir, as his parliamentary patron, to write the *Researches* and to campaign for the liberation of the Khoisan.

Meanwhile the tide of reform forced Somerset out of the governorship by 1826. His successor, Acting Governor Sir Richard Bourke, following the recommendations of the commission of enquiry, carried out a virtual political revolution in the colony. For Walker, the year 1828 was an *'annus mirabilis'*.²¹⁰ Bourke did away with remaining monopolies and all restrictions on free economic activity. He established new taxes and devalued the rixdollar. He remodelled the civil and judicial establishments, creating a new system of administration, an independent judicial system, and a Legislative Council with changed composition, and displacing the Dutch notables from government. The legal system was not only reworked, but partly Anglicised. By 1829 freedom of the press was also firmly established, creating an important new arena of public discourse. From January 1827, as a measure to encourage British immigration, English became the only official language in terms of a Somerset proclamation of 1822.²¹¹

Moreover, Bourke secured the passage of the famous Ordinance 50 of 1828, which removed from the Khoi all pass laws, compulsory service, and summary punishment without trial. At the same time, as Crais emphasises, it reaffirmed "the virtues of private property and wage labour."²¹² Bourke had just promulgated Ordinance 49, which encouraged Xhosa migrant labour into the colony. Though abolition of passes for the Khoi had been floated from early 1826, according to his biographer Bourke felt it particularly unjust to favour extra-colonials when indigenous people within the colony were oppressed.²¹³ Hence Ordinance 50. Recent historiography has tended to downplay Philip's role in the passage of this. What he did achieve however, in London, was its constitutional entrenchment. The victory, such as it was, belonged to Philip and the humanitarians, who had created the climate for it.[214]

The actual measure was prompted by a memorandum of April 1828 from Andries Stockenstrom, now Commissioner-General on the Eastern Frontier.[215] Stockenstrom had been rapidly influenced by the views of the humanitarians. In 1819 he had defended the Boer view that all 'Kaffirs' were enemies as "natural and well grounded."[216] In 1820 he had commented favourably on Philip's views on the role of the missionaries in defence of the colonial frontier.[217] Visited at his home by William Wright, Philip, and Thomas Pringle in 1825, Stockenstrom wrote that there was "little to be disputed between my guests and myself as to the past" [of the indigenous people] "but they certainly tried my temper by the virulence with which they persisted in denouncing the present generation of the Colonists and refused to make any allowance for their actual position, which rendered self-defence often absolutely necessary." He believed that they were "tolerably satisfied that I was not so hostile to blacks or missionaries as I had been represented."[218] Stockenstrom was to be an influential actor in the Colony for the next ten years, and again in the late 1840s and early 1850s.

Recent historiography has tended to warn against exaggeration of the effects of the Ordinance. Ross, for example, regards it as a "non-event".[219] For the Khoisan, though, it precipitated a 'flight from the estate' with an "astounding number of desertions", a flight to towns and to the missions (whose populations rocketed): it provided 'a taste of freedom'.[220] Even on paper it was a charter of rights - that could be mobilised for by the Khoi, possibly more in the eastern than the western Cape.[221] It may not have been primarily, as was argued at one time, brought about from considerations of labour shortage, though Keegan concedes that for Stockenstrom at least the ordinance "was not unrelated to issues of labour needs."[222] "The enemies of the Hottentots are enraged", wrote Read of the reaction to Ordinance 50, "and what is strange, the English settlers are most reluctant for the Hottentots to enjoy their liberty."[223] The whole revolution, in fact, created a backlash among both Boer and British settlers, preparing the way among other things for the Trek of 1834-1837.

Save for the continued patrol system and the opening up of trade, the revolution within the colony distracted attention from relations with the Xhosa. During the 1820s Maqoma, having returned to the Kat River area, became the most important chief west of the Kei. His father Ngqika's power was eroding. In 1825 Ngqika even lost the sole recognition he had enjoyed from the colony, in favour of a policy of recognising different chiefs.[224] He died - as did Ndlambe - in 1828. Thomson described Maqoma at the time as a "very active enterprising young man" who had "a considerable body of Kaffirs attached to him of a similar description."²⁵⁵ The tragedy for Maqoma was that though Ngqika's first son, he was not his first son by the Great Wife, whom Ngqika had married later, for diplomatic reasons. He could not succeed Ngqika but would have to leave the succession to the physically handicapped and frail Sandile.²²⁶

Preoccupied with Khoisan issues, the LMS did not take the opportunity to consolidate their position among the Xhosa, or with Maqoma. Selective moderniser as Maqoma was, he wanted a missionary, and the LMS did not oblige.²²⁷ Moreover none of the missionaries entering Xhosaland in the 1820s, writes Peires, picked up "any of the threads indicated by Nxele [Makana], Ntsikani, or even van der Kemp."²²⁸ Thomson, official government agent, stationed at Tyumie (6 miles north of the present Alice) introduced other Glasgow missionaries to the area, such as John Bennie (from 1820) and John Ross (with Ngqika from 1823). In 1824 they established Old Lovedale near Tyumie, which became in time an important education centre. (Tiyo Soga was the first black southern African to be educated and ordained there, in 1856.)²²⁹ In 1823 the Wesleyans were directed to the Gqunukhwebe by the LMS and GMS and established a station, Wesleyville (William Shaw).

As early as 1821 Read had pointed out to Shaw "the need of Missionaries far up the east coast; and I [Shaw] unhesitatingly join with him in opinion, that if a number of zealous and prudent Missionaries were allowed to enter Caffraria, the disturbances occasioned by that untutored, but noble race of men would soon terminate."²³⁰ Taking up the idea, the Wesleyans drove eastwards across Xhosa territory in a chain of stations that went in tandem with the trading pulls among British settlers to Port Natal: to Ndlambe (Stephen Kay, 1824); among the Gcaleka of Hintsa across the Kei (William Shrewsbury at Butterworth, 1827); among the Mpondo (from 1829/1830) and among the Thembu. Meanwhile the Glasgow missionaries reached Maqoma, with a station at Balfour in 1828. They also established Pirie and Burnshill before 1834. In the 1820s all these missionaries had to report periodically to Thomson. Brownlee returned to the LMS in 1825 and established a station at the later Peelton on the Buffalo River with the old Bethelsdorp convert Jan Tshatshu's people, the amaNtinde. He was joined by Friedrich Kayser in 1826. In 1827 Moravians established a mission with some Thembu.²³¹

The Wesleyans arrived along with the 1820 settlers, had congregations among them and drew financial support from them and, over time, were to have a crucial role in shaping their identity. They were both pro-settler, and highly conservative, quite different from the LMS.²³² As early as 1833 Read complained to Fairbairn of the years-long "close connection between the merchants, traders and Wesleyan missionaries"²³³ Neither the Wesleyans nor the Glasgow Society worked among the Khoi in the colony. And, while they "liked the [Xhosa] people themselves, admired their courtesies and conceded their intelligence", the missionaries among the Xhosa, concludes Mostert, "regarded practically every aspect of Xhosa life with revulsion and loathing. Their adjectives were the sharp ones of disgust and contempt."[234] In fact until much later the missionaries failed in Xhosaland in their work of evangelisation: conversions were few and limited mainly to outcasts from society.[235] Despised by the Xhosa, feeling ineffectual in his role as government agent, Thomson resigned in 1828 - but the government refused to accept this.[236]

Disturbances further north and east of the Xhosa affected the Colony-Xhosa frontier in the late 1820s, driving refugees - often termed 'Fetcani' or 'Mantatees' - to work in the colony. It was a part of what has been called the *mfecane*. In 1828 a colonial force, alerted among others by the missionary Shrewsbury, invaded Mpondo territory to attack 'invading Zulus' who turned out to be the Taung of Matiwane. Cobbing has argued that the reason for the invasion was the desperate desire of the colony for labour, but the evidence points rather to the official preoccupation with military security.[237]

Chapter 6

The expulsion of Maqoma and the Kat River settlement, 1829

In 1829 Maqoma, then probably with more than 16,000 subjects, was expelled by colonial forces from the Kat River area. It was a turning point in Xhosa-colony relations, adding greatly to Xhosa mistrust. In Maqoma's place Stockenstrom established a settlement of 'coloureds': the Kat River settlement. His main aim was, as he put it, to turn "the better and more efficient part of the Hottentots into a breastwork against an exasperated, powerful enemy in the most vulnerable and dangerous part of our frontier"[238] At the same time, for the humanitarians, paradoxically, it was the culmination of their dreams for the Khoisan.

Though Stockenstrom had wanted Maqoma out of Kat River as early as 1822, it was probably the advent of a new tough governor, Sir Lowry Cole, in 1828 which provided the impetus.[239] The opportunity came in January 1829 when Maqoma attacked Thembu who had settled north of his area, driving some into colonial territory.[240] Maqoma, stated Stockenstrom later, had been treated with "mistaken lenity and vacillation, which he misinterpreted as weakness", and he had recommended his expulsion. After negotiations, military force was sent in early May (with the endorsement of Ngqika), torching the kraals of Maqoma's people, compelling them to abandon the area and move eastward.[241] The consequence was the flight of some into the colony, joining the many Xhosa who had already entered it as pass-bearing (or pass-evading) labourers in the late 1820s, and an increase in the elementary resistance of cattle theft.[242]

A frontier settlement of 'coloureds' was a 10-year old humanitarian idea: in October 1823, for example, Thomas Pringle had written a paper titled "Hints of a Plan for Defending the Eastern Frontier of the Colony by a Settlement of Hottentots"[243] As Philip put it in 1836: "Ever since I have formed fixed opinions on the subject I have always considered it of the last importance to have belts of civilised natives between the colonists and their less civilised neighbours. The people in [the] immediate neighbourhood [of the Colony] who have worked themselves up to a knowledge of our character and power, and who have acquired any portion of the civilisation of Europeans without losing their sympathy with their uncivilised neighbours, would unite the colonists and the uncivilised tribes by internal bonds, and operate in preventing collisions taking place between them."²⁴⁴ The activity of freeing, civilising and uplifting the Khoisan would, he maintained, relieve the labour shortage, causing the cessation of commandos and "all classes will shortly be seen mingling together, in one common fraternity, without bloodshed and without fear."²⁴⁵

Together with this, as Stockenstrom emphasised, the Kat River Settlement "gave practical effect" to Ordinance 50 by providing land for Khoisan/coloured settlement.²⁴⁶ The Kat River settlement was pivotal to the creation of a coloured peasantry.²⁴⁷ Conditions at missions in the eastern part of the colony were poor by the end of the 1820s, with indebtedness, alcoholism, and social despair.²⁴⁸ In showing that the freed Khoisan could succeed economically, it was also intended as an example of much importance for the cause of slave abolition.²⁴⁹ As Philip expressed it on his first visit in 1830, it was an experiment in determining whether the Khoisan were "fit for freedom, whether they would work except under the lash of a master - and the failure of this experiment would have deeply affected the future condition of the colonial population at large."²⁵⁰ For the Khoi, as Elbourne puts it, its advantages were the promise of justice and of equal access to the white colony in return for becoming 'civilised'. Access to the land also offered some hope of national regeneration, when linked with literacy and education.²⁵¹ Andries Stoffel, a founder settler, stressed one side of this when in Britain in 1836: "When the missionaries came, then we began to breathe...the Hottentot has no water, he has not a blade of grass, he has no lands, he has no wood, he has no place where he can sleep; all that he now has is the missionary and the Bible"²⁵²

Philip was still in Britain when the expulsion of Maqoma took place and the Kat River settlement was established. Stockenstrom toured the LMS mission stations enlisting coloured settlers.²⁵³ In June 1829, wrote the missionary George Barker from Theopolis, Maqoma "became a troublesome neighbour to the Colony, and in consequence has been ordered backward": indeed, he had "forfeited all claim to favour from the Government". "And strange as it may be to you," he continued, "that part is now offered to the Hottentots, on the same terms as other lands are possessed by the colonists."²⁵⁴ To the LMS at the same time, Read seemed equally unconcerned about the expulsion of Maqoma. Stockenstrom, he wrote, had proposed that the neutral territory "be given to the Hottentots and at last Govt. [agreed] to it, accordingly Capt. Stockenstrom came down again about two months ago to put it into execution after arranging with the Caffre chiefs one of which (Makomo son of Gaika) had to be driven over the Keiskamma....The country given in the first place is at the source of the Cat River Konap River which 30 years ago was in possession of a tribe of Hottentots called Heintemas. It never was considered part of Caffreland." Read added that it was "considered the finest part of

Africa yet known for water, wood and soil" - and indeed it was widely regarded, by the settlers and missionaries, as the most fertile part of the eastern Cape east of Kei, well-watered by 12-13 branches of the Kat River flowing out of the Winterberg.[255] In an 1831 letter Read showed equal lack of concern about the expulsion of Maqoma: "I rather think you are not yet much acquainted with our new settlement on the Kat River. The Hottentots on receiving their civil liberty became anxious to obtain also some property. On application to Government to grant them some unoccupied land to cultivate and to erect habitations upon, on the neutral ground lying between the colony and Cafferland... It was inhabited by Makomo the son of Gaika, a powerful chief, who had no idea of its being connected with the neutral ground, but Government considered him only on suffrage - and this ground was granted to the Hottentots." [256]

In June 1829 Barker made clear that Stockenstrom was "importunate that no time should be lost in taking possession"[257] - before it could be occupied by Boers or other Xhosa chiefs. 101 able men, with women and children numbering 400, had volunteered and some had left already. Read added that "among those that have been residing with Boors etc... many more will go... and hundreds are pouring down from Graaff Reinet."[258]... "I was very glad", concluded Barker, "to see Capt. Stockenstrom very anxious to have one of the Missionaries with the first party and he proposed Read, if it takes with Read the Hottentots will flock there and I defy the Government to draw back.[259] Read wrote modestly: "Stockenstrom expressed a wish for me to follow them... but I felt no liberty to take any step till Dr P[hilip]. arrives. My leaving Bethelsdorp might affect the station as many Hottentots probably would follow. The Hottentots that have left Theopolis are very anxious that I should follow them and I suppose they expect it but I have no particular desire nor should I except it might be the opinion of others that my labours could be more useful there and that it is my duty to do so."[260] Around this time he wrote to Stockenstrom that the Kat River settlement should be called Stockenstrom.[261]

Strangely enough the first complaint to government at Maqoma's expulsion came from the estranged government missionary William Thomson. "Their removal", he wrote has produced a considerable degree of irritation and hostility, in the minds of those particularly, who have suffered by it; and it is likely to cause an unfavourable impression upon the natives generally." This was particularly because the precise boundaries were under dispute in the area. "Under these circumstances it is not probable that the natives will perceive or acknowledge the claim which the Government now makes to the country in question."[262]

Cole did not want Read at the Kat River - causing Stockenstrom to reverse his encouragement to Read to go.[263] Philip returned to from Britain in October 1829 and visited the settlement in April 1830. "On my arrival in the Colony" he was later to write, "I had the intelligence conveyed to me by various respectable individuals that the Government had determined that no missionaries should be allowed to settle in that district... my acquiescence was inferred from my silence."[264] Of the establishment of the settlement he wrote in December 1830,"had I been in Africa when it took place, it would not have taken place in the way that it did. Almost all the wealth and respectability at our Institutions have been removed to that new station... When the scheme was in preparation, the Institutions were visited by [Stockenstrom etc]... as if they... had been recruiting sergeants, and the missionaries were so far duped as to bond themselves fully to his scheme. A few months after the people were settled in their new locations they were visited by yhe Governor... and now we heard of nothing but the superiority of the Hottentots at the Kat river under the direction of Government to those at the Missionary Stations. The fact that these people having been at our Missionary Stations was [ignored?] by the friends of the Government... While the people on the Kat river were praised and our institutions condemned, it was confidently reported on every side that no missionary from the London Missionary Society was to be allowed to settle amongst them."[265]

When he visited in April 1830, continued Philip, "I had previously received an application from the people signed by the heads of all the [families?] praying for a missionary from our society... On visiting them the application was repeated, and the people were unanimous. Mr Read was with me, from his long acquaintance with them it was natural that they should wish for him. To their proposal on this subject I concurred and when it was heard at head quarters the rage of our great father [Cole] was indescribable. Brownlee and the missionaries in Kaffirland who had jobs [with] the Government, said that had such a result been contemplated, the locations in the Kat River would have never taken place. The Colonial Government however could get hold of nothing tangible against me in the business, and they are obliged to digest their mortification the [best?] way they can. They talked of ordering Mr Read away... that is a thing they are not likely to do. If these people have the rights of other colonists they have a right to choose their own minister."[266] "From the time that the Government intimated that no missionary was to be allowed to settle among them", wrote Philip later, "the doom of the settlement was considered as sealed, by their enemies and themselves. On three sides of them were hostile Caffres and on the other were the White colonists, who made sure of having all their lands within 18 months, and the principle on which their anticipations were formed were correct."[267]

The Government appointed Thomson as official missionary at Kat River and he was inducted on 13th July 1830 and settled at Balfour, the previous GMS station to Maqoma.[268] Meanwhile, Read had arrived at the Kat River as minister to those who had called him.[269] Philip in Cape Town learnt that Cole was irritated by the "schism" and threatening to order Read's removal, and told him that he the governor was the cause of the schism and that he had no more power to remove Read than to remove Philip from Cape Town.[270] "As there is plenty of work for a number of ministers in the district," wrote Philip, "I requested Mr Read to go forward peaceably in his work as if no such thing had happened and to co-operate with the government's minister as far as in his power, doing nothing to counteract any good he may do..."[271] The hatred of the colonists for Read, said Philip at this time, "was not from the moral obliquity into which he had been led [his adultery] but for his uncompromising stand against oppression."[272] In contrast to other missionaries Read did not keep social distance from his charges, but "associated himself indistinguishably" with them.[273]

When, after the 1834-1835 war, Read was accused by the Wesleyan William Boyce of complicity in the expulsion of Maqoma, his response was to "disclaim" it: "I knew at the time nothing of Macomo nor the country he inhabited, nor had I ever corresponded with Capt. Stockenstrom upon the subject... I had [heard] that the neutral territory was to be given out to the colonists as it had been ceded by Gaika and I considered in that case the Hottentots had the first claim... Capt. S proposed it to the Hottentots themselves...[other] missionaries... accepted the offer much to our surprise and regret especially after becoming acquainted with the real state of the affair, on this account I was most reluctant to agree to... following them as Missionary and did not do it until nearly a year after the settlement was established. The Hottentots all knew my mind upon this subject."[274]

The original settlers of the Kat River included, besides 144 families from Theopolis and Bethelsdorp, Gonaqua who had been living in the area as clients of Maqoma's people, who were placed under the Gona leader Andries Botha, 70-80 families of Basters from the Somerset and Graaff Reinet districts[275], placed under Christian Groepe, and others from Enon and elsewhere. Some were converts, from the LMS, the Wesleyans and the Glasgow Missionary Society. In 1853 some inhabitants were still using a Khoi language. Read in about 1831 mentioned 33 locations - some named after abolitionists such as William Wilberforce, Stephen Lushington, Thomas Buxton and Johannes van der Kemp - with on average 100 persons in each, 21 of them occupied by LMS people. By 1834 there appears to have been 5000 inhabitants. By then the LMS dominated the settlement, with Thomson's congregation confined largely to Basters.[276] The structure of the settlement is described by Kirk as "semi-feudal", with clientage prevalent. There was considerable differentiation of wealth and property. The aim was to turn it into a prosperous cash-crop community. As among the Xhosa, the agriculture was carried out by women.[277] In 1831 Read wrote, "I expect our improvements will be rapid, as we have from our stations all kinds of mechanics: masons, smiths, carpenters, sawyers, wheelwrights, shoemakers, etc. We have excellent forests of timber, extensive markets in the colony, and easy of access." As at Bethelsdorp earlier, the settlement served as the centre of a 'coloured diaspora' of traders, transport riders, artisans and teachers. And up until the 1834-1835 war at least it prospered.[278]

The rest of the ceded territory was distributed by Stockenstrom to Boers and British settlers "at least, three or four times as much as was allotted to the Hottentots". When land was sold by government near Kat River, the coloureds were prohibited from buying it. This area was soon to become the "wealthy wool-producing district of Fort Beaufort."[279]

Philip soon extended the frontier defence concept of the Kat River settlement into concrete proposals for the statelet at Griquatown which had been nurtured by the LMS since early in the century and to which his protégé Peter Wright had been transferred in 1825 as missionary. In 1830 he recommended to government the appointment of a magistrate to the Griqua who would form "a kind of frontier militia" to prevent aggressions by the Boer farmers who were moving into Transorangia. He was, in other words in favour of their incorporation in the colony.[280] In the ensuing decade he would promote Griqua expansionism from Griqatown and Phillipolis in Transorangia, exerting hegemony over Sotho-Tswana peoples. At the same time Philip supported in the area the state of increasing size and wealth built by Moshoeshoe around the valley of the Caledon river through the *mafiso* [cattle-loaning] system since the 1820s. In 1833 he sent French Protestant missionaries to establish themselves with Moshoeshoe. In the same year, since government did not support annexation, he and Wright worked out a proposal for a treaty arrangement between the colony and the Griqua chief Andries Waterboer.[281]

Thus the realisation of Philip's vision in the Kat River Settlement was used to promote the interests of 'coloureds' on the northern frontier as well. All this had been at the expense of the Xhosa (and, would be, for a period, of the Sotho-Tswana). Mostert asserts that the "Boer frontiersman" took over from the "philanthropist" in Stockenstrom when he expelled Maqoma.[282] In reality the contradiction was inside philanthropism, between forcible civilisation and upliftment. The "more civilised" were set against the "less civilised", and the LMS missionaries at this stage favoured the emerging 'coloureds' at the expense of Bantu-speaking peoples.

Meanwhile the settler reaction at the liberation of the Khoisan was growing apace. In fact the ideas of 'freedom' became a two-edged sword. As taken up by Dutch farmers and British settlers in contrast to the humanitarians, they became principally for more settler self-government, based on a system of labour coercion. In the Dutch case at least it included a defence of the property rights of slaveholders. Agitation for representative government began in the 1820s but recieved a setback when Fairbairn withdrew his support for it in 1832, after Boer farmers met and passed pro-slavery resolutions, on the grounds that the settlers could not be entrusted with it. (There was also mistrust between British settlers and Afrikaners).[283] Settlers found voices in the *Boer De Zuid Afrikaan* (from 1830) and the British *Grahamstown Journal* (from 1831). Both these newspapers denounced Ordinance 50, for which they held Philip and Fairbairn responsible. Afrikaners in particular resented the merchant-humanitarian alliance because of the removal of their role as agents of the Somerset autocracy.

From early on, the British settler elite had discarded the use of white free labour as had been intended, and turned to employ unfree black labour, particularly when in the late 1820s the economy was picking up.[284] As Read wrote, "tis strange to tell but so it is that the chief opposers have been the English settlers. When they found the Govt. was unshaken with the ordinance, they did all they could to get vagrant acts made".[285] The *Grahamstown Journal* with Robert Godlonton as editor came to represent the interests of the rising agrarian capitalists of the Eastern Cape, desiring racial subjugation of labour and dispossession of the indigenous from their land.[286] It denounced Fairbairn's *South African Commercial Advertiser* as the "Hottentot Advertiser", representing the interest of "vagrant Hottentots and heathens" over "whites, Christians and property owners", and maintained that the African was a "creature of uncontrolled volition" who required and even desired domination.[287] Crais has stressed the 'construction of the Other' by British settlers at this time. "Instead of a positive projection there emerged a discourse of condemnation situated around a chain of signifying dichotomies: 'white' and 'black', 'civilisation' and 'barbarism', 'us' and 'them' and so on... From the end of the 1820s Africans were increasingly represented as libidinous, uncontrolled, lazy and disrespectful of established authority."[288] This discourse, for Crais, not only served to legitimate the development of racial capitalism but underpinned an emergent colonial identity.[289] In its specific racism, it was a post-Enlightenment reaction to the Enlightenment.

In the constructed identity of British settlers, equally, Ross has perceived the development of an English nationalism, particularly from the 1840s, as "the prime nationalism of South Africa, against which all the subsequent ones, whether Afrikaner or African, reacted, either directly or at a remove... Through much of the first half of the nineteenth century, and indeed later, Englishness was the major symbol used to determine what was right and acceptable in the political life of the Cape Colony."[290]

Settlers complained of desertion of labour, vagrancy, insolence and theft inside the colony. Blacks were 'thievish' and 'indolent'. Godlonton wanted not only rapid returns on land: "His objective also presupposed easy access to cheap labour. This would require a vagrancy law, to prevent coloureds from evading participation in the colonial labour market."[291] In 1834, a draft anti-vagrancy act proposed by Acting-Governor Colonel T. F. Wade was passed by the Cape Legislative Council, but vetoed by the British government. Significantly, as Elbourne notes, the 'resolutions' which accompanied this act were couched in the language of 'civilisation' appropriated from the humanitarians.[292] The attempt to pass it, together with the failure to do so, provoked opposite reaction from Khoisan and settlers.

On the one hand, the Act's disallowance intensified settler demands for self-government. On the other hand its passage in the Cape served to sharpen the identity of the Khoi. They "were the chief lobbyists against the Act. This was the first instance in their history of a widespread petitioning movement."[293] At public meetings at the mission stations they recalled their harsh treatment by farmers, and claimed the act would be a forced labour measure which would "seal the[ir] degradation" and "defeat the end of the labors of missionaries"[294]. "If Khoi had not been greatly excited by Ordinance 50 in 1828", writes Keegan, "in 1834 it was the touchstone of their agitation." Plaatje Jonker at Bethelsdorp said "Every nation has its screen: the white men have a screen, the colour of their skin is their screen, the 50th ordinance is our screen". While the language of the Khoi was self-consciously liberal, with reference to rights and liberty, the protests also served to crystallise what Trapido has called 'Hottentot nationalism'. 'Hottentots' embraced not only indigenous Khoi but persons with white, Xhosa and San ancestry and even slaves - an identity which James Read was accused of brokering. As Esau Prince at the Kat River put it, "I am a Boor's child, although I had to sit behind the chairs and the stools, as my mother was a Hottentot woman and therefore I consider myself a Hottentot also. Men say I have Christian blood in me, but I know only of one blood that God has made. The so-called 'Christeman' steals the name!" Only the Baster supporters of William Thomson at the Kat River petitioned in favour of the Act.[295] The opposition of British settlers to their rights changed the perception of the Khoi towards them. However the disallowance of the Act by the British government reinforced Khoi perceptions of British justice.[296]

In the same year, 1834, slavery was abolished as from 1 December - though with a four-year apprenticeship period so the full effects were not apparent until 1838. The some 3000 Boer slave-owners had resisted many amelioration measures, and wanted gradual abolition.[297] As with the disallowance of the vagrancy act, abolition increased their discontent and sowed the seeds of the Trek in which many left the colony. In their eyes the 'proper relations between master and servant' were being disturbed.[298] However the goals of emancipation for the colonial government, asserts a recent study, "were clearly revealed: the replacement of slaveowner arbitrary tyranny by a more powerful state regulation of labour but one which would continue to ensure the maintenance of social hierarchy and inequality of race and class."[299]

Keegan points out as well that the humanitarians, particularly Philip, were "relatively reticent" on the issue of abolition, because of their defence of the rights of property. Philip welcomed the idea of monetary compensation to slaveowners, and did not oppose the four-year apprenticeship period.[300]

Philip made his first journey to Xhosaland proper, with Fairbairn and Read, on a five-month tour in early 1830. As the 'architect' of Ordinance 50, he was received with acclaim at Bethelsdorp in February. Men on horseback accompanied him into the station from 12 kilometres out, and he was accorded a lavish public feast.[301] His aims, however, were not just among the Khoi, but to restore and establish relations with the Xhosa, particularly in view of the expulsion of Maqoma.

He had contact with the chiefs and with GMS as well as LMS missionaries. He observed "The Caffres are not the savages one reads about in books. They are intelligent and are not afraid of conversing with strangers; they are, moreover, well acquainted with their own history and study mankind, if not books; at ten years old, they are politicians!... They have humour and are clever at giving characteristic nicknames; they are not generous, but they say they are poor. They acknowledge the white man's superiority in science and arts, but do not individually feel inferior to those they meet; though they despise the contempt of the colonists, yet it rankles in their minds and degrades them in their own estimation."[302] In a well-known letter to missionaries in America in 1833 he wrote that: "in point of abilities and good feelings, I consider the Caffres on the borders of the colony as most decidedly superior to that portion of the refuse of English society that find their way to this country."[303]

Maqoma and other chiefs told him of their grievances of loss of land, the wrong done by the 1819 treaty, the patrols seizing their cattle, and the expulsion from Kat River. Philip criticised the expulsion as unjust and promised to take it up with government. Subsequently Fairbairn's paper published editorials and letters condemning colonial aggression against the Xhosa.[304] Philip also predicted "slavery or extermination" for the Xhosa on the basis of the existing policy on the border, and commented that "Frontier Boers, Field Cornets, magistrates, friends of magistrates want new grants of land, and these grants must be taken from the Caffres."[305]

Opposition to Maqoma's expulsion became further publicised in Saxe Bannister's Humane Policy in 1830, and Pringle's African Sketches in 1834, but the Wesleyans would later try to use the initial acquiescence of the LMS in the expulsion of Maqoma against them.[306] At this time, indeed a Wesleyan who met Philip wrote of his visit: "I did not thinkt that the proceedings of the doctor were at all calculated to lead to any good; he seemed to strengthen the idea that they had been unjustly dispossessed of it [the Neutral territory] and pledged himself to do all in his power to have it restored", and tried to negate Philip's impressions among the chiefs. According to Seton, the rift between the "pro-Xhosa" LMS and the pro-settler WMS began as a result of this visit.[307] Shortly after the visit Maqoma met Stockenstrom at the Kat River Settlement where his appeal for a location in the colony was denied and he was told the Rharabe would soon lose more land. He "now began to perceive the extent to which the Europeans wanted to conquer and absorb Xhosa territory" writes Stapleton."[308]

As colonial pressure on his land and cattle followed, Maqoma made a request to the GMS for a missionary to replace those at Balfour, though at the same time witch-hunting Christians at GMS's Burnshill mission.[309] It was the LMS, however, who would eventually provide a missionary for Maqoma. Philip's 1830 visit, followed up through trips by Read, strengthened the relations between the LMS and Maqoma. In particular, as Philip wrote, the "appointment [of Read] changed the face of things in the new Settlement among the Caffres and within the Colony. To the Hottentots at the Kat River it was like life from the dead, Macoma and his expelled Caffres were conciliated." This was inter alia because Read's name was "associated, among the Caffres, with the name of Vanderkemp."[310] Maqoma and Philip met again at the Kat River settlement in September 1832 when Maqoma, according to Philip, "begs hard for a missionary."[311] As a result Friedrich Kayser of the LMS installed himself at Knapp's Hill near to Maqoma's Great Place.[312]

In October 1833 Maqoma visited the Kat River settlement again. He told his entourage that "These Hottentots were once as oppressed and despised as we are, but see what the Word of God has done for them... I must see the same things in Caffreland as I now witness here." Maqoma had entered the colony without a pass, and was arrested at the settlement by soldiers and deposited across the colonial border. "From that point on", claims Stapleton, "Maqoma became the favorite of most of the missionary community" - and certainly of the LMS. "What our Society has been able to effect for the Hottentot nation" wrote Read, "gives us great influence with the Caffres, and they are looking up for assistance as formerly the poor Hottentots did, and in fact still do." Correspondingly, Maqoma became hated by British settlers.[313]

By 1833 Read's attitude to Maqoma's expulsion was totally altered. Western Xhosaland was so crowded, he wrote, that "they eat up one another and where Makomo [Maqoma], Eno and Congo will go I know not." Many Xhosa "were in a State of Starvation."[314] "The country had been taken from the Caffres in a very unsatisfactory way, and it was like occupying a stolen country - but God has been pleased to clear up the black Cloud by causing this settlement to prove a blessing to the caffres thus their minds have been reconciled to the Hottentots occupying this land... If the Hottentots had not occupied it the Boers would have taken possession of it, in which case nothing but war and bloodshed would have resulted; whilst the Hottentots generally have been on the most friendly terms with the chiefs and their people, so that they appear rather pleased than otherwise of having the Hottentots as their neighbours." He was perhaps over-optimistic. At the same time he wrote that " **[W]e have [become] acquainted with** their true situation with the colony and the abominable commando and Patrole system carried on" (my emphasis) - indicating that this knowledge was only recent.[315]

Colonel Wade took over from Cole as Acting Governor, in August 1833 and before the next governor arrived ordered the military on the frontier to push Maqoma (and his brother Tyali) further east. Maqoma withdrew, and then dictated a letter to Kayser who sent it to Philip: "As I and my people have been driven back over the Chumie River without being informed why - I should be glad to know from the Government what evil we have done? ... When shall I and my people be able to get rest... When my father was living he reigned over the whole land, from the Fish River to the Key... Yet both I and my brother Tyalie have almost no more country for our cattle to live in. Good Sir, I do not know why it is that so many Commandoes come into this country and take away our cattle and kill our people without sufficient reason. We do no injury to the Colony, and yet I remain under the foot of the English." As Stapleton comments, "Maqoma hoped that his influential missionary sympathisers could arrange the return of Rharhabe land before the radical elements of his kingdom decided to take up arms."[316]

Early in 1833 Stockenstrom took leave from his post as Commissioner-General to travel to Europe to try to persuade the Colonial Secretary to entrust him with the powers necessary to implement his frontier policy.[317] In January 1834 Governor Sir Benjamin D'Urban arrived, with instructions to enter alliances with the principal Xhosa chiefs.[318] Philip and Fairbairn at the same time were canvassing a policy of formal treaties with the chiefs, and placed high expectations in D'Urban. Indeed D'Urban at first appeared humanitarian: he wrote to Colonel Henry Somerset on the frontier that lack of land caused the Xhosa "to be Suffering within their own Borders."[319] At this time Philip would have had "no objection to the annexation of the Caffre country tomorrow, provided the people are not robbed of their cattle and deprived of their country" - but did not trust the colonial government to secure this.[320] Maqoma, allowed to pasture his cattle west of the Tyumie in January but driven across the river again in March, was infuriated.[321] In April Read reported that Maqoma was thinking of leaving the eastern Cape altogether. But Read presented to Maqoma and other chiefs the proposals of Fairbairn and Philip, to which they responded favourably.[322] Between May and August "relations between D'Urban and Philip were intimate", asserts Macmillan though they "never reached any real understanding."[323] In July, in the midst of the agitation against the Vagrancy Act, Read could claim that D'Urban "has we believe got all the necessary information... to enable him to judge of the evils flowing from the policy hitherto pursued towards the Caffres and a new era will we trust commence for the Caffres as well as for the Hottentots."[324]

Philip left Cape Town for the eastern frontier in August, expecting that D'Urban would soon follow him. He wrote to the LMS that "I am setting off [early] that I may met the Governor on the Kat River, to try, if possible, to introduce a new system... I am the only person in the Colony who know's the Governor's mind on this subject". D'Urban was later to confirm that he saw Philip as an official emissary, detailing "the nature of the agreements which I should be prepared to enter" with the chiefs.[325] Though Read was preoccupied with the Vagrancy Act, Philip saw Maqoma, Botomane, Kama, and Tshatshu in September, waited in vain for the Governor's arrival, and on October 27 decided to return to Cape Town, seeing Maqoma again in early November. On his way coastwards from the Kat River Settlement, Philip passed along the west ridge of the Tyhume basin, and "during a ride of perhaps twenty miles... did not find a single Kaffir kraal or hut which had not been burnt or otherwise destroyed by the military." Yet he still advised Maqoma to comply with official demands and trust in the Governor's coming to correct the situation."[326] Philip, who witnessed early trekking by Boers, was inclined to blame them for all the problems of the frontier, and was blind to the land-grabbing mentality developing among British settlers.[327] D'Urban had dallied in Cape Town to receive instructions concerning the regulation of slave-apprentices, and in the end did not get to the eastern frontier until 20th January 1835, by which time war had broken out.[328]

While Philip was still on the frontier, his Griquatown protégé Wright had accompanied the Griqua chief Andries Waterboer to Cape Town where, on 11 December 1834, D'Urban signed a treaty with him, which declared him a 'friend and ally' of the colony, required him to return fugitives and assist against external enemies, gave him a salary of £100 a year and arms and ammunition. Wright (secretly) accepted the post of government agent. The treaty did not specify any northward limit to Waterboer's territory.[329] Philip attempted to secure a similar treaty with Adam Kok of Philippolis, but when Kok visited the colony in 1835 D'Urban was preoccupied with the war with the Xhosa, and Kok died. It was not for some years that a treaty with his son Adam Kok III was signed.[330]

Chapter 7

Maqoma's war, or the war of Hintsa, 1834 to 1836[331]

The Sixth Frontier war, writes Peires, "burst beyond all previous constraints and charted new depths of slaughter and destruction... and it raged unabated for a full nine months."[332] For Crais the crisis was one internal to colonial society, because of labour demands and resistance to them, which was projected by the settlers onto the Xhosa.[333] On 21 December 1834, three weeks after the abolition of slavery in the colony, 12-15,000 Xhosa divided into small guerrilla units invaded the Cape colony along a 90-mile front from the Winterberg above the Kat River to the sea.[334] For the first time the Xhosa used substantial numbers of firearms. The war was sparked off by the wounding of Tyhali's brother, chief Xhoxho, by British troops. "I am a bushbuck", stated Maqoma to Kayser on 22 December, "for we chiefs are shot like them, and are no more esteemed as chiefs."[335] Maqoma's tactics were governed by the failure of Ngqika's attempts at collaboration with the colony, and equally the failure of the frontal assault of 1819.

Behind the war lay the Xhosa grievances of loss of land, expulsions from the Ceded territory, the patrol and reprisal system, and all the other oppressions and indignities heaped upon them. As Philip understated this to the LMS, Maqoma and the Xhosa 'felt that they had been unjustly treated in being deprived of the fine and beautiful country of the Kat River, but when they saw the Hottentots in possession of that country they had the magnanimity to forgive the injury they had sustained and to feel a satisfaction in seeing their beautiful country given to a people who had been as much oppressed as themselves, but the conduct of the frontier authorities in constantly harassing them and in refusing to allow them to occupy a small part of the country which has been taken from them of which we made no use were to them a constant source of irritation."[336]

For Keegan, the war and its consequences were a crossroads: "Was settler militarism to prevail in securing state support, or were countervailing priorities to stabilise the colonial society as a low-cost outpost of merchant capital? Was imperial power to be mobilised in pursuit of settler speculative profit and accumulation of resources, or were African peoples to be incorporated as free producers and consumers into the colonial embrace." In the end, for him, the motor of the war was "the fundamental compulsion which came in the 1830s and 1840s to dominate all others... to shake resources free for settler accumulation from the neighbouring African peoples. This project required... military intervention. Bellicosity, repeated war panics, exaggerated reports of Xhosa depredations and spoliation, became the stock in trade of settler propaganda. An imperial commitment to the militarisation of the frontier would mean expanded markets, potentially massive war profits, and the ultimate promise of accumulation through subjugation and dispossession of the indigenous African farmers."[337] Exerting pressure upon pressure on the Xhosa until they launched into war was one of the means, followed by putting pressure on the governor to exact retribution.

Hintsa of the Gcaleka Xhosa across the Kei had been consulted by the Ciskeian chiefs, and, at least clandestinely approved of the war.[338] Of the principal Xhosa chiefs west of the Kei only Pato of the Gqunukhwebe, among whom the Wesleyans had a station, stood aside. He was later to send forces to join the colonial side - although many of his men fought on the Xhosa side.[339] The Xhosa initially hoped that even the Khoi in the colony would join them.[340] In the event the 'coloureds' marched off to war, from the Kat River settlement and elsewhere, with the encouragement of Philip.[341] As Read said of those of the Kat River during the war: "As a political body they were moderate, and their attachment to the British government unquestionable."[342]

Stockenstrom praised their courage at the time and later: "when panic had seized the whole country, including many a stout warrior, when a detachment of the bravest troops in the world had to abandon such a fortress as Fort Wilshire then was, under cover of the night, and when the Kat River settlers had received positive and threatening orders to abandon their all and retreat upon Graham's Town, to save their lives - the latter despised community had indignantly set authority at defiance - sworn to die on the land so lately bestowed on them before they should cede an inch - kept their ground throughout the war, and thereby covered the Winterberg, East Riet River, Baviaans River and Somerset districts, which must otherwise have given way as far as jungles extend, whilst strong contingents were constantly drawn from these Hottentots to reinforce the army in the field." He singled out in particular the Gonaqua leader Andries Botha who "by his valour, activity, and zeal, gained such general approbation" that he was appointed field-cornet.[343] The Kat River settlement was however devastated by the war.[344]

The colony's defences were at first in disarray, and settler paranoia, according to Stapleton, exaggerated the extent of the Xhosa attacks.[345] On January 1 Maqoma put out feelers for peace but these were rejected by the brash Lieutenant Colonel Harry Smith, who, arriving on the frontier on the 6th, drafted all available Boers and British settlers and the Cape Mounted Rifles (as the

Cape Corps had been renamed in 1827) to join the some 1500 British soldiers then in the colony.[346] The Xhosa aimed at a limited war to force a negotiated settlement of their grievances. As Xhosa detachments retired with captured cattle across the Kei, they established their main positions in the Amatolas and the Fish river bush from where they pursued harassing guerilla tactics. Colonial forces made an initial unsuccessful attempt to clear the Fish River bush followed by unsuccessful invasion of the Amatolas.[347] Thereafter (in April) Smith and D'Urban led a British army for the first time across the Kei, which declared war on Hintsa and seized many cattle. Eventually, after coming voluntarily to the British, Hintsa was taken prisoner and on 11 May murdered when trying to escape and his body mutilated - an act which the Xhosa have never forgotten.[348]

D'Urban arrived in Grahamstown on 20 January. His views had been strongly modified there by the British settler lobby led by Robert Godlonton of the *Grahamstown Journal* - he became, in Keegan's phrase, a "rogue governor".[349] Many prominent settlers (as well as Wesleyan missionaries) attached themselves to D'Urban as advisers.[350] When Fairbairn, Philip and Read denounced the war, Godlonton accused them of fomenting it, and the government banished Read to Bethelsdorp for its duration. John Centlivres Chase of Port Elizabeth, an 1820 settler who had become a pioneer trader beyond the Orange, also wrote three pamphlets attacking Philip and Fairbairn between 1834 and 1836.[351] "It was of the greatest importance to them [the settlers] that the Xhosa be seen as bloody savages who had to be subjugated and displaced before civilisation could triumph."[352] D'Urban "became convinced that he had been entirely misled by Philip about the situation on the frontier and that the war was due not to Somerset's police measures, but to a conspiracy of the chiefs, with Hintsa the ringleader."[353] In January 1835, explaining the war to Buxton, Philip wrote: "The frontier colonists have long set their hearts upon Caffreland - they already calculate upon having it given them as sheep-farms and the general cry is 'blood! Blood!'"[354]

On May 10th, still in Hintsa's territory, D'Urban, publicly blaming the Xhosa for the war, declared the 'ceded territory' the district of Victoria and annexed Xhosa territory between the Fish and the Kei as Queen Adelaide Province, and simultaneously described the Xhosa as "treacherous and irreclaimable savages." He demanded the expulsion of all Ciskeian Xhosa across the Kei, out of the new province. But Maqoma and the other chiefs immediately rejected this, and British forces could not achieve it against Xhosa resistance.[355] They continued their scorched earth tactics, destroying homes, grainstocks, crops, and stock, ensuring that the Xhosa were unable to plant new crops and began to face starvation. Meanwhile in Britain, Buxton's Select Committee on Aborigines (originally recommended by Philip, but with its terms of reference broadened from South Africa to consider indigenous peoples throughout the Empire) started its hearings on 31 July - in an atmosphere of atonement for the evils Britain had committed against aboriginal inhabitants 'by introducing the blessings of civilisation and Christianity".[356] The Commission was eventually to prove influential on events on the eastern frontier.

In August, Maqoma again rejected British terms to deny him the Amatolas. The next month, however, D'Urban abandoned his May policy. A peace agreement signed by D'Urban and chiefs on 17th September left the Xhosa within Queen Adelaide Province as subjects of the crown with resident agents.[357] The Wesleyan missionaries had played a part in brokering the peace.[358]. Maqoma had shown himself to be a skilled tactician. Even though against British power the Ngqika had been driven back once again, they retained land in the Ciskei, including their defences in the Amatolas. "Aristocratic control over Xhosa commoners, cattle and land was maintained" However, increasingly there was a loss of Xhosa commoners to labour in the colony.[359]

In what Keegan characterises as "the single most important consequence of the war", some 16,000-17,000 'Mfengu' were resettled from Hintsa's territory to the Fort Peddie area and made British subjects, to act as frontier buffers against the entry of the Xhosa to the Fish River bush. Ultimately they were drafted into the colonial forces in the later stages of this war.[360] They were also intended to provide a labour supply to the colonists, and, indeed, their introduction brought a downturn in wages.[361] (Stapleton maintains that from the time of their establishment on the frontier, the 'Fingo camps' were a pole of attraction for nearby Xhosa.)[362] For the next forty years, the Mfengu performed these roles admirably - and a core of them became successful peasants and the vanguard of a new African elite.[363] As a part of Cobbing's re-evaluation of the mfecane there is considerable dispute about the nature of the 'Mfengu' For Webster the term is a pure colonial construct, used to disguise the forced removal of Xhosa into the colony as labourers. In a conspiracy by the Wesleyan missionary at Butterworth, John Ayliff, with the government, the move of the Mfengu was falsely presented as the voluntary exodus of peoples from the Shakan wars who had sought refuge with Hintsa's Gcaleka, become a 'tribe' and been oppressed by them. There is however considerable evidence that at least some of the Mfengu were refugees from Natal, and the idea of a conspiracy has been strongly challenged.[364] What is certainly the case is that the Mfengu, 'liberated from slavery among the Xhosa' and becoming 'civilised' under British rule were set ideologically against the resistant and barbarous Xhosa, who had to be dominated to be reformed.[365]

Of Queen Adelaide Province D'Urban wrote to Colonel Hare: "The whole is an experiment - It has never been tried before and we must give it a fair trial

- If it fails - it is vain for the future to talk of any other Relation with these people [the Xhosa] than the Bayonet's point."[366] Smith declared that he viewed the Xhosa as "irreclaimable savages... whose extermination would be a blessing" - though were he compelled to deal with them, it would be "for their information, improvement, and consequent happiness."[367] As well as 18, 500 Mfengu, there were 56,000 Ngqika, 9200 Ndlambe, and 7500 Gqunukhwebe to be ruled as British subjects.[368] D'Urban hoped that the "system of clanship... will be at once broken up and its spirit and feeling will be rapidly subdued and forgotten, as the power of the Chiefs shall be seen to have ceased and passed away, and the whole will be brought under the power of the several Colonial laws".[369] Colonel Harry Smith was appointed Civil Commissioner. He placed the tribes in defined 'locations', gave the chiefs the title of magistrates - with Maqoma as 'Chief Magistrate' - and inteded to teach them to administer English law and live off salaries rather than fines. Witchcraft executions were banned. The territory was to be filled with schools, missionaries and trade commodities to 'civilise' the Xhosa. A new military headquarters was established at King Williams Town.[370]

Wesleyan and GMS missionaries were appointed, together with secular officials, as commissioners to the tribes they had their stations in - a precedent established with John Ayliff among the Mfengu in July 1835 and Theophilus Shepstone among the Gkunukwebe.[371] By June 1836, with characteristic self-glorification, Smith was writing: "everyone kisses my hand and greets me, not by outward show but inwardly, with his heart and voice, as his *Inkosi Inkulu*... and never was the authority of the Normans more thoroughly established over the Saxons, than the British over this mass of human beings from the Keiskama to the Umzimvooboo; for it is not only on this side of the Kye but beyond it that I am looked up to as the Great Chief".[372] However, as Keegan points out, the chiefs were not yet conquered: Smith's pipe-dreams were illusory.[373] Yet the results of the war were widespread dispossession and proletarianisation. In 1836 an LMS missionary, surveying the area around Maqoma's Great Place, wrote: "The finest valleys and rich pastures which were formerly numbered with kraals and cattle are now empty and whol[l]y without them...And the Kaffers are now very much seeking work to get food."[374] "At some point in the 1830s", Peires writes, "Xhosaland became unable to provide for its population"[375]

Settler identity, it has been argued, had already crystallised into 'Othering' the Xhosa before the war. For Alan Lester, however, it was predominantly the experience of the war and the debates to which it gave rise, "which prompted most of the settlers to close ranks and to forge an unprecedentedly clear and embattled political identity." Certainly attitudes hardened. William Shaw, the Wesleyan missionary, away in Britain during the war, returned to find "a great revolution in the sentiments of the British settlers in reference to the Caffre race". Even Harry Smith noted "a spirit pervading all classes of society... to teach everyone to view and treat the Kafir as a beast".[376] British settlers had welcomed the May settlement, but regarded the September peace as a retreat by D'Urban and objected to 'locations' of blacks in territory they coveted for their growing herds of sheep. A prominent settler, T. Holden Bowker, who had first seen the land beyond the Keiskamma during the war, said it would "make excellent sheep farms" and was "far too good for such a race of runaways as the Kaffirs"[377] D'Urban reassured the settlers that "large tracts are still left vacant for the occupation and speculations of Europeans"[378] He intended to sell the territory to settlers and land speculators to recover the expenses of the war. Godlonton and Smith provided the ideological justification: the Xhosa were recent usurpers from the Khoi and the Boers, had been possessors by right of conquest only and could be ejected by the same right. It was to become a commonplace idea among the settlers.[379] By mid-1835 "the whole settler agenda seemed set fair to materialise": it seemed " a turning-point had arrived and humanitarianism was a beaten force."[380]

In fact Buxton and the secretary of the LMS, fed with numerous letters from Philip, had been putting pressure on the liberal Colonial Secretary, Lord Glenelg, a sympathetic "scion of an evangelical family" who had come to office in April with the Whig Melbourne government.[381] The opening of the hearings of Buxton's Select Committee on Aborigines in late July allowed Stockenstrom, already in Europe, to testify to it and give damaging evidence against D'Urban's and previous policies. Philip left for Britain early in 1836, intending to take Maqoma with him. "If Macomo can see the state and power of the King of England," he wrote, "he would never afterwards think himself degraded by giving up his independence to become a British subject, and the treatment he would meet with in England would firmly attach him for ever to our own interests."[382] For some reason, however, Maqoma did not go and instead with Philip went Andries Stoffel from the Kat River settlement, and Jan Tshatshu, the Christian Xhosa chief as well as James Read (who arrived later) and his son. They all testified to the Buxton Commitee, as did more than forty others.[383] All of them gained confidence, and a faith in the British people, through their visit. While there Read wrote: "In Africa we appear half-devils; here people treat us as half-angels."[384]

Under the influence of the Committee, on 26 December 1835 Glenelg, the Colonial secretary, sent a dispatch ordering the retrocession to the Xhosa of Queen Adelaide Province (unless D'Urban could justify his actions).[385] This arrived at the Cape on 21 March 1836, though Glenelg had to send another dispatch in August to insist it should be implemented. Glenelg's dispatch was the "pivotal event of the nineteenth century".[386] It condemned the entire policy conducted towards Xhosa since 1811, the unsatisfactory nature of the 1819 'treaty' with Ngqika, and the injustices of the commando system. It insisted it had been wrong to deprive the Xhosa of land between the Fish and Keiskamma. In "the conduct which was pursued towards the Caffre nation by the colonists, and the public authorities of the colony, through a long series of years... the Caffres had ample justification of the war into which they rushed with such fatal imprudence... The extension of His Majesty's dominions in that quarter of the globe, by conquest or cession, is diligently and anxiously to be avoided."[387] This was to be the high point of humanitarian achievement in South Africa - and it was also a big victory for the Xhosa.[388] Read wrote exultantly: "What will Godlonton etc now say? They will surely be confounded. Everything is going as we could wish it", and, later "our cause and that of the Native tribes has been hastened by the Caffre war and our coming to England, 50 years."[389] Read's faith in a benevolent Britain was confirmed. Yet, echoing through the words of Glenelg and, behind him, of Buxton and Philip, were the voice and the arguments of the absent Maqoma.

Philip, however, regarded retrocession of Queen Adelaide Province as a second-best solution. In May 1835 he had written that he "did not object to any of the countries beyond us becoming part of the Colony, provided the natives have their land secured to them and are governed as the Hindus are": it was the system of "extermination" - starting with colonisation of indigenous lands by white settlers, that he opposed.[390] Though Buxton and Ellis in London believed that Philip favoured retrocession, it was this "Indian model" of annexation that he supported - indeed, "up to the tropics".[391] The war of 1834-5, he told the Aborigines Committee, had convinced him that the Xhosa would not "ultimately be exterminated", as were the San or the indigenous people of Australia. However, was the policy of land expropriation to be continued, he feared that "the name of the Cape of Good Hope" might be "blot[ted] out... from the list of British colonies." On the other hand a policy administered by an "able governor" might "in twelve years, influence the continent of Africa as far as the tropic; influence it for good, make every tribe to know its limits; to be content with its own, to respect its neighbours, and to drink with eagerness from the fountains of our religion, civil policy, and science."[392]

Between Philip and the LMS on the one hand and the Wesleyans on the other, sharp and rancorous exchanges had broken out in the course of the war, initiated by an address of loyal support submitted by the Wesleyans to D'Urban in June 1835. In this they agreed with D'Urban and the settlers - in total contrast to the LMS view - that the Xhosa were to blame for the war, stated that the settlers has only desired the "welfare and prosperity" and that the war had been conducted "in accordance with the principles of justice and mercy."[393] Philip regarded the letter as sycophantic and responded that he had regarded the Wesleyans "for some years past as the eulogists of the Commando system and the servile tools of the men who are the most deeply stained with the blood of the Caffers", and that their claims were totally false.[394] On 13 June Fairbairn's *Advertiser* attacked the Wesleyan William Shrewsbury for a letter he had written in January to Smith, with proposals on frontier policy, including the idea that chiefs who had invaded the colony should lose their chieftainships, and the people their lands, that 'murderers' should be executed on the spot - a letter which even a sympathetic biographer regarded as "brusque, and even harsh."[395] Shrewsbury was then chief local officer of the Wesleyans, acting for William Shaw who was in Britain. His letter was passed by the Colonial Office to the Wesleyans in Britain, who disavowed it, expressing their "deepest regret and disapprobation" at Shrewsbury's views.[396] Earlier in his life Shrewsbury had been hounded out of Barbados by slaveowners because of his abolitionism. But now abolitionism was not incompatible with a standpoint of 'civilising through conquest.'

The exchanges between the LMS and WMS resulted in a vigorous correspondence eventually published by Shaw as A *Defence of the Wesleyan Missionaries*.[397] In the same year the Wesleyan William Boyce published his fiercely pro-colonist *Notes on South African affairs from 1834 to 1838*.[398] On Boyce's book, Read wrote: "There is a general feeling against Boyce's book by all our missionaries and the Scotch Brethren. Before the war Boyce said to Brownlee, 'Nothing can be done with the Caffres till all their cattle are taken from them and the half of the nation be hung.'"[399] Paradoxically, the pro-colonist Wesleyans also supported the claims of the Gqunukhwebe to the Zuurveld, and blamed the LMS for the expulsion of Maqomo from the Kat River area. Settled as they were, among the weaker chiefs, both in Xhosaland and in Transorangia, they could perhaps be accused of playing the tactics of divide in order to rule. In addition, they published the first Xhosa periodical, a newspaper titled *Umshumayeli wendaba*, which appeared fifteen times between July 1837 and April 1841.[400]

Nor was a pro-D'Urban and therefore pro-colonist view confined to the Wesleyans. In September 1835 the Glasgow missionary James Laing wrote in his journal: "The Governor has made the most ample provision for [Xhosa] settlement in the new province [Queen Adelaide] ... Few governors have done so much for the native tribes as Sir Benjamin D'Urban... I hope and pray that these humane but just deeds will be attended with the happiest results."[401]

Seton has written an account of the Wesleyan side of these exchanges, presenting a picture of the differing views among them showing, for example, that some, just like the LMS's John Philip, opposed land grants to settlers.[402] He nevertheless concludes that: "What is indisputable is that the Methodists emerged as supporters of D'Urban's policy while their opponents [the LMS] claimed to be the Xhosa's friends. As is so often the case, neither judgment is completely true though each contains truth."[403] Other historians have also commented on the moral authority given to settler views by the Wesleyan missionaries, who wrapped their support in the discourse of 'civilisation'.[404]

Chapter 8

The treaty period 1836 to 1844

Sir Andries Stockenstrom (then in Europe) was appointed Lieutenant-Governor of the Eastern Cape by Glenelg, and returned to Cape Town on 25 July 1836 with a policy of signing treaties with the Xhosa chiefs as a substitute for the patrol and reprisal system. Treaties were signed in December. The whole of the 'ceded' territory was restored to the Xhosa, making the Fish and Kat rivers the boundary. Xhosa were permitted to return to the area between the Fish and the Keiskamma, though the British insisted that the Mfengu remain in their settlements in the 'ceded' territory - where they would be challenged and partly ousted by the returning Maqoma, as well as by Pato.[405] Queen Adelaide Province was formally de-annexed on 2 February 1837.[406] Stockenstrom also (in his common model with Philip) intended to settle "as dense a population as possible... in villages in the territory between the said boundary and the Kat and Fish Rivers, upon the same principle as the new Hottentot settlements, the advantages of which were demonstrated during the late contest", and made some initial attempts to do so.[407]

The treaty system, writes Peires, "never had a chance. Trade, missionary activity and labour migration had already bound the Xhosa inextricably to the Cape Colony."[408] At any rate the land-hungry British settlers, their appetites whetted by D'Urban's annexation in May 1835 and extremely frustrated by the retrocession, were determined that the treaty system should not succeed. The settlers gained strength from the fact that the humanitarian-merchant alliance which had characterised the 1820s had begun to break up - precisely on the issue of policy towards the Xhosa. The Cape Town merchant elite and Afrikaner professional and business class (save, at first, for Fairbairn) were now beginning to see more opportunities in colonial capitalism built on racial exploitation than in an independent brown and black peasant-artisan economy. Cape Town capital was flowing eastward into the new wool-based economy. Slave abolition hastened this shift in the centre of gravity to the Eastern Cape: money paid as compensation to indebted slaveowners passed to merchants who used it to promote the wool economy. Significantly, the first private commercial bank was established in 1837.

The period after the war was one of prosperity, as Cape wool production increased in response to the demand created by the expanding textile industry in Britian. Governer Sir George Thomas Napier wrote in 1841 that "No merchant of any importance in Grahamstown has not within the last few years invested considerable sums of money in the purchase of farms along the immediate border, and in stocking these farms with sheep."[409] Already nearly 1 million pounds (lb) at the end of 1830s, wool production was 5.5 million pounds (lb) a decade later, dominated by a small number of wealthy farmers.[410] Wool production, moreover, as Crais has pointed out, was more labour intensive than earlier forms of agricultural production, and created a huge demand for labour.[411]

The climate was hardly conducive to welcoming Stockenstrom. From before his return, the settlers led by Godlonton mobilised against him, and after he returned they succeeded in bringing his administration to a virtual standstill. "The Stockenstrom years", writes Le Cordeur, "were the most tempestuous in the history of eastern Cape politics."[412] Stockenstrom and D'Urban clashed on almost everything: frontier policy, the Mfengu, Khoi locations, the appointment of magistrates. D'Urban, discredited in London, tried all means to undermine Stockenstrom with the British government. The final straw was the attempt by leading settlers to pin a charge of murder on him from 1813, when he had shot a young black on commando. Stockenstrom sued the Civil Commissioner of Grahamstown and lost, causing the celebratory all-night illumination of houses in towns throughout the Eastern Cape. There followed an official enquiry which exonerated Stockenstrom of the charge, but he went to Britain in mid-1838 to clear his name with the colonial office.

Read wrote at this time that Stockenstrom: "had established the best system we had ever had on the frontier. He has been proof against all bribes or insinuations. He has gained the good will and confidence of the Caffre chiefs who very reluctantly granted consent to his leaving even for a time... The Hottentots were very much alarmed when they heard that the Lieutenant Governor was going to leave."[413] Arriving back in South Africa in mid-1838, Philip complained to the LMS: "I do not always look at the bright side of things more than you do yourself, and my views were never so gloomy with respect to the colony as they have been since my late return to it. We have through mercy gained victory after victory, and we seem at this moment as far from the end of our warfare as we were. We all move to the end of our journey, but one difficulty is no sooner overcome than another rises, and the last appears more unmanageable than the first."[414] After visiting the Xhosa frontier later in the year Philip wrote that all the chiefs were anxious for the return of Stockenstrom, and if he did not, there was the danger of another war.[415]

While in Britain, however, Stockenstrom was relieved of his post by Glenelg's successor in 1839 because he was regarded as too controversial, and awarded a baronetcy in compensation. In the meantime Colonel John Hare had been installed as acting lieutenant governor in August 1838. He nominally supported the treaty system, and at first reported to the governor on the falsification of the frontier situation by the settler camp. Formally, the system remained, with minor modifications by Governor Napier in January 1841, but the removal of Stockenstrom and its progressively desultory administration by Hare essentially defeated it.[416]

From about 1834 some of the Boers who opposed the reforms of the 1820s began to trek out of the colony to preserve their old practices and seek new opportunities beyond the colonial boundaries. This movement (the 'Great Trek') reached its peak in 1836. Settler propaganda at the time blamed the Trek on Glenelg's decision for retrocession of Queen Adelaide Province. D'Urban even blamed the Trek on Stockenstrom. Stockenstrom was scornful - the trekkers, he declared, were "perfectly indifferent" about the Province, and were moving off "long before the Glenelg Treaties had been heard of."[417] Stockenstrom had previously dismissed as a field commandant, Piet Retief, who became a Trek leader. But Stockenstrom was in the 1840s to become a popular leader of the Boers who remained in the colony, and even at this time, maintains Keegan, he was popular: "Reportedly, great affection was evinced by the mass of Boers on his return to the eastern Cape as lieutenant-governor in 1836, in the face of massive propaganda from British settler sources opposed to his appointment."[418] Of Retief Stockenstrom said scornfully, "I might indeed have soothed Retief and his associates with the promise that the slaves should not be set free; that the 50th ordinance should be repealed; that Kaffraria should be divided amongst the colonists, the missionaries hanged, and the Blacks extirpated."[419] However, for Keegan, these were not the aims of most frontier Boers.

Recent historiography sees the cause of the Trek as lying in the political revolution of the 1820s - Ordinance 50, the abolition of slavery, Anglicisation, etc. Since their arrival and crushing of frontier rebellions, the British had successively demolished most of the institutions of 18th century Boer society. Writers such as Keegan portray the sense of resentment, powerlessness, bewilderment and alienation felt by many Boers because of the breakdown of their personal rule over their 'servants'. At the same time Keegan also emphasises the possible frustration of the Trek leaders as a levelled-down elite still anxious for accumulation, and for exploring the frontiers of trade and opportunity - though the Boers, unlike British settlers, were not generally agitating for military expansion against the Xhosa. While the early treks were inclined to break ties with Britain, those who left from 1836 continued to cling to colonial trade links: they were not fleeing but carrying the colonial nexus into the interior. Later Afrikaner nationalist ideologists depicted the Trek - and the depiction is frozen into the friezes of the Voortrekker Monument -- as a heroic flight from British oppression, taking the ideals of Christian civilisation into a barbarous and unknown interior, and helping to forge the Afrikaner nation. But as Keegan writes, a "self-conscious sense of national mission" was "absent." Moreover most of the territory into which the Trekkers moved - Transorangia and Natal - was already well-known to white traders and missionaries. Mercantile and British settler agitation around Natal as a possible colony of settlement "reached a peak on the eve of the Boer emigration" and "new heights" during and after the 1834-5 war.[420] The propaganda of the *Graham's Town Journal*, on Philip's assessment at the time as well as for Keegan, contributed greatly to the Trek.[421]

Paradoxically, the real effects of emancipation came in 1838, when the Trek was already over. 25, 000 slaves were freed and fled from the farms - to vacant land, to missions, northwards to the Griqua, and above all into town - joining the already-'emancipated' Khoi. Broken slave families were reconstructed with men as head, and ex-slave women and children were largely withdrawn from the labour market. On farms over this period and after, a whole variety of social relations developed. Many people became labour-tenants. By the 1840s a 'bifurcated division of labour' had developed - on the one hand permanent workers and on the other seasonal workers with a resident base outside the farm, a division which has persisted to the present.[422] "The most obvious change in productive relations on the land... was the shift to short-term, task, or daily work arrangements - although the limited availability of land for independent existence hardly provided much scope for discretion in entering such arrangements."[423] By the early 1840s the local state, under the control of settlers, was attempting to dispossess squatter and peasant communities. Rural resistance, particularly of squatters and peasants, increased from this time, according to Crais. Indeed, 'squatting' itself was a rejection of primitive accumulation and colonisation. Prevalent was the theft of livestock. "Theft, as Engels put it, the 'most primitive form of protest', constituted a basic rejection of settler capitalism."[424]

British intervention north of the Orange in the 1840s was, once again, partly pioneered by Philip. Mainly in the first part of 1842, he and Read (sr) toured Transorangia. Boers in Transorangia were encroaching more insistently on the territory of the Philippolis - while Griqua at Griquatown and Philippolis had been attempting to consolidate their hegemony over the southern Sotho-Tswana.

Since the signing of the treaty between Waterboer and the colony in 1834 the Griqua had been attempting to expand the range and depth of their authority in Transorangia. Wright, their missionary, justified this in terms of the military capabilities and duties of the Griqua, allowing them to be dependent on the agricultural production of Sotho-Tswana peoples.[425] This expansionism was accompanied by a "Griqua nationalism" not dissimilar to that displayed at Kat River in 1834. "Look at the American nation", railed a Griqua at an unfriendly missionary in 1838, "what a powerful (or able) people they are and if our first teachers had done their duty, we should have been as advanced in civilisation and knowledge as they... but now we have able teachers who teach us and we also are now able to teach the inhabitants of the whole country including the Bechuana tribes."[426] Those imbued with this nationalism at Griquatown and stations in the Colony were of a similar type - 'native agents.' There is some evidence that the desire for the removal of missionaries was being urged on the Griqua from the Kat River.[427]

Robert Moffat, the LMS missionary at Kuruman among the Tlhaping had from soon after his arrival in 1817 opposed the van der Kemp/Read idea of 'baptism by profession' and the 'native agency' associated with it. As Read complained in 1840: "Few of the Brethren think as we do respecting Native Agency in any way and I fear the feeling respecting colour is retrograding. With us we are pushing on to raise the people in the scale of society; others are for leaving them behind or pushing them back... Tis a thousand pities that by conversion Hottentots and others do not get white skins and long hair. I think wigs would be a good substitute for the last, but for the first there is no remedy. I think the Hottentots should get a number of peruke-makers out immediately. What the missionaries were concerned about was the difficulty and danger of bring[ing] them to a state of equality!!"[428]

Moffat now took the lead among non-Griqua Town missionaries in Transorangia in opposing Griqua expansionism through the 'native agency'.[429] By 1840 Moffat was in Britain, trying to get Philip removed as superintendent of the LMS mission and his replacement by an area-based committee system. Read commented that,"I fear there is a majority of our Brethren here who are of the same feelings and who would rejoice to see him home tomorrow. I am not one of those, nor James either... I would not lose him for any advantages the cause would gain (of which I am not sanguine) by our having the affairs in our own hands."[430] When on tour with Philip in 1842 - and a part of the reason for the tour was to examine Moffat's complaints about Griqua behaviour - Read took care to extol the LMS work at Griqua Town: "The French missionaries are doing great things but Wright is overdoing all, and that with Native Agents. Perhaps in the whole range of modern missions there is nothing to exceed, if any thing to equal, the work carrying on under the eye of the Brethren at Griqua Town, both as to the extent and genuineness of the work."[431]

Philip's answer to the problems of Griqualand - Boer encroachment at Philippolis and the Griqua-Sotho-Tswana problems - was for the replacement of treaties by annexation of Griqualand - and Moshoeshoe's territory. The Lesotho kingdom was strategically situated between the Boers in Natal and in Transorangia, was the strongest power in the area, and as Philip realised, "held the key to the future of Transorangia."[432] Instead Governor Napier in 1842 issued a proclamation warning the Boers not to molest 'native tribes' or take their lands, and in 1843 treaties were signed with Adam Kok III at Philippolis and with Moshoeshoe.⁴³³

Under pressure of local mercantile and land-speculative interests publicised as usual by Godlonton, the 'destabilising' effects of Boer rule as the Republic of Natalia were used to justify the annexation of Natal by Britain in 1842. "Land speculation by merchant interests on a massive scale followed" (Keegan). Many Boers moved back to the highveld during the 1840s. Meanwhile the new colony strengthened its trade links with the Cape colony along the land route through Xhosaland to Grahams' Town. As in the eastern Cape, settlers and Wesleyans established a special relationship, including in the promotion of immigration to the new colony.⁴³⁴ Theophilus Shepstone, son of a Wesleyan missionary and 1820 settler, who had been an interpreter in the public service since 1835, in 1839 had replaced Bowker as agent to the Mfengu, and assumed the role of 'paramount chief' in 1841.⁴³⁵ In 1846 he was appointed 'diplomatic agent to the native tribes' in Natal and, as Keegan comments, was compelled to recognise existing settlement realities when he 'segregated' the Africans in 1846/1847.⁴³⁶

Retrocession of Queen Adelaide Province allowed Maqoma to reclaim his lands on the east bank of the lower Kat River, establishing his own kraal near the colony at the junction of the Kat and Blinkwater rivers. Meeting Governor Napier in May 1838, however, Maqoma complained "with great force and pertinacity" that the lands around the upper Kat River (where 'coloureds' were settled), had not been returned to him. Despite settler instigations against him, he also made serious attempts to co-operate with the colony, including strenuously implementing the terms of the treaties until 1844. In January 1839 he took a case of theft of his horse by a settler to the court in Grahamstown, and was delighted to win. While in general the Xhosa turned away from the missions at this time, Maqoma preserved his relations with the LMS, sending two of his young children to be cared for by the mission.⁴³⁷

Initially it had been the LMS missionary Kayser who had re-established himself with Maqoma, at the old station of Knapp's Hope. While in Britain, however, Read had met the young Henry Calderwood, about to enter LMS work in South Africa, and been very impressed with him. From Cape Town Read wrote to Bethelsdorp on his return of "a Mr Calderwood, a Presbyterian but [an] excellent man, almost a radical. The Grahams' Town people will not like him. He has made himself acquainted with the whole of our and the Caffre affairs."⁴³⁸ Later he commented that Calderwood "will soon be stinking as much as Dr Philip and myself, for he is most determined."⁴³⁹ Calderwood was deployed to Blinkwater (previously a Kat River out-station, and very close to Maqoma's kraal) on the Kat River, and personally introduced to the chief by Read.⁴⁴⁰ Why was Calderwood appointed to this key post, rather than Read himself? The available evidence does not answer this question. Instead of strengthening his own relationship with Maqoma, the modest Read remained at the Kat River, living in the same 'wattle and daub' house to which he had moved in 1830, and devoted his energies rather in establishing new stations further north, among the San and the Thembu.[441]

The decision to send Calderwood was a fateful one. Calderwood was rapidly to fall out with Maqoma - and with the Philip/Read perception of the situation on the frontier. In an early letter from the station he referred to an incident when he had remonstrated with Maqoma for ordering his wife to bury alive a baby she had given birth to from an adulterous affair.[442] "I have been involved in much trouble with him and at one time I began to think that I should be compelled to leave Cafferland... I am now truly thankful to be able to say that Maqomo appears now to be perfectly convinced that I am his real friend and he appears now to have implicit confidence in me." He referred to Maqoma giving "testimony of his confidence in the teachers of the word of God and his estimation of the great truths he was hearing from day to day" in a public meeting with Hare. "By the way I may here state that when I was striving with Maqomo about his sins, a Wesleyan Missionary who knew of it, came and offered his services. Maqomo nobly said 'My people may do as they please but I will hear my own Teacher.'"[443] It was the last praise he would bestow on Maqoma.

In July 1840 Maqoma reluctantly relinquished his position as regent, and the club-footed and young Sandile was installed as paramount of those now termed the Ngqika.[444] In May 1841 Calderwood could write, "As to Maqomo I do not think I can say anything favourable except that he still attends the Chapel on the Sabbath... His public word is with us. His character, and I sometimes fear his private word is against us", and took issue with his drinking 'addiction'.[445] Maqoma's penchant for alcohol was remarked on frequently at the time, and was used to demean him by both settlers and, later, Harry Smith, though Stapleton defends him at length against the charge.[446] By December relations between Maqoma and Calderwood were so bad that the latter had left his station and gone to Cape Town. Read Jr, at Blinkwater in his place, reported that Maqoma "says there is not one of the Caffreland missionaries he would like to have here if I do not remain excepting Mr Laing" of the GMS.[447] Calderwood, much to Maqoma's annoyance, had 'abducted' Maqoma's sister and "one of his concubines" as his domestic servants. Read jr was at Blinkwater in his place. While Calderwood was in Cape Town, moreover, he published an article in which he complained that the condition of the Kat River 'coloureds' was 'degraded' and that they had a 'low state of mental cultivation.' Also attempting to poison relations between Maqoma and the Reads, Calderwood was failing to live up to Read's initial expectations of him.[448]

Almost a year later, however, Calderwood returned, on the urging of the LMS directors. In the meantime a 'smelling-out' intrigue in 1842 against Suthu,

Sandile's mother had been instigated by Maqoma with the intention of discrediting Sandile which was however foiled by colonial intervention.[449] In March 1843 Calderwood wrote: "As to Macomo I am deeply grieved that I can say so little that is good of him. About 6 months before our return from Cape Town he had moved to the immediate vicinity of Fort Beaufort for the sake of intoxicating drink... since, he affects to be angry with me. I shall do everything I can consistently do, if not to reclaim him, at least to keep on good terms for the sake of the poor people."[450] Of missionary attitudes to him, Read sr commented in the same month:"Some have become very distant... and Calderwood tries to keep up friendship, but is not open and free. They are watching for my halting."[451]

Although initially Calderwood had opposed the removal of Philip, by now he was firmly in the anti-Philip/Read camp.[452] Not only was he critical of the 'coloureds' at mission stations but was remarking on the "still very low intelligence among the Caffers".[453] In 1840 he took issue with an LMS missionary allegedly baptising 'on profession' - the standpoint which Moffat opposed.[454] In 1843 Moffat returned to South Africa and, travelling to the Kuruman via the Eastern Cape, in June summoned a meeting to establish a regional "Cafferland" LMS committee. Read commented: "Moffat is, I suppose, to be the leader on the opposite side of the Great River, and Calderwood I suppose on this."[455] By June Dr Philip had had enough, and offered his resignation to the directors of the LMS. Of Moffat and the native agency Read wrote: "I suppose Saul of Tarsus was not more enraged against the Christians than he [Moffat] is against Dr Philip and myself ...I never took any party, but now shall declare myself to be an Independent or Congregationalist, as I perceive the object is not to have Native Agents or native churches to have a voice in anything."[456]

Particularly after the war, the situation of 'coloured' mission stations in the colony deteriorated, with entire families going out to labour. In 1838 Bethelsdorp inhabitants were unable to pay taxes for the first time.[457] Hankey was viewed in the 1840s as the model mission to succeed Bethelsdorp.[458] By the 1840s the fertile area of the Kat River settlement (very suitable for sheep) was surrounded by the farms of wealthy settlers, with whom there were occasional flare-ups.[459] At the same time, "from 1839 to 1846... fixed as well as moveable property was greatly accumulated in Kat River" - the fixed property valued at £36,000 to £40,000, despite the fact that Khoi had little access to credit.[460] In 1842 it had some 4876 inhabitants, and was quite diversified by wealth and descent, particularly reflected in the prevalence of clientship relations. Those dispossessed by conquest or the growth of capitalist agriculture from all over the Eastern Cape flocked to the area. After the 1834-1835 war, D'Urban granted a part of the Blinkwater to Hermanus Matroos, son of a deserted slave and a Xhosa woman, who now had a mixed ethnic following, largely Gqunukhwebe. Over time the Blinkwater became a 'halfway house between the Colony and Kaffirland" - to which Xhosa women came to return with maize to Xhosaland. Government officials began to try to enforce the signs of 'civilisation': stone or brick houses, fencing, and the planting of trees. Aspirations to 'respectability' among the residents coexisted with a certain simmering rebelliousness among the poor, who were growing increasingly destitute. "Some prayed to a Christian god, some struggled to reproduce the social and cultural world of the *umzi*, others occupied a reality where Christ and the ancestors and the capitalist market and pre-capitalist exchange all had their increasingly uncomfortable place."[461]

What was the character of Khoi-Xhosa relations at this time? Calderwood, writing later of the early 1840s, claimed it "was then a fashion with the Hottentots to despise the Caffre, while the Caffre in his turn looked upon the Hottentot with the most sovereign contempt."[462] Read, in contrast, remarked with pleasure at the time how at the Kat River settlement, despite the losses of the war, he had not "heard a single expression of revenge against the Caffres"[463] Indeed the settlement was an area of intermingling of all the peoples of the Eastern Cape (save whites), including Maqoma. Thus are our views of Khoi-Xhosa relations filtered through the eyes of missionaries with different standpoints on colonisation.

Chapter 9
The road to war, 1844 to 1846

The 1840s saw a high-point of British settler power in the eastern Cape, driven by wool production for export. The decade "witnessed both an enlargement of the state and a massive capitalisation of settler agriculture."[464] By 1851 Fairbairn could report that "A large proportion of the money in Cape Town is derived from mortgages on frontier farms and frontier estates; a large proportion of the trade of Table Bay is connected with the frontier, and a great many people in Cape Town have an interest in estates in the eastern province."[465]

As Crais points out, capitalism in South Africa took a predominantly landlord-dominated 'labour-repressive' mode rather than a black peasant road, "in which massive state coercion went hand in hand with capitalist development."[466] Settlers "discovered that the making of a working class involved more than simple dispossession and, while the land might be conquered, the minds of Africans remained uncolonised...settlers had not only to produce and control but also attempt to deracinate a working class from what increasingly was viewed as a culturally repugnant society. They needed the colonial state to "strive to control the time, space and cultural practices of an 'intimate enemy' and to seek to redefine the body of the African as a metonym of a dominated life."[467] "What Marx called 'primitive accumulation' became for farmers such as George Gilbert the more culturally determined 'deadly feud' of 'civilisation' and 'barbarism'. Most crucially, however, it was this very same elite who constructed and disseminated the discourse of the Other."[468]

All this required that the Xhosa come under direct imperial rule, along with the expansion of European settlement. Confident in the growing world ascendancy of Britain, settlers called vociferously for military advance to acquire the resources of land and labour for accumulation, and for the crushing of the Xhosa, on the basis of a new racist ideology of dispossession. Appropriating the language of 'civilisation', the *Graham's Town Journal* declaimed, that if Xhosaland was annexed, "Colonisation would then be synonymous with Civilisation, and the natives instead of being depressed or destroyed, would be raised from their wretched grovelling condition, and participate in all the advantages which civilised government is calculated to bestow."[469] The speeches of John Mitford Bowker summed up the philosophy of the British settler elite. In August 1844 he said of the Xhosa: "I know that rapine and murder are in all his thoughts, and I see them in his looks, and hate him accordingly... and I begin to think that he too, as well as the springbok, must give place, and why not? Is it just that a few thousands of ruthless worthless savages are to sit like a nightmare upon a land that would support millions of civilised men happily? Nay, heaven forbids it." And, again, the Xhosa were "no more than would be required by an industrious population as its hewers of wood and drawers of water, and such they ought to be made."[470] The settler elite tended now to equate "civilisation" with labour.

British settler identity reached its maturation with the 25th anniversary in Grahamstown of the launching of the scheme to colonise the Zuurveld in 1844. The celebrations have been described as the "self-conscious beginning of the cult of the 1820 settlers."[471] The Wesleyan William Shaw set the religious seal of approval on settler endeavour: God had brought them to prosperity because they had always shown 'Christian forbearance' in their relations with Xhosa and Khoi. As Le Cordeur writes, "The British settlers came perilously close to seeing themselves as sent by God to civilise Africa."[472] Lester brings out how, though the discourse of "British settlerness" and racism was largely male-generated, settler women also contributed to its elaboration and implementation in the home (to which they were confined by the new ideology of domesticity).[473] The combination of British power, settler drive, and the resilience of the colonial economy provided the force and the means over the decade after 1846 to conquer and subdue the Ciskeian Xhosa, to destroy the Griqua states in Transorangia and consolidate new white states there and in Natal.

The contradiction between the free labour ideology promoted by Britain and the need of the Cape economy to subordinate and control workers was exposed by the passage of a new stringent Masters and Servants Act passed in 1841. Liberal historians like Macmillan were uncritical of this law because of its 'non-racial' character, but in reality it was directed at binding the new 'coloured' and Xhosa labour force to the farms. Workers were to receive contracts, but in return were bound with severe criminal sanctions for breaches thereof; thus deference, corporal punishment for desertion or subordination, long working hours, poor living conditions and low wages were promoted by criminal law. Women were subordinated to men as 'head of the family.'[474] As Crais writes: "The assumption that the intrinsic character of the African in colonial society demanded compulsion, for example, justified the promulgation of coercive legislation and ultimately legitimated the development of a racial capitalism....Racial capitalism as an economic system was also the foundation for a cultural and colonial order in which the black remained a perpetual outsider."[475] This was the more the case the more that settlers controlled the local state. The establishment of the Fort Beaufort magistracy in 1844, for example, went along with a "dizzying increase" in the destruction of squatter communities, extension of private property rights over African-held land, and enforcement of requirements for building proper houses and fencing.[476]

The passage of the Masters and Servants Act, viewed by Fairbairn as removing the inferior status of coloureds, was the reason he gave for recommencing agitation for representative government. He had allied with the merchant interest in the expansion of a racial colonial capitalism - which wanted representative government because it believed that the fiscal conservatism of officialdom (and the lack of power of the legislative council on spending matters) was preventing the investment necessary for development.[477] By the 1840s also the colony's "Afrikaner elite... had been reconciled to the essentially bourgeois view of the British middle classes; at the same time the liberal reformers of the 1820s (such as Fairbairn) had lost their humanitarian optimism". By the time of the 1846-1847 war with the Xhosa, Fairbairn had become an "ardent militarist". He wrote that the Xhosa had to be "put down or expelled, though it should require 10,000 regular troops to accomplish it... not victory but conquest is to be the end of this outbreak." He saluted Governor Sir Peregrine Maitland as proceeding to war "not to exterminate savages, but to subdue anarchy, and to establish the reign of justice on a foundation that no barbaric arm can shake."[478] Significantly he compared the Xhosa to the Chartist movement, the "mob" struggling for democracy in Britain. However, as Keegan points out, "Fairbairn's later commitments were not inconsistent with his earlier adherence to humanitarian prescriptions. After all, acculturation and incorporation of the native peoples as a dependent class was always the humanitarian vision, and if that could not be achieved by moral suasion, then conquest and dismemberment of African societies might be presented as alternative means to the same end."[479]

The British government had yet to be convinced about representative government. In 1842 British colonial secretary Lord Stanley had replied to a petition from the Cape Town municipality fearing that it could be "perverted into a means of gratifying the antipathies of a dominant caste, or of promoting their own interests or prejudices at the expense of those of other and less powerful classes." As Le Cordeur writes, six years were to pass before Governor Harry Smith answered Stanley's question.[480] In the meantime, the colony was re-organised administratively. It had built up a big debt as a result of the 1834-1835 war, and the imperial government bore almost the whole cost of the military between 1836 and 1842 as well as part of civil spending. The situation was turned around thereafter (as the result of wool), particularly under the administration of John Montagu, who became Colonial Secretary of the Cape Colony in 1843. He paid off the colonial debt in two and a half years, professionalised and streamlined the civil service, and organised posts, harbours, and a program of road and pass-building by means of convict labour, establishing lines of communication for the wool economy.[481] Montagu shared the viewpoint of the settler elite on the Xhosa: when he paid his first visit to the frontier in 1844, "on beholding the Chumie valley... he observed "*it's a pity such black Devils should have such a fine country*" - this soon became the catchword in Albany."[482]

In May 1843 Maqoma had told Charles Stretch, diplomatic agent among the Xhosa, "I will hold by Stockenstrom's word until I die and my people put me in the grave. If the treaties are forced from us, nothing can preserve us from war."[483] However in September the following year, under settler pressure, the new governor, Maitland, did abrogate the treaties unilaterally and imposed new 'agreements' on the Xhosa chiefs. In particular, the hated patrol system was reintroduced. Also, Xhosa living at mission stations were no longer to be subject to traditional law. At first Maitland treated with the lesser chiefs, even refusing to see Maqoma and the other Ngqika chiefs, and then merely 'informed' them of the abrogation.[484] The settlers rejoiced, and burnt an effigy of Stockenstrom. The lieutenant governor, John Hare, offered his resignation in February 1845 because he said he was left with nothing to do: it was accepted in September 1846.[485]

"As Rharabe regent", writes Stapleton, Maqomo "had interacted intelligently with the powerful colony and was responsible for a long period of peace along the frontier. However, with the rise of the inexperienced Sandile to the paramountcy and Governor Maitland's abrupt cancellation of the treaty system in 1844, the situation deteriorated."[486] Stretch, the diplomatic agent, saw the Xhosa begin war preparations.[487] At the same time Maqoma's mistrust of missionaries, fuelled by his breach with Calderwood, increased - because they weaned people away from traditional law and customs. Maqoma's mother Nothonto, who had been friendly to the mission since the 1820s, reacted against "civilisation" and became a rainmaker. Maqoma told Laing that it had been a mistake to allow missionaries into Xhosaland because "they were stealing people and becoming chiefs and magistrates." This was what the Wesleyans had already been doing in Queen Adelaide Province, and what was to come again after the 1846-1847 war.[488]

The mistrust of missionaries came about because missionaries had urged on Maitland the abandonment of the old treaty system. As Philip wrote, "This alienation of the chiefs from our Missionaries has been growing for years past. It may be traced to various sources and late events in connection with the Governor's recent visit to the Eastern frontier since brought it into public notice. The chiefs blame the missionaries for the active part they took in recommending to the Governor (which they did as a body) alterations in the amended treaties which the chiefs consider as adverse to their views and interests and (as coming from the Missionaries) in some instances insulting to them. The chiefs from some time back have ceased to regard them as their friends. They have been in the habit of considering the missionaries as always leaning too much to the side of government and as occasionally their interests with the Government and since the unfortunate affair of the treaties to which reference has been made they have been in the habit of regarding the missionaries as disguised or open enemies."[489]

Philip's remarks were occasioned by a bitter quarrel which had erupted between the majority of missionaries led by Calderwood on the one hand and the Reads and their allies on another. It was symptomatic of the times, as Calderwood was converted to the majority Wesleyan-Moffat missionary view. "It was in fact an attempt to destroy the influence which it was believed the Reads wielded in London and Cape Town. By branding them as untruthful, their critics hoped to discredit them."[490] For Bank the quarrel signified a "fundamental challenge to James Read's egalitarian vision of the evangelical mission among Africans": it was "at heart a dispute about racial politics and attitudes towards indigenous peoples."[491] Mostert writes of Calderwood's "deep, biting jealousy of Read's relationship with Khoikhoi and Xhosa."[492]

A meeting of 12 GMS and LMS missionaries (including the government missionary William Thomson) was called at Block Drift (the later Fort Hare) to reopen the case of the dismissal of a GMS missionary. Read "disapproved of the way the meeting was got up, and of its being held, as not all the parties were present, also of the document being read."[493] After the meeting, the other missionaries alleged, Read wrote to the Secretary of the GMS in Britain "to contravene what Reverend Calderwood was directed by the meeting to communicate to the directors."[494] Calderwood 'discovered' a letter at the Fort Beaufort post office written by Read to the GMS. Read admitted "he had written a private letter to the Secretary of the Glasgow Society, who is my friend, and they have heard that I have written to controvert what had been done at the meeting. I declare I have not."[495] The other Xhosaland missionaries refused to believe Read. From here this petty affair escalated into a complaint to the directors in London against Read in which the existing matter was regarded as merely a "specimen of what we have to complain of".[496] At the same time they wrote a memorial against the system of superintendence.[497] Calderwood also confided to a military acquaintance at this time that he wanted to separate the Xhosa mission at the Kat River from the Khoisan part: "I am disgusted with much of what has lately come to light in Kat River". He wanted to go into "the very centre of Maqomo's people" or else go back to Britain.[498] The GMS missionaries were also involved. They wrote that Read's behaviour was characteristic and "has had the effect of producing a distressing want of confidence in him in the minds of the Missionary Brethren who knew him best".[499]

Read wrote that "I have fallen into the hands of the philistines...They will use all their might to injure me", and added later "I am at present an outcast among my Brethren ...I think I am not made to act with these white men. I am too much of a Hottentot."[500] In July he wrote of the motives of those behind it: "I may thank my Brethren Kayser and Calderwood for the whole. From my favourable attachment to the Doctor and opposition to some proceedings at our meetings and other things they have had an eye upon me, and have long been digging a pit, and now a favourable opportunity 'twas thought offered to throw me into it... The Doctor pities them and other Brethren consider that I have not acted wrong, but a broken, shivered reed against eleven cedars is as the Caffres say, no joke."[501] In September he added: "Brother Calderwood told Arie and Valentyn Jacobs that Shaw had said to him, if old Mr Read was out of the way then all the missionaries would be united."[502]

However it was what Read told the church deacon Arie Van Rooyen that really inflamed the Calderwood faction. When the faction discovered that Read had written a letter to Van Rooyen criticising some of them, they regarded this as treason. "Considering the circumstances and the natural disposition of the Natives generally all who know this country will admit that a more serious offence against the souls of the people and the comfort and influence of his Brethren could scarcely be committed than that which Mr Read had many a time committed on speaking and writing to the Natives in the manner of which this letter is a sampler."[503] Van Rooyen was one of the 'native agents' despised by the Calderwood faction, and it is small wonder that later in the 1840s they objected to his ordination as pastor of Blinkwater.[504]

Philip travelled to the frontier in mid-1845 to mediate in the quarrel, but his efforts were cut short when, soon after arriving at the Kat River, he was told that his eldest son Wiliam, missionary at Hankey, and one of his grandsons had drowned in the flooded Gamtoos river, a blow from which he was never really fully to recover.[505] In 1846 however he did withdraw his resignation offered in 1843.[506]

The quarrel within the LMS had its reaction, in turn, upon relations with the Xhosa chiefs. Philip, forwarding the correspondence to Britain, lamented on the "baneful effects of such a state of things on the Caffre Missions": "The Reads are more popular with the natives of the country than those that oppose them and Captain Stretch adverts broadly to that fact and to the pernicious influence it will have upon the labours of the Caffre missionaries."[507] Read remarked how he had had to "work to reconcile the [Xhosa] people to" Calderwood: "Macomo was most anxious for his removal... 2 captains upon one place would not do. I did all I could to pacify him."[508] Later Philip added that the differences among the missionaries "have done much injury to the minds of the Caffres. And this is not all. You must know that the

Cafferland missionaries have lost the confidence of the chiefs.... This is a lamentable state of things and one which cannot be defended. The Reads form the only party among our Missionaries in whom the chiefs have confidence and this is one cause of the hostile feelings manifested against the Reads and the reason why they (Reads) find it necessary to give up holding intercourse with the chiefs."[509] Indeed the fact that Read imagined that the new treaties imposed by Maitland on the chiefs in September 1844 "will please for the moment" is interpreted by Mostert to show Read's lack of contact with the chiefs.[510]

By the 1840s, the attitude of the majority of missionaries towards the Xhosa "had settled into one of severe and unqualified censure for their attack upon the colonists, intensified disgust for most of their customs, and firm support for any colonial initiative that would help stamp out their most offending of them."[511] Rather than regarding the black mind as malleable, the missionaries engaged in settler-like assertions of inherent racial difference. They were responding to what as they saw as the failure of their enterprise, in the limited conversions and the 'clinging to barbarism' of the majority. Philip wrote at this time: "Such has been the want of success in the Kaffirland Mission, that some of our Missionary societies have for years been on the point of abandoning it wholly."[512] The response of most missionaries was to demand British rule, not in the quasi-benevolent sense proposed by Philip, or on the Indian model of indirect rule with recognition of indigenous systems of government, but British rule to forcibly impose 'civilisation' (i.e. British culture) on the Xhosa. Repression could be justified to inculcate responsibility and obedience, and conquest justified as the only way to implant Christian civilisation.[513] Humanitarian liberalism had given way, in Keegan's terms, to utilitarian liberalism, for which results were more important than the state of people's souls, in which efficiency and discipline were necessary for progress and coercion could be employed to impose them.[514]

Shortly after the next war began, Philip wrote to the LMS: "You will remember that, while I was opposed to the last war as a war of extermination, I was also decidedly of opinion that the Kafirs having given in their adhesion and taken the oath of allegiance to the British government, ought to have been retained as British subjects, and that the expense of such a measure was the only objection urged against it. Every one here is now of my opinion, but the result might have been no better had it been acted upon."[515] He wanted Xhosa land holding protected, based on the Indian model. In a book written later, Calderwood sought to explain the reason why the Indian model could not work in South Africa:

"In India, the British power had only to contend with another government and a standing army. When the opposing army had been overthrown, the work was done - British supremacy was proclaimed, and there was at once a revenue to meet the expenditure - the old government was supplanted - the great mass of the people until now have not been disturbed, or even generally interested..."

"In Caffraria, this has not hitherto been the case. There was no revenue that could at once be made available for the expenses of the war or government. There was no government in the ordinary acceptation of the term, and no standing army. A whole population was to be dealt with... Here, then, lies the grand difficulty - a whole population, or nearly so, numerous and warlike, and in the highest degree predatory in their habits, are to be dealt with and punished for past offences, or at all events effectually restrained from future aggression, and improved in their own condition, as well as the colony protected. These ends can only be attained in one of two ways - either by driving the culprits from a country peculiarly adapted to their predatory practices, or by an adequate force, justly and mercifully, but ably and firmly handled, so as to restrain or coerce them in their own country, as circumstances might require."[516]

"An adequate force" - to "restrain or coerce them in their own country, as circumstances might require" - this was what the missionaries, no less than the settlers, urgently required.

Writing on this period, Bank has drawn attention to the apparent "premature demise" of humanitarian attitudes in comparison to the rest of the white English-speaking world. Historians of this have generally traced the transition from humanitarianism to racism in the 1850s and 1860s, the consequence of the Indian mutiny of 1857 - and of the 'post-emancipation backlash' induced by the Morant Bay rebellion in the West Indies in 1865 because of the failure of slaves to turn into productive labourers. Bank explains the earlier transition at the Cape as because "wars with the Xhosa bred a rising racism amongst those who had once been self-styled champions of the African cause."[517] In my view the cause was not simply 'war'. In the colony there was a combined 'post-emancipation backlash' against the apparent 'failure' of ex-slaves and Khoisan to become 'productive workers',[518] a settler land and labour hunger directed at the Xhosa, and a burning missionary desire to 'civilise' the Xhosa under British rule - all against Xhosa resistance and recalcitrance.

Hence, when war broke out in 1846, there was no humanitarian opposition to it. The Glasgow missionary Laing wrote that the Xhosa were being "called to account for their abuse of the mercies [of] God and for their rebellion against him" - thus putting God on the side of the British. Philip, under attack within the LMS, was a spent force. On 23 October 1847 his wife Jane died at Hankey, further compounding his personal losses. Though they tried to stand apart from the mainstream still, neither Philip, now aged 71, nor Read, now aged

69, could resist the stampede. Philip wrote that the 1846 war was a "great" undertaking and must succeed. With Moffat and his future son-in-law Livingstone now influential, LMS focus had turned to northwards expansion. In addition, as Mostert points out, both Philip and Read were influenced in favour of the war by Xhosa raids on the Kat River settlement. In July, during the war, James Read senior wrote of the "national antipathy" of the Khoi against the Xhosa on account of "aggressions by their ancestors."[519]

Chapter 10

The War of the Axe [520] 1846 to 1847

By the mid-1840s there was virtually no productive farming land remaining to be granted in the colony, and the attention of the British settlers was the more urgently directed to the lands of the Xhosa.[521] In late 1845 there arose what Le Cordeur calls the first political movement in the history of eastern Cape separatism. Significantly it was catalysed around the issue of the 'leniency of frontier policy', or, in other words, the settler desire for labour and land. What they wanted was more direct access to British military power, the means of subjugation of the Xhosa.[522]

In mid-January 1846 a party of military engineers provocatively crossed the Keiskamma to survey a site for a fort at Block Drift, on the later site of Fort Hare. Sandile objected and a military confrontation threatened. The British withdrew, and Maqoma attempted to restrain Sandile.[523] At this stage Maqoma "was angry with both the whites and the young Xhosa warriors for destabilizing what he considered an acceptable frontier system"; at the same time he was lacking "a sympathetic ear within colonial circles and [was] unable to discourage Sandile's confrontationalist policy".[524]

The pressures built. In February Governor Maitland contemplated a pre-emptive strike against the Xhosa.[525] On 7 March the *Grahamstown Journal* demanded annexation of the old 'ceded territory'.[526] "At meetings held throughout the Eastern Cape in the early months of 1846, the characteristic war hysteria reached new heights."[527] On 16 March a member of the Dange was arrested for theft of an axe, but the party escorting him to Grahamstown for trial was ambushed by Xhosa warriors and the culprit released. The chiefs refused to deliver up the Xhosa responsible. On 21 March Lieutenant-Governor Hare announced his intention to march into Xhosaland and this was backed up by a declaration of war by Maitland on 1 April. Maqoma asked Stretch for land for himself and his people further north in the colony, among the Thembu, where they could sit the war out, but Stretch unwisely refused.[528]

The British ordered the missionaries out of Xhosa territory and three British columns invaded Xhosa territory on 11 April, aiming to camp at the foot of the Amatolas.[529] The Xhosa, with firearms and horses in significant numbers for the first time, attacked the columns' baggage trains at Burnshill (an abandoned GMS station) and captured 65 wagons. "At one stroke the Xhosa had stripped the invading army of the bulk of its supplies, together with the baggage and kit of officers and men, the hospital and veterinary supplies, the mess plate and china of the 7th Dragoon Guards, two wagonloads of wine for the officers mess... and currency... It was by far the worst humiliation the British army had yet suffered in its campaigns in South Africa."[530] As the British withdrew, the Xhosa - appealing to the Boers to stand aside - swept into the colony, burning farms and missions, and besieged Fort Peddie.[531] The "barbarians of the mountain completely outgeneraled the English officer", wrote Calderwood, "A new thing this in Caffer warfare...The whole Eastern province of the colony is already overrun by the Caffers."[532]

Every chiefdom in Ciskeian Xhosaland joined with Sandile's forces, including the Gqunukhwebe of Pato, who attacked the Mfengu settlement around Fort Peddie which was on their former land.[533] Jan Tshatshu, early chiefly convert and pride of the LMS, joined as well, asserting that it was the British and not the Xhosa who had broken the treaties.[534] Sarhili of the Gcaleka was also supportive.[535] The unity was a remarkable achievement, given the Xhosa history of separatism, of feuding chiefs, of being driven back onto each other's land, of feuding missionaries with different groups.

Only the Mfengu, shaped as collaborators, took the British side. They began the war fighting with assegais but ended it with guns. While at first the British tried to impose their own fighting methods on the Mfengu, they later recognised their skills in hand-to-hand bush fighting with the Xhosa.[536] The people of the Kat River settlement also fought on the British side throughout the war. James Read Jr later wrote that their "heroism and gallantry... is well known to the public in the colony." Some 1100 served as garrisons at Elands Post, Fort Armstrong, and Blinkwater, and in the field.[537] Stockenstrom highlighted the role of Andries Botha in the battle of Burnshill - who, "with 250 of his Kat River settlers, came, forced his way through retreating friends and pursuing enemies - seized upon the ammunition - carried it triumphant through the fight - covered the retreat, and was mainly instrumental in saving what was saved."[538]

Despite criticising the conduct of the war, the Read family actively participated in it. Joseph Read was commissioned and led Khoi, Mfengu and San, including into the Transkei. James Read junior justified the family's participation with reference to the activities of Moffat in the Griqua battle at Dithakong in the course of the *mfecane* in 1823.[539] Le Cordeur and Saunders maintain that Joseph's "activities caused his father much heartsearching."[540] Read senior did indeed write to the LMS in March 1847 of Joseph that "the situation he has been called to fill has given me great uneasiness of mind, for I hate war with my whole heart - but Joseph knew not what to do otherwise than to yield as the Government might be thwarted in their plans - he is often ailing and speaks of resigning - I am in trouble about him."[541] However in Read senior's letters to a brother missionary at Bethelsdorp it is rather an embarrassed pride that comes across: Joseph had "given an opportunity to show that the Reads can not only preach and pray but also fight if necessary." Read wrote also of being "an enemy to war in every sense of the word, but when I make war I make [it] in earnest, not as our rulers and commanders have been and are doing", and, again, "you consider that I and my Brother Calderwood are fallen Brethren as far as the Peace Society is concerned, as we professed to be members: I suppose this must be admitted, for my son Joseph is an officer, they say a first rate one (not with my sanction). Both James and [I] are not a little involved: at this moment I am partly Commandant".[542] At the same time Read senior could write to Bethelsdorp: "I would say it was an unjust war... an unnecessary and a most untimed and precipitate war, unnecessary because I conceive means by police and proper position of the military might have prevented the thefts of the colony and also to prevent the import of arms and ammunition... As to the precipitancy of the war, the colonists are much to blame. Their meetings, speeches, and memorials hurried it on, and our valued friend Fairbairn for once committed himself greatly, and now approving of all".[543]

The Xhosa besieged Fort Peddie until 28th May, when they launched an attack on it which the British deployed the Mfengu outside the fort to repulse, while all whites retreated inside. The Xhosa seized many cattle. Some ten days later a cavalry force led by Somerset killed several hundred Xhosa in an unusual open battle, called the battle of the Gwangqa.[544] Meanwhile Maitland had taken command, declared martial law, and ordered burgher commandos to be called up from all over the colony. The Boers would have none but Andries Stockenstrom to lead them - and even his British settler enemies such as Godlonton, Bowker and Chase supported him as more competent than the British military leadership.[545] The commandos took months to assemble, but by the end of June Maitland had at his disposal 14,000 men - 3200 British regulars, 5500 burghers, 800 Khoi levies, and 4000 Mfengu and Khoi labourers. "But it was a force weakened by shortages of supplies, and demoralised by the apparent lack of any semblance of organisation or strategy."[546]

Much of the next phase of the war was a British attempt at an anti-guerilla campaign in the Amatolas, attempting to starve the Xhosa out. Learning from previous wars, however, the Xhosa captured stock to ensure their food supply once the British had burnt their crops, and targeted British supplies.[547] In the course of this Stockenstrom found the Xhosa to be "quiet [ie quite] a different people to what they were 20 years ago."[548] Four months into the assault on the Amatolas, Read wrote "we seem as far from peace as we were at the beginning. The Dragoon horses and the horses of the Boers are all knocked up very many dead - no forage to be found - and from one of the severest droughts we have ever had there is no grass - where there was any, the Caffres have set fire to it - so that the oxen that have to drag the wagons have been dying by hundreds so that the troops cannot get supplies. And then in many cases the Caffers have succeed in capturing the wagons taking to themselves their contents and the oxen and burning the wagons - a thing quite unknown in former wars - at this instant the Troops are suffering greatly from want of supplies of Bread and Meat etc etc - the Caffres have sent all their own cattle and what they have taken from the Colony - far into the interior".[549] For the first time in war the Xhosa inflicted huge suffering on British wounded - Xhosa women, apparently, tortured them to death.[550]

In June 1846 the *Grahamstown Journal* editorialised: "These antagonistic powers ['civilisation' and 'barbarism'] are now brought into collision, and are engaged in deadly feud; it is a conflict of light and darkness - of truth and error - of order and confusion." Only British supremacy over Xhosaland and a strong state within the colony in the hands of the landed and wealthy could resolve it. Such was the Manichean language of struggle in which British settlerdom understood the situation.[551]

To avoid giving an impression of failure, Stockenstrom in August proposed an offensive across the Kei against Sarhili's Gcaleka, and Maitland eventually agreed to this. He wanted Sarhili to acknowledge British conquest up to the Kei.[552] Stockenstrom and his force met Sarhili at his Great Place where they reached an agreement peacefully. However when Maitland heard of the agreement, he immediately repudiated it and demanded that Sarhili pay reparation for the damage his people had done to missions and trading stations. Stockenstrom, in frustration and anger, then decommissioned his burgher force and resigned from his post. The Boers were simply not interested in conquest of the Xhosa or land expansion there.[553]

Maqoma had been reluctantly dragged into the war, and indeed his biographer finds it hard to reconstruct whether he participated or not during the first five months of it.[554] He wanted a brief war, and indeed by September he was suing for peace - at a time when the colonial army was "virtually prostrated and unable to pursue the war any further."[555] The Xhosa meanwhile were adopting, in the face of Maitland's threat of mass resettlement, a sit-down strike which Mostert calls 'passive resistance" - "the first example in South Africa" of such a strategy.[556] Maitland had enlisted the aid of the Wesleyan Shaw and the LMS Calderwood to advise him, and he now sent Calderwood to negotiate with Maqoma.

Calderwood had now replaced Philip as the main 'confidante' of governors. Already he had told the LMS that "the salvation of the Caffres themselves requires it, that they be made subjects of Britain. I think this might be done with advantage to all - if it be not effected I fear the result will be much suffering to them and ultimate ruin to the other party. But if they are to be made subjects to Britain it must be done with much wisdom and mercy - they

JOHANNES VAN DER KEMP

JAMES READ

VIEW OF A XHOSA HOMESTEAD

LORD CHARLES SOMERSET

NXELE (MAKANA)

NDLAMBE IN 1820'S

JOHN PHILIP

JOHN FAIRBAIRN

GRAHAMSTOWN IN 1823

MAQOMA AND WIFE

THE HON. ROBERT GODLONTON.

ROBERT GODLONTON

SIR BENJAMIN D'URBAN

HINTSA

SIR ANDRIES STOCKENSTROM

SANDILE

BATTLE IN WAR OF THE AXE, 1846

SIR HARRY SMITH

KAT RIVER SETTLEMENT

ATTACK ON FORT ARMSTRONG

FIGHTING IN THE WATERKLOOF, 1851

XHOSA ATTACKING WAGON TRAIN IN 1850-1853 WAR

BLINKWATER AND THE WATERKLOOF

BLINKWATER
(and Waterkloof Heights)

ANDRIES BOTHA

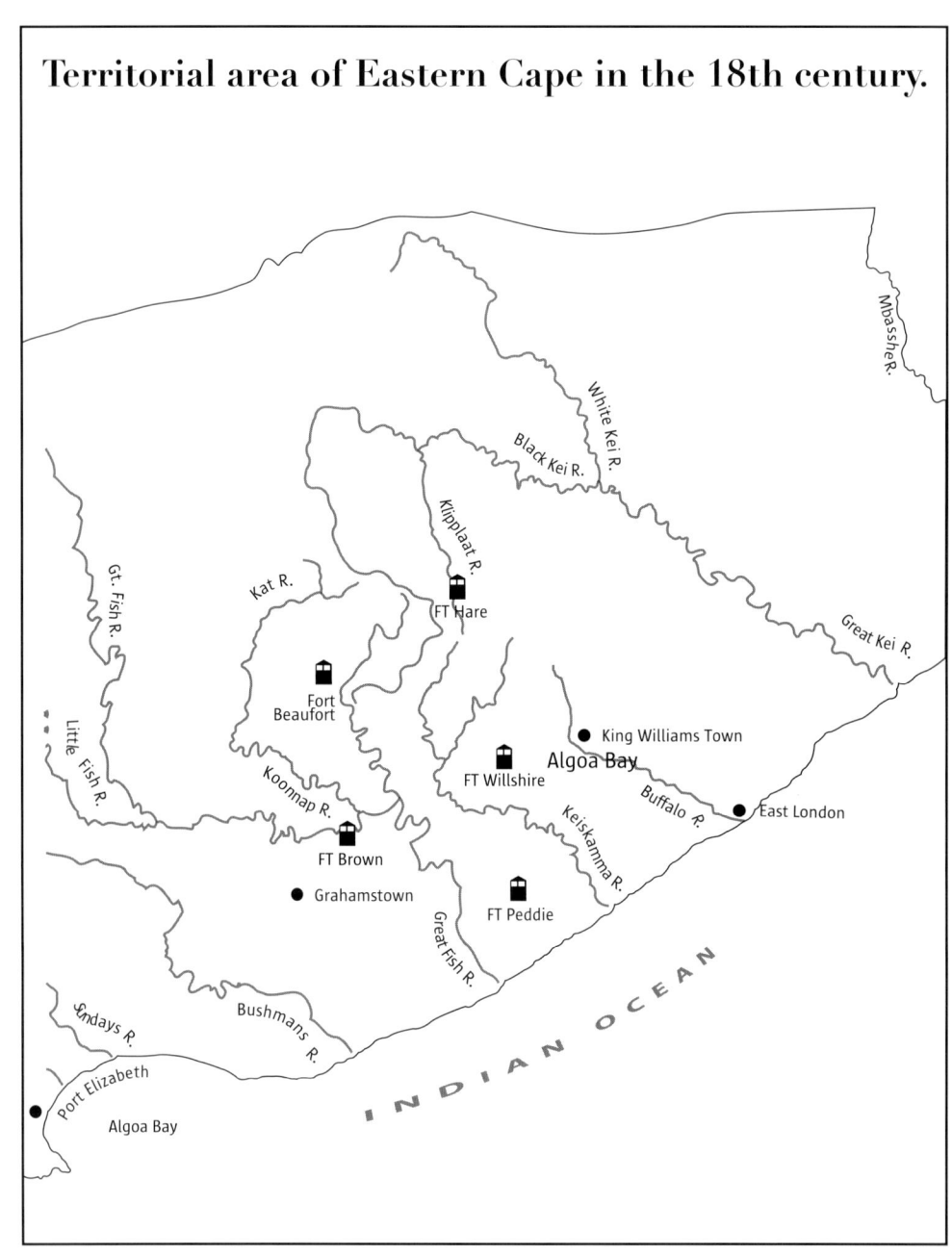

must be made to feel that it is intended for their advantage".[557] He now wrote: "The Governor has declared his determination to restore British authority over the whole country on this side of the Kei river... I have thoroughly urged the importance and justice of retaining the Caffres in that territory. The Governor sees the importance of this and entirely agrees to it. He proposes the immediate boundary shall be occupied by Caffres connected with the various missions - Hottentots and Fingoes and other coloured people subjects of the Colony - *white* men are not to get any of the country."[558]

He met Maqoma and other Ngqika chiefs near Block Drift, commented that "Maqoma has much influence", but that the chiefs refused to give up their firearms as Maitland demanded. "But they desire peace on their own terms. They are evidently heartily tired of the war... The seed time of the Caffers has come and they are anxious to sow. But they are not willing to give up anything." His aims, he said, were "to prevent the Caffers, however guilty, and they are guilty, from being driven beyond the reach of the gospel - I wished therefore to persuade Maqoma for the sake of his people to submit to the terms offered by the Governor as the only likely means of saving himself and people from ruin and the colony from violence."[559] The negotiations having failed, the chiefs returned to the kraals to plant crops. In October Maqoma surrendered, led his people out of the old ceded territory, and settled himself at Block Drift (Fort Hare). Sandile even returned the axe thief to the British, but to no avail. Maitland wrote that "the sowing season has been passing by unemployed owing to the scouting of the country by the troops. Great scarcity among them has been the result; many of them are much wasted, and the women have extremely suffered the horrors of famine."[560] A sort of stalemate set in in the war, "both peace and war" (in Calderwood's terms) and in January Maitland - on a renewed expedition against Sarhili - received a dispatch recalling him. He immediately revoked martial law.[561]

On the peace negotiations Read wrote to Philip "Does Sir Peregrine [Maitland] still think the Caffres are children or idiots?... We have in no ways subdued the Caffres...And then... proposing terms that anyone might foresee the chiefs under present circumstances would not submit to... and as for Calderwood, they hate him."[562] However in one of his last actions before hearing of his recall Maitland appointed Calderwood as Commissioner to the Ngqika, essentially replacing Stretch, but no longer a diplomat among an independent people, rather as "satrap over a subject people"[563] In his letter announcing his appointment and resigning from the LMS, Calderwood wrote that "The Governor ... proclaims the supremacy of the British government over the county to the west of the Kei - that is the country of the Gaikas, Slambis, Tambookies and Patos... all Caffers who will submit to the British government will be allowed to remain in undisturbed possession of their lands... The chieftainship as it now exists will be abolished and chiefs and influential men will be heads of sections of country - they will decide all cases among themselves subject to appeal to a British Commission." [564] He had taken the post of Commissioner to further the general cause of missions in Xhosaland, he argued, which was being obstructed by the chiefs. Moreover, under his influence, Maitland was opposed to the release of further Xhosa land to whites.[565] Philip, in fact, was in enthusiastic support of the proposal.[566] It failed because Maitland did not have the power or the will to impose it.

In Britain, because of delayed communications, the war was essentially dealt with by Lord John Russell's Whig government which replaced that of Peel in June 1846. The new government set about dismantling the final bulwarks of protectionism on the basis of the ideology of free trade. Russell and his colonial secretary Earl Henry George Grey were influenced by the ideas of Edward Wakefield on colonial affairs - responsible local government by free settler communities, with financial self-sufficiency as the goal. This left little room for humanitarianism, and the general attitude was that British settlers would 'play fair with the natives.'[567] At the time, even the Wesleyan Shaw expressed his concern to his erstwhile foe Philip: "You are not ignorant that there is a strong and growing party at home who look upon colonisation as the panacea for all the evils of the new and old world with Earl Grey at its head. This party embraces much talent has much influence and is supported by a great portion of the public press, and they have found out that missionaries stand in the way of their plans and they do not wish to see the aborigines of barbarous countries converted to the Christian faith but they wish to see those countries we see now evangelising emptied of these inhabitants and in the possession of white men."[568]

However "civilisation" did indeed enter into Grey's vocabulary - because, for him, stabilising the Xhosa frontier once and for all was the necessary condition for conceding representative government to the Colony.[569] And peace demanded British conquest. If peace could be maintained, by a "strict and even severe system of government", religion, education and commerce would gradually civilise the Xhosa. With all the confidence of a mid-19th century British politician, he wrote: "The authority of the British Crown is at this moment the most powerful instrument, under Providence, of maintaining peace and order in many extensive regions of the earth, and thereby assists in diffusing amongst millions of the human race the blessings of Christianity and civilisation."[570] This was, in Mostert's words, "the moral justification that would serve British self-interest during the second half of the nineteenth century."[571] As Lester comments, "Thus was a humanitarian discourse of Christian intervention appropriated and moulded into a settler and official discourse of active colonisation in the Cape."[572]

It was to stabilise the frontier that Grey replaced Maitland with Sir Henry Pottinger, whose colonial experience was mainly in India, but who had lately obliged the Chinese to open up their ports to trade. Grey instructed Pottinger to pacify the frontier by proclaiming British sovereignty up to the Kei and subjugating the Xhosa. His legal experts pondered over how to exercise British rule without giving the Xhosa colonial citizenship rights and came up with the idea of a 'protectorate.' Grey also called for a report on whether the colony was prepared for constitutional advance to representative government. Pottinger, who arrived on 27 January as the first British civil governor, also became the first to hold the post of High Commissioner, giving him powers to act across colonial boundaries. Sir Henry Edward Fox Young was appointed as the new lieutenant governor.[573] Pottinger had asked for a temporary appointment only, wishing to return to India. He was apparently a man of great intellect, but also great rage and impatience.[574]

The stalemate had frustrated the settlers. "Having failed to win the war in 1835 because of (in their view) a lily-livered, humanitarian-inspired failure of nerve, they were determined it would be won this time round."[575] At a meeting in Bathurst Godlonton spoke of the "mission" of the Albany settlers together with British power: "the task of colonising Kaffirland: that was a work allotted to them evidently by Providence."[576] In Xhosaland there was "a wide and most fertile tract of country which must, to preserve the advantages the British forces have gained over the Kaffir tribes, be occupied by British subjects".[577] In the minds of the leading settlers, separatism was the political response - though not at the expense of releasing the western districts from an obligation to pay for frontier 'defence', i.e. expansion.[578] The east was however by no means united on these questions. Godlonton wanted the "whole of South Africa" under British rule. The new lieutenant-governor, Young, championed the separatist cause and appointed J.C. Chase as his secretary. Even Stockenstrom wanted a separate government for the east. In mid-1847 however Young was transferred to Australia.[579]

When Pottinger arrived, the Xhosa were not fighting. The Ngqika "continued to insist they were at peace without admitting that they had ever been defeated." Sandile refused to open discussions with Pottinger "saying that he had already made peace and there was nothing more to talk about."[580] Responsive to the settlers, however, Pottinger reported to Grey that the "natural anxieties and feelings of the inhabitants of this colony (and especially its eastern frontier) have been totally disregarded."[581] In the end, according to Mostert, it was Calderwood who convinced Pottinger to take up the war again, because the Xhosa had not been sufficiently 'humbled' and there was the need for a more decisive surrender on their part. At the time Philip wrote how, because of his government post, Calderwood had "brought upon himself the inveterate hatred of Caffreland and not only upon himself but upon the missionaries in general... Sandile the head chief has declared in his own name and the name of the other chiefs in league with him that there never can be peace between the Caffers and the Colony while Calderwood has anything to say in the affairs of Cafferland", and, again, that Calderwood "is so hated by the Caffres that he never can be again a missionary among them... the Caffres say that they never thought that a missionary who came out to teach them the way of peace would leave his accredited office and apply for a secular one - merely to have the gratification of oppressing them".[582]

While like his predecessors, Pottinger aimed to expel the Xhosa across the Kei, unlike D'Urban and Maitland, he did not want to abolish the Chiefs.[583] The *Graham's Town Journal* ardently supported him: "Let the war be made against Kafir huts and gardens. Let all these be burnt down and destroyed. Let there be no ploughing, sowing, or reaping. Or, if you cannot conveniently, or without bloodshed prevent the cultivation of the ground, take care to destroy the enemy's crops before they are ripe, and shoot all who resist. Shoot their cattle wherever you see any. Tell them that the time has come for the white man to show his mastery over them."[584] Pottinger's aim was to settle matters with Pato of the Gqunukhwebe and Sarhili, in order to put pressure on other chiefs, particularly Sandile - whom Calderwood was zealous to bring to heel. However he was handicapped by the disinterest of Boers in pursuing the war, which made mass Xhosa expulsion impossible.[585] The pretext for resumption of the war was the theft of 14 goats by a follower of Sandile in June - which led soon to the declaration of Sandile as a rebel. Pottinger was disgusted by the war profiteering among the British settlers. But, to raise the necessary forces, he proclaimed that Mfengu, Boers and coloureds could take whatever cattle or other booty they wanted.[586] The aim was to clear the Ngqika out of the Amatolas. On 20 September the offensive began - in time to prevent the Ngqika from sowing, with Calderwood urging again and again more pressure: "I would say give it a few turns more - the people are not subdued."[587] The war ended in October when Sandile allowed himself to be taken into custody on the understanding that he would be treated as a negotiating equal, but was instead made a prisoner. At the same time (September) Maqoma was exiled by the government from Block Drift to Port Elizabeth. Pottinger wound up the war by attacks on Pato and by a further campaign across the Kei against Sarhili. However by the end of September the governor knew that he was leaving for a coveted post in Madras in India.[588]

Under Pottinger the government also launched a serious assault on the Kat River settlement. Kat River residents had played a major role in the first part of the war - providing 90% of its males for service when every other area of the colony provided at most 3%. Somerset wrote that "their services were absolutely necessary to enable us to compete with the enemy in this peculiar warfare."[589] Even at the end they played a major role in the clearing of Xhosa from the Amatolas.[590] However in the meantime Pottinger had been angered by their reluctance to rejoin the military, because they had been badly treated by Maitland. His attitude resonated with that of the settlers, who coveted the fertile Kat River pastures for their sheep. Godlonton and others had for a while been attacking the settlement for locking up land and labour. Pottinger appointed Thomas J. Biddulph, a leading settler figure, as magistrate to the settlement and Biddulph soon produced a scathing report on the settlement which was eagerly publicised by the *Grahamstown Journal*.[591] Biddulph wrote that the Kat River was the "abode of idleness and imposture" and that the settlement "from beginning to end, has been nothing but the most transparent piece of humbug ever practiced upon the public, to serve the purposes of unscrupulous, intriguing people."[592] Pottinger endorsed the report and told Earl Grey that residents of the settlement were "a concourse of rebellious, idle paupers" who wished to "wallow in filth in idleness at the expense of the government."[593] Biddulph, wrote Read, wished to see the settlement destroyed because he believed "that black men should not possess property in the soil, but rather become slaves of, or disappear before, the White Man." His report, he added exaggeratedly, "met with repulse from one end of the Colony to the other". However it was criticised in at least three newspapers.[594] Stockenstrom, appalled because of the strategic importance of the Kat River settlement, attacked it in the *Eastern Province Herald* (27/11/1847).[595]

Matters were not helped when, in another break from the humanitarian tradition, in late 1847 William Elliott of the LMS wrote a long letter to the Directors arguing for the breaking up of the mission stations and the conversion of their land into freely transferable individual ownership - a letter then published in *Evangelical Christendom*. His rationale was the cost of the stations, and the fact that the law now extended "protection to the black man as well as the white." Heavy use was made of his arguments in the settler press in their campaign against the Kat River settlement, for here "was a leading experienced missionary exposing the institutions to be what the settlers of the eastern province had always asserted, havens for indigent paupers who would be better elsewhere."[596] Moreover, despite Philip's opposition to it, Elliott maintained his stance, even going to Britain in February 1849 to press his case.[597]

Chapter 11

Smith's Governorship: the first years, 1848 to 1850

Sir Harry Smith arrived as Governor on 1 December 1847, "his overwhelming arrogance further bloated by victory in India [in the Sikh war] and by the favour of Wellington."[598] In the first Anglo-Sikh war Smith had led British troops to victory against the Sikhs, a principal adversary, in the battle of Aliwal, allowing the British occupation of Lahore and the declaration of a British protectorate, the prelude to the annexation of the Punjab. Indeed in Britain he had been adulated as the "first authentic military hero of the Victorian age."[599] He assured Earl Grey that he could achieve the subjugation of the Xhosa while reducing military forces and spending. He was in time to reap the fruits of victory in the war against the Xhosa. Within three weeks he had set out on a grand tour, first to the eastern frontier - where he was met with huge celebration by the settlers - and then north into Transorangia and to Natal. By February 1848 he had annexed the former 'ceded territory' as the district of Victoria (East), established the new 'protectorate' of British Kaffraria between the Keiskamma and the Kei, extended the colonial boundary in the north-west to the Orange river, and annexed Transorangia up to the Vaal River as the Orange River Sovereignty - as well as instructing William Porter, the attorney-general, to draw up a memorandum on representative government.[600]

Smith had come with the mission of reimposing the D'Urban system with which he was intimately associated, and that Glenelg had rejected. In his first address in Grahamstown he told a settler audience that: "The first act of my government will be to bring the savage Kaffir hordes prostrate at your feet."[601] So far as the chiefs were concerned, he meant it literally. Behind Smith was all the pride and panache of mid-19th century Britain. Earlier, on landing in Port Elizabeth, he had seen Maqoma outside his hotel through the window and went out to meet him. He "approached Maqoma in a friendly manner but at the last minute... grabbed his sword and drew it partially from its scabbard. Startled by this sudden menace, [Maqoma] pulled back and was ridiculed loudly by the crowd of settlers. With a sarcastic smile, Sir Harry retired in silence to the hotel."

"That afternoon, Smith summoned Maqoma and an interpreter to the

Phonenix [Hotel]. When the chief offered to shake hands with the governor, the latter knocked him to the floor... Placing his boot on [Maqoma's] throat and brandishing a sword over his head, Smith yelled 'This is to teach you that I have come hither to teach Kaffirland that I am chief and master here and in this way I shall treat the enemies of the Queen!'. Although terrified, the chief snarled in retort: 'You are a dog and you behave like a dog. This thing was not sent by Victoria who knows that I am of royal blood like herself.' Applying more pressure to Maqoma's neck, Her Majesty's representative stated that because of the war the chiefs had forfeited everything they possessed."[602]

Members of the settler elite were soon appointed to official positions: Richard Southey, for example, close colleague of Godlonton, became Smith's secretary.[603] In Grahamstown Smith treated Sandile as he had Maqoma. Asking Sandile who was the great chief of the Xhosa and getting the natural reply "Sarhili", Smith shouted "I am your Paramount Chief, and the Kaffirs are my dogs! I am come to punish you for your misdoings and treachery. You may approach my foot and kiss it, but not until you repent the past will I allow you to touch my hand."[604] On 23 December Smith met in King Williams Town with all the chiefs save Maqoma to announce, in a threatening speech, the establishment of British Kaffraria.[605] At the end "Each of the chiefs once more had to come forward and, as a final gesture of submission, kiss Harry Smith's foot in the stirrups. That done, Smith hurled the stave of war to the ground and cried, 'There is the end of war.' "[606]

On 7 January Smith met again with the chiefs (save Maqoma) and 2000 of their followers. Following a Wesleyan missionary's prayer asking God's forgiveness on behalf of the Xhosa, Smith launched into another tirade "offering an alarming series of pronouncements on every vital aspect of their lives, customs, and existence." In British Kaffraria everyone was to learn English, ploughing and the 'art of money'. Cattle-keeping would be discouraged in favour of sheep. *Lobola* and witch-finding were banned. He, Harry Smith, and not Sarhili, was now the *Inkosi Inkhulu*, the Great Chief of the Xhosa - though Sarhili retained independence in the Transkei. 'See what I will do if you make war' he threatened the assembly as a "wagon packed with explosives... parked a safe distance off...blew skywards in spinning fragments. Then, tearing a piece of paper into fragments and hurling them into the air, he yelled, 'There go the treaties! Do you hear? No more treaties". "I make no treaty. I say this land is mine".[607] Smith was exercising a power that he did not have, and subsequent events were to bring this home in full force.

Read senior attended this meeting with all the missionaries to Xhosaland: "We were all requested to stand in the Front of the meeting and allusion was made to us continually in the address Sir Harry made to the Caffres." His reaction indicates Smith's magnetism: "God has however we hope thwarted the intentions of those who rose up against us - and has sent us a deliverer in His Excellency Sir Harry Smith who came at a crisis both as respects ourselves, our Settlement, our people and the cause of the Hottentots generally, the cause of Missions and the cause of the Frontier especially and thus of the whole Colony... Scarcely was Sir Harry Smith on the Frontier but a feeling of confidence was inspired, and peace was the result." Read was further taken in by Smith's visit to the Kat River settlement, where he made Commandant Groepe a Justice of the Peace - "a man of colour... the first instance of the kind in the colony" - praised Stockenstrom, Thomson and Read for their roles in the settlement, and told Read that he was "perfectly satisfied" with the Kat River Settlement and "that the progress of the Hottentots in industry and general conduct exceeds my most sanguine expectations". Read even believed that coloureds would be allocated more land.[608] As we shall see, Read was to be sorely disappointed by Smith.

The Xhosa were finally expelled from the new Victoria East district, which was allocated mainly to settlers, and in addition to some Mfengu (and Thembu) 'locations'.[609] Land speculation and absentee ownership flourished, while some British settlers established wool farms in the northern areas of Victoria East where Maqoma and Sandile had once lived.[610] Maitland had not only promised the Mfengu their lands in perpetuity but more land for fighting in the 1846-1847 war, but this had been forgotten by the end of the war. Only late in 1848 did Smith make some additional provision for Mfengu to settle on land taken from Xhosa in the war.[611]

In British Kaffraria itself, Queen Adelaide Province "had been reborn".[612] Smith ruled it now though as High Commissioner, not governor. This was to prevent the 'complications' of directly incorporating thousands of Xhosa into the colony. It was also because British Kaffraria was to be ruled militarily and to do this in a part of a single colony would have been anomalous. British Kaffraria was ruled, therefore, as a protectorate until 1865 when it was incorporated into the Cape. At the outset Colonel George McKinnon was appointed Chief Commissioner.[613] The rebuilt town of King Williams Town and the new port of East London were settler enclaves within the territory. King Williams Town was the "pivot for a grid of forts in and around the mountains" - Fort White, Fort Cox (Burnshill), and so on. White villages were also established at Woburn, Auckland and Juanasberg in the foothills of the Amatola.[614]

In 1848 a census was taken of the protectorate's newly permanent British subjects. The Ngqika - who still were in possession of the strategically significant Amatola mountains - numbered 27,179 - in contrast to 56,000 in 1835. The rest were in the colony or in Gcalekaland. Of those in British Kaffraria Sandile had 14,915 followers and Maqoma 2066. Maqoma had been allowed to return from Port Elizabeth to his people around Fort Hare, though his request for land at Blinkwater was denied. Most cattle among the Ngqika were concentrated in the top quarter: the bottom quarter owned only 5%. There were 35,179 Ndlambe. Those absent from all the groups were estimated at 20-25000. The Gcaleka of the Transkei numbered 70,000. A tax of £1 was levied on African plotholders, to try to induce labour and a system of fines was established to suppress traditonal customs, and of rewards for promoting 'European attitudes'.[615]

In contrast to his ignoring of the missionaries in 1835-1836, Smith tried to co-opt them to promotion of his plans. Early in 1848 he sent them - even including Philip - a circular asking for their advice on methods of 'civilising' and 'Christianising' the Xhosa - in particular through buying European goods. The missionaries were "barely able to contain their excitement", they thanked God for Smith, they were "happy...that in a work in which we hitherto laboured alone and unassisted encouragement will be given us."[616] Smith managed even to get assistance from the Aborigine's Protection Society in Britain, which, secretly, he hated. By 1850 the Wesleyans had launched a renewed Xhosa newspaper, *Isitunywa sennyanga*, of which however only five issues appeared before it was interrupted by the renewal of war.[617] The missionaries took the opportunity to wage an assault on polygamy and *lobola*, central structures of Xhosa patriarchy.[618] As Mostert points out, however, Smith's plans for the transformation of agriculture were unrealistic, and would have required big state inputs to succeed.[619]

The war and the settlement drove large numbers of men to take up the 'womens' work' of agriculture. At the same time increasing numbers of Xhosa - perhaps half the Ngqika population - sought work in the colony, some moving to the Mfengu locations to 'pass as Mfengu' on the way.[620] Calderwood, first magistrate of Victoria East and stationed at Alice, as well as being a zealous flogger of Xhosa for minor offences, became "Smith's principal recruiting officer."[621] He wrote that "There is indeed great suffering now in Caffreland and the opportunity should not be lost of scattering the people far into the Colony where they can find food and be useful." "The colony was awash with widows and orphans, suffering from crippling shortages of land and cattle.... For the majority, bridewealth for one son... was virtually unattainable. Xhosa society had once revolved around marriage and female fertility, but abortion was now allegedly universal... The fabric of peasant lifestyles was unraveling."[622] Calderwood sent many women and children to labour, pointing out that "the women will be as useful as the men... and many of the children will soon be useful."[623] There was, adds Peires, "an enormous demand in the Western Cape for the labour of little children aged between eight and ten years." Terms of labour contracts were altered: instead of entering the colony and seeking work on the free market, Xhosa were now indentured to particular employers, at unspecified wages, even before they entered the colony.[624]

Smith also intervened in Transorangia. Here tensions had been building up during the 1840s, threatening the Griqua statelets, particularly at Philippolis, and even Moshoeshoe. Boers in the south tended to make arrangements with Moshoeshoe to secure land, but in the north the hard-line Potchefstroom Boer axis (what Keegan calls the *maatschapy*) was more confrontational. Their demarcation of states ignored the areas defined in the treaties between the colony and Kok and Moshoeshoe. Maitland had crossed the Orange to meet the chiefs of Transorangia at Touwfontein in 1844 and reached agreements for the establishment at Bloemfontein of a British Resident, Major Warden. Griqua and Sotho land was also divided into "alienable" and "non-alienable" areas, a provision which was unenforcable and unworkable. By the time Smith arrived, moreover, land speculators from the Eastern Cape were already active in the Caledon valley.[625]

British settlers desperately wanted annexation of Transorangia: "land purchases had little legitimacy without state authority to enforce them against counter-claims, and the credit that was part and parcel of the commercial system could only be secured by such authority."[626] In Bloemfontein, Smith - already under the illusion that the Boers could easily be won back to British authority - received deputations which gave him the impression that most Boers also wanted annexation.[627] He assured Boer and British settler alike that "you shall hold your lands from the Queen of England and from no native whatever." Promptly, he altered the treaty with Kok to the Griqua's disadvantage and wrote to Earl Grey that the Griqua were "mere squatters, and have no more hereditary right to the country in question than the Boers themselves." Against Moshoeshoe's protests, he confirmed Boers in permanent possession of all the land they claimed. Proceeding to British Natal - where 5000 new British settlers would arrive between 1849 and 1852 -- he proclaimed the annexation of the Orange River Sovereignty on 3 February.[628] At this point the enthusiasm for Smith extended to the ex-humanitarian Fairbairn, who called in the *Commercial Advertiser* for the erection of an equestrian statue of Smith in the centre of town because he had been able to pacify South Africa in fifty-eight days.[629]

Smith argued to Earl Grey that the new colony would pay for itself, on the basis of an influx of settlers and capital. No sooner, however, had he returned to Cape Town than a Boer rebellion threatened in Transorangia under Andries Pretorius, who sought an alliance with Moshoeshoe. Pretorius charged that the extension of British rule north of the Orange would turn blacks with whom the Boers had previously lived in 'peace and security' into their 'enemies and persecutors.' The rebels were however defeated at the battle of Boomplaats in August, though this required denuding the Xhosa frontier of troops.[630]

Land in the Orange River Sovereignty was gobbled up by the Eastern Cape elite, including Godlonton, who bought five farms, and speculators from

Natal. 139 people, mainly from the Eastern Cape, bought up over 2,5 million acres of land in the new colony. Absentee ownership was rife. By September 1850 land prices had risen 400% since the Pretorius rebellion. Godlonton established a new newspaper in Bloemfontein, *The Friend of the Sovereignty*, to promote landed interests. The economy became more closely tied to the larger colonial economy in the Cape and Natal. Grain from Lesotho fed the town of Bloemfontein and even rural parts. T.J. Biddulph, now magistrate at Winburg, together with the Wesleyan William Shaw, supported the weaker communities of the eastern part of the colony in an attempt to undermine Moshoeshoe's previous role as the pillar of British hegemony and the strategy was taken up and pursued by Major Warden. Many Boers continued to look to Moshoeshoe as the hegemonic force. But, under British settler pressure, land in the southeast was arbitrarily removed from Lesotho in a new 'boundary definition', opposed by Moshoeshoe, which increased tensions. "The truth... is that a strong, independent Lesotho had ceased to be a useful instrument of imperial policy in the southern African interior. It was now increasingly an obstacle to British hegemony and to the further development of colonial capitalism." Though Smith moved cautiously at first, the "drive to break Sotho power and expropriate Sotho resources, most obviously the fertile arable land of the Caledon valley, had become a dynamic force shaping imperial policy at the mid-century."[631]

Meanwhile, within the Cape colony, pressures on the 'coloureds' mounted, particularly at the Kat River. In 1848 British settlerdom and Smith agitated for a new vagrancy law, but it was disallowed by the imperial government.[632] At the Kat River - now no longer straddling the border with Xhosaland or functioning as a buffer - Smith had replaced the unpopular Biddulph with another settler, T. Holden Bowker, who was to become equally unpopular. He wrote off the "Kat River experiment" as a failure: for the Khoi and Xhosa to become "civilised... he must [first] become a good servant before he can raise himself to be a master." Later he described the area as a fine district that had become a "lazarette and a receptacle for the refuse of Kaffirland". The residents "beggared and starving, anxious to relieve themselves from Government and charity-rations, took to the hardest work that this country knows - timber-felling and sawing! In a couple of weeks upwards of 90 saw pits were at work"[633] - but Bowker promptly raised the tax to six shillings a load, double that charged to whites. Settlers - including Godlonton - were allocated portions of the Kat River land, while Bowker waged a campaign against the impoverished Xhosa clients ('squatters') who had flocked there, sending in troops to burn their huts in the Blinkwater areas and expel them. When their field-cornet, Andries Botha, protested, he was suspended. All this was done in the name of 'civilisation', and in support of the 'Baster' element of the population.[634]

In 1849 eight Kat River residents petitioned the Aborigines Protection Society in Britain for deliverance from the "insatiable thirst of colonial oppression." In 1850 an oppressive Squatters Ordinance was passed - to prevent 'idle and ill-disposed persons' from 'refusing labour for their livelihood' (a forced labour measure) - though it was eventually withdrawn. Meanwhile the campaign of vilification of the residents continued in the *Grahams' Town Journal*.[635] Eventually Bowker resigned and Andries Botha was reinstated. Yet by 1850 Arie van Rooyen, of Gonaqua origin and the first ordained coloured after James Read junior, could write to the LMS' Freeman: "If things go on, the inhabitants will find it impossible to remain any longer. There is nothing but violent oppression." At about the same time Philip's son-in-law, George Christie, toured the LMS stations in the colony and reported that treatment of 'coloureds' in the last few years had been such as to create among them "a deep and painful impression that the Government had no disposition to consider their claims and do them justice or even preserve their liberty."[636] The tinder was there for rebellion, and the spark was soon to come in the War of Mlanjeni.

Chapter 12

The struggle for representative government and the war and rebellion of 1850 to 1853

In 1848 a constitution drafted by the Attorney General, William Porter, had been sent by Smith to London. It was based on a non-racial qualified franchise: all adult **males** occupying property worth £25 for at least a year were eligible to vote. Porter was a (utilitarian) liberal, not a democrat. Two years later he denounced the alternative of universal manhood suffrage as threatening the colony with 'communism, socialism and red republicanism which had caused so much mischief in France" in the 1848 revolution there. Smith's dispatch to London, however, crossed at sea with a dispatch from Grey which proposed sending Irish convicts to the Cape.[637]

This proposal, made public on 8 November by Smith, aroused a storm of agitation in the Cape Colony against the government, which intersected with and popularised the struggle for representative government. "Behind the single issue of convict transportation lay the wider fact that gubernatorial oligarchy was unacceptable to the emerging local bourgeoisie." A meeting in May 1849, probably the largest held up to then in Cape Town, launched (however) a 'mere' Anti-Convict Association, which for about a year "became the most formidable political force yet to emerge in the colony."[638] "Working together for the movement were Afrikaners, akkerboer and trekboer, the English settlers of all opinions, ranging from a Scots radical like Fairbairn to Godlonton and the Grahamstown merchants, the Cape Folk at Kat River and the institutions, together with the missionaries led by the old Doctor himself."[639] For the bourgeois, the convict labour was said to represent a threat to the desire for 'respectability', though the real challenge was to hierarchies of race and class. Poor coloured workers, on the other hand, who also participated, were threatened by convict labour in the midst of an economic depression. It was a cross-class movement, led by the bourgeoisie. Comparisons were drawn locally with the revolutions of 1848 in Europe.

Dissatisfaction with the Legislative Council had been simmering since 1843. Members of the Legislative Council were now ostracised. The consequence was that "the Legislative Council effectively collapsed, local officials in the districts began to submit their resignations, and government was paralysed." In the midst of the crisis, on 19 September, the ship *Neptune*, carrying the convicts, arrived in Simon's Bay. The Anti-Convict Association, now under the leadership of Fairbairn, organised a boycott of supplies to the government. The *Neptune* was left stranded for five months, until eventually it was ordered onwards and left for Australia on 21 February 1850. Conservative reaction started: those such as Montagu, alarmed by the radicalism of the movement, demanded that Smith asserted the government's authority. On the grounds that the movement was anti-English, Smith secured a delay for representative government.

Very soon two tendencies had crystallised. On one side were the 'conservatives" represented by the Goverer and most of the executive council led by Montagu, the big merchants of Cape Town and the Eastern Cape settlers led by Godlonton - together with the newly arrived Anglican, Bishop Gray. These established a new conservative newspaper, the *Cape Monitor*, in October 1850. On the other were the 'radicals' led by John Fairbairn, Christoffel Brand, Francis Reitz - and Andries Stockenstrom - both English and Afrikaner.[640]

Stockenstrom had re-entered politics to oppose Smith's frontier policy, and supported representative government to get rid of militarist autocracy and restabilise the frontier - in contrast to Grey who had wanted to restabilise the frontier to create the conditions for representative government! Stockenstrom spoke for the Boers of the eastern districts - including those he had led into action in the 1846-1847 war. Maintaining that it was impossible permanently to cow the Xhosa, despising Smith's insistence on foot-kissing, he advocated a return to the old treaty system of Glenelg. He on one side, and Fairbairn, Brand and Reitz on the other, differed on this issue, because the latter supported conquest of the Xhosa - but Stockenstrom was allowed to put his position in the pages of the *Commercial Advertiser* - and of the *Cape of Good Hope Observer*, edited by F.S. Watermeyer, established in January 1849 as a new crusader against the corruption and nepotism of oligarchy. When war broke out again in 1850 Fairbairn's position at least came closer to Stockenstrom's: as a peg on which to hang the campaign against autocratic government, he criticised Smith's frontier policy as serving the interests of a war-profiteering elite of merchants and settlers.[641]

In the Eastern Cape, the Godlontonians were not only disliked by the Boers, but also by increasing numbers of British. Port Elizabeth for example was coming into its own as the main commercial rival of Grahamstown, and a "midlands axis' was arising, aligning Afrikaner Graaff Reinet and English Port Elizabeth against settler Albany. Godlonton's diehard support for Smith further discredited him in the east.[642]

Early in 1850 Grey submitted his constitutional proposals to Smith and instructed him to summon the Legislative Council to fill in its details. But even Smith could see that the existing Legislative Council was discredited, and he turned to municipalities and district road boards (the only elected institutions in the colony) to nominate new candidates for it. Those thus unofficially 'elected" overwhelmingly represented the popular party - Stockenstrom in particular enjoying overwhelming support in the east, as well as support in the west. Smith, however, appointed Godlonton to the fifth seat on the council, though he had not received the fifth largest number of votes. The four 'popular' members soon resigned from the council. Smith promptly accused them of "wanting to be without any government whatever." Together with the Cape Town municipality, they drew up a popular draft constitution and promoted it.[643]

The conservatives argued for a fully nominated second chamber with weak powers together with a strong executive authority. Godlonton wanted no domination by Afrikaners and separate government for the east. They all came to demand stiffer property qualifications for the franchise and stiffer still for membership of representative institutions.[644] Around this time Godlonton criticised the low franchise because it would let in "the untutored aborigines of the Kat River", though Ross argues that he turned against it only as a result of the Kat River rebellion from early 1851.[645] Certainly then his position was clear: the low franchise placed "the Kat river settler with his sheepskin blankets and his hut on the same platform with the burgher... The dunghill and the mansion are to stand side by side on the same dead level, while 'Jack is as good as his master' is to be the standing political maxim for this country."[646] Montagu endorsed the view that the low franchise would mean a "body of ignorant coloured persons, whose mere numbers would swamp the wealthy and educated portion of the community, would enjoy votes which would be turned to account by political partisans."[647] The editor of the pro-government *Cape Monitor* (15/5/1853) bewailed that the new constitution would "raise up an immense black constituency comprising almost every Negro, Hottentot and Malay within the colony... and it will completely swamp the British population. The knowledge of this constituency... does not rise much higher than the instincts of brute beast - and that of three fourths of the Boers is not much superior"[648]

The popular party defended the low franchise. Bank calls their ideas "a new racial conservatism", but perhaps he goes too far. Porter, the Attorney-General who had originally proposed it, attacked the British settlers, who feared 'Dutch preponderance", and "whose strength might be in the support of the coloured population" but who were throwing the Coloureds into the arms of the Afrikaners "by depriving the Coloured population of those privileges which our liberal-hearted Dutchmen hold forth with a free hand... It seems to me suicide."[649] At the same time, defence of the low franchise was not necessarily philanthropic. Du Toit and Giliomee comment on the change in 20 years among Afrikaners from "seeking self-government for slave-holders, as a means of staving off threats to their property rights and traditional privileges, to support for a popular movement for representative government that would include the extension of political rights to subordinates and former slaves."[650] Others, however, suggest the popular party supported the low franchise in the interest primarily of enfranchising Afrikaners to ensure "white security and solidarity" (with the consequence that a minority of coloureds acquired the vote also).[651] What was the attitude of coloureds? Some at the Kat River expressed a mixture of "foreboding", but "satisfaction" at the £25 franchise. Probably the dominant feeling, however, was the fear that any form of representative government would entrench in power their oppressors - and establish vagrancy laws and other coercive legislation on labour. Such viewpoints were expressed even at conservative missions like Genadendal.[652]

Fairbairn left in October 1850 for Britain, deputed to put the case of the popular party. Stockenstrom joined him there the following spring after touring the colony to assess opinion.[653] In London Stockenstrom intended to try to get a repeat of 1836-1837: the retrocession of Xhosa territory and the reintroduction of treaties, in a situation where this was no longer possible. Before he left the colony, there had broken out in December 1850 not only war again with the Xhosa, but a rebellion among coloureds originating in the Kat River settlement.[654] The conservatives sent a spokesman to London to try to delay the onset of representative government - an argument strengthened by the outbreak.[655]

Representative government was one crisis for Smith. The resumption of war with the Xhosa - in many senses merely the resumption of the war of the Axe - was another. The war was precipitated by Smith's decision to depose Sandile. It was launched on the Xhosa side under the patronage of the war doctor Mlanjeni.[656] Though, as Crais points out, Smith was unable to 'abolish' the chieftainship as he would have liked, the chiefs had experienced social demotion: in British Kaffraria they had lost their two main levers of social control - cattle repossession and witchcraft execution - so that their power and legitimacy had declined rapidly.[657] Living under military rule, claimed Sandile, had "emasculated him". "By 1848, many a chief in British Kaffraria was no longer regarded as a 'father' of his people. Instead he was seen as 'an old wife', bossed around by Englishmen. The undermining of elites is a key cause of millenarian movements - and figurative castration extended beyond chiefs. Patriarchal privileges - cattle, land, political power - haemorrhaged away. So did lives. By definition, casualties were concentrated among the most militaristic men; 'all our best men are dead'".[658] This, together with a terrible drought, was the context for the rise of Mlanjeni from January 1850 as a prophet, and eventually as a war leader in place of the discredited chiefs. "Religious leadership from within the common masses aimed to seize the initiative from the impotent aristocracy."[659]

Mlanjeni was "a teenager [of 18 years], dying of tuberculosis, virtually living in a river" who "proclaimed a new message from God. Bloodshed should end; sorcery [witchcraft] should be eradicated, by new methods of purification. Since almost all deaths were ascribed to witchcraft, he was effectively promising eternal life."[660] In August, the British attempted to arrest Mlanjeni, but failed. By early October, through a 'whispering campaign', the message had spread to the Thembu, to Lesotho, among the Gcaleka - and among the Xhosa on farms in the colony. Fortified by the prophecies, farmworkers deserted their jobs and returned to Xhosaland: one farmworker told a settler (as he reported) that "their strength was superior to mine".[661] While servants deserted in one direction, white farmers fled their farms towards Port Elizabeth: interestingly, Xhosa and Khoi servants warned Boers but not British settlers of the danger to come.[662]

Crais comments that: "The prophet spoke to issues of ethnicity and community and not directly to class, but the resistance which centred around the witchdoctor took on proletarian overtones and the emergent working class took the lead in the war which was about to begin."[663] However Maqoma, together with Sandile, tried to "co-opt the national hysteria" by encouraging Mlanjeni to "mobilise the masses in a rebellion against colonial hegemony that would remove restrictions on cattle-based feudalism and restore royal legitimacy."[664] It was Maqoma, argue both Mostert and Stapleton, who made the military plans, and, indeed, once the war started, Mlanjeni's influence tended to decline.[665]

Smith came to the frontier to call a 'Great Meeting' with the chiefs and, when Sandile and Maqoma did not attend, deposed Sandile and appointed the 29-year old Charles Brownlee, son of the missionary, in his place. Mlanjeni ordered the killing of cattle. Smith sent out a force to hunt for Sandile which was attacked and virtually routed by the Xhosa on 24 December - with the coloured Cape Mounted Rifles again saving the day by covering the retreat. Shortly before this Maqoma met Smith, who confirmed he intended to strip Sandile of power. Maqoma then enraged Smith by complaining of his unjust expulsion from the Kat River in 1829. Smith boasted in return that "you know all about ships - you have been at Algoa Bay and know I can bring them there." To this Maqoma's response was to ask if Smith had "any ships that can sail into the Amatolas."

By the end of December the Ngqika had overrun the frontier as far as George, and destroyed the new settler villages of Woburn, Auckland and Juanasberg: "the rage seemed particularly against the English", reported Read.[666] Governor Smith was left besieged in Fort Cox. "It is doubtful if any other civil or military commander found himself in such an embarrassing situation of his own devising throughout the span of empire. Sir Harry Smith's bombast had failed spectacularly. His governorship of the frontier had produced a shambles that was remote from his intentions, but which many had predicted would be the consequence of his policies."[667] An attempt to relieve Fort Cox on 29 December was forced into a four-hour bloody retreat under assault from the Xhosa forces. Smith escaped on 31 December, escorted by 250 Cape Mounted Riflemen - by "putting on the clothes of a private Hottentot soldier".[668] The Xhosa, said Godlonton, were "masters of that whole country". Moreover "Mackinnon's account of the organisation, intensity, and ferocity of the two battles in the Amatolas showed that this differed from his own experience of Xhosa warfare."[669]

Sandile blamed the war on the oppression of the English: "You English come to rob me of my people... Some white men come and say the Kaffirs steal; but the white men are the robbers. God made a boundary by the sea and you white men cross it to rob us of our country... Englishmen make promises about the land and then break them. They make a boundary and then take it away."[670] His sentiments were echoed by the rank and file: one Xhosa met by missionaries at the start of the war explained: "The English have always been making war and saying it is we who are seeking war. This is now the fifth war we have been in with the English, and though we lose our country by every war, we are regardless of that, and will fight."[671]

Just before the war started, a missionary was told by a Xhosa that the missionaries would not be spared "on account of what Mr Calderwood has done to them."[672] It reveals their hatred of Calderwood. In similar vein, Maqoma said to another missionary a little later "You are a teacher. You say that it is your object in coming among us, to teach us the word of God. But why do you always give over teaching that word, and all leave your stations and go to military posts when there is war! You all call yourselves men of peace; what then have you got to do at any of the forts, there are only fighting men there? I am doubtful whether any of you be true men of peace; Read, I think he is, but look at Calderwood; what have you to say about him - did he not come as a teacher? Now he is a magistrate - one of those who make war."[673] "What are the teachers?," said another Xhosa, "I do not care about them; it is them who have killed the country... we look on all white people as our enemies."[674] Sandile burst out to another missionary: "Who are these teachers? Are they not men who at home have no people of their own, and they come here to take my people from me!...They only take my people and give them to government... I have always spared the teachers, but now I think I will just kill them too! What did they do? - only teach men that they are not to fight, even although their chiefs be in danger... The white men! The white men put the Son of God to death, although he had no sin: I am like the Son of God, without sin, and the white men seek to put me also to death."[675] It is clear that from the top to the base of Xhosa society there was a deep-seated and determined common fury against the white man.[676]

Smith's problems were compounded by mutiny among the "Kaffir Police" (who had been founded in 1835) and by the great majority of the Kat River coloureds, who joined with the Xhosa in rebellion, and spearheaded a far wider uprising of coloureds within the colony. The initial leader was Hermanus Matroos (aka Nguxukumeshe), who renewed the relationship he had with Maqoma at the Kat River before 1829. While Matroos, like other leaders of the coloureds, was an independent peasant, his "rag-tag army of the disinherited - Khoikhoi, ex-slaves, Gonaqua, Mantatees, Xhosa - by and large were also squatters and rural workers."[677] Writing in January to the LMS, Read expressed his shock that: "scarcely was war broken out before he (Hermanus) ...began to press and compel the Hottentots of Tidmanton [formerly Blinkwater] to join him who had no arms and ammunition to protect themselves they applied to the magistrate and commandant at Hertzog but little aid was given and the consequence was that the most of the Hottentots at that... place were compelled to join... we found to our great grief that the minds of many others were disaffected... many Hottentots were flying from their masters in no way connected with Kat River to join those who were now considered rebels - we wrote letters and sent messages to try to stay the torrent but in spite of all we only saved a few." Read, his son, and Van Rooyen visited the rebel camp, found many there not from the Kat River, and made desperate attempts to turn their flock away from the "evil of war and especially... the evil of rebellion".[678] James junior wrote how his "heart sunk within me... It seemed to be the breaking down of the work of fifty years."[679] These were, after all, not the pagan serfs of the revolt of 1799-1803, but a supposedly model Christianised and literate community. Not a few of them were in the tradition of the 'native agents' so assiduously fostered by Read (and opposed by Moffat).[680]

The revolt continued to gather strength. Residents of the Moravian missions at Enon and Shiloh joined, as did some from Bethelsdorp and all but two from Theopolis. Besides these, Cape Mounted Riflemen deserted, or in some cases, mutinied to join it, and Mfengu refused to re-enlist for military service.[681] Summing up its causes at the start, Read wrote to the LMS: "There were as you know irritating circumstances which were creating very generally an underground feeling - an idea that the Whites, especially the English, were trying to enslave them again - they said they were insulted almost by every low Englishman, the attacks upon the Missionary Stations, constant breaking of Vagrant Act at the Institutions, the sending of the Magistrates to catechise them, read, etc, irritated them, as they never heard that anything of the kind was done to white men - then in the Kat River the conduct of Biddulph, Sir Henry Pottinger, Bowker the magistrate of Fort Beaufort trying to get the peoples lands from them, the wood taxed, etc".[682] Read junior too mentioned the "greater dread of the English than of the Dutch community": that the rebels said "the English must leave the country, and go away in ships."[683]

When Read, a frail 74-year old, visited the rebel camp, he "pointed out that they ought to seek redress if they had grievances in a lawful way - but not by force of arms and by violence." The rebels replied, significantly, that Read "had been seeking redress for them 50 years and that instead of things getting better they were getting worse and worse." Read remonstrated defensively that the "late Dr van der Kemp found their fathers and grandfathers...50 years ago without property without clothing without education without means of grace compared to what the advantages and privileges they now enjoyed - it was as light from darkness" The rebels, however "did not seem inclined to listen to our remonstrances and advice" though they wished it to be made known "they had nothing against the Dutch Boors".[684] One rebel said "This land is our land; what portion of it is in the possession of the Hottentots? Strangers inhabit it, while the real owners have only this ostrich nest, the Kat River; and this is called giving a nation land!" His son James related how it was "in vain" to explain the proposed constitution to them, that "by the low franchise which had been fixed, the coloured people would largely share in the boon of self-government. They plainly told us that we were only hushing their fears. They sometimes seemed mad with rage."[685]

Other evidence suggests the same: the treatment of coloureds by British settlers, the devastation caused by the frontier wars (with no or belated compensation); the fierce desire not to return to a condition of slavery; the fear of representative government; the fact that they had little to lose.[686] As Elbourne intimates, while many rebels had lost faith in the government of Queen Victoria in Britain, others still looked to it as the fount of justice, their natural protector against the dangers of representative government.[687] "The...rebels say they will not and do not fight against the Queen", wrote Read in July 1851, "but against those who wish to enslave them, this of course is folly, but so it is, the war may become one of races".[688] As Crais points out "even the most committed rebel failed to fully comprehend that the London of the first three decades of the 19th century no longer existed. Few accepted that the influence of Exeter Hall was very much on the decline, and none seemed to realise that many policy makers in London entertained views almost as racist as those held by the colonial farmers they attacked."[689] The aim of many seemed to be to establish a "separate district... in which they would live by themselves."[690]

At this stage, having reduced the Cape garrison, Smith was faced with a chronic shortage of troops on the frontier to quell the coloureds and the Xhosa. Immediately after his escape from Fort Cox, he called on the colonists to "rise *en masse*... to destroy and exterminate these most barbarous and treacherous savages, for the moment formidable."[691] But he could not mobilise the necessary forces. Boer farmers had already abandoned the frontier and intended to leave the fighting to the British army.[692] Godlonton actually asked Smith to call on Stockenstrom to lead the Boers, but Smith refused. Godlonton later complained of the Boers not fighting, to which they replied (according to Read): "You people on the Frontier supply the Caffres with the munitions of war, then pick a quarrel with them, and then you expect us to come and fight your battles, while many of you sit in your shops and make more money."[693] In January already Calderwood wrote to Godlonton in frustration at his fears that the Xhosa were "doing their utmost to separate *all* classes from the English"[694] In mid-1851 William Southey confided to Godlonton "It would be easy to subjugate all Kaffirland and take it for ourselves for ever **if men would generally turn out for the work**... All Kaffirs, even to Natal, must be subdued, their lands conquered from them and they themselves made *servants*. This will however, not all be effected at once, but I shall live to see it." (my emphasis)[695]

While waiting for reinforcements, because of the desertion of Boers and coloureds, the British were compelled to place a greater reliance on Mfengu troops. Some 400 Mfengu participated. Hostility between Mfengu and coloured rebels was sharp, with coloureds acting out their resentment of Mfengu labour undercutting and pressure on land.[696] In July, moreover, Read noted: "The Fingoes have done great service for Government, and the Colony in this war, but have made themselves odious to the Caffres, and should there be an opportunity the revenge will be fearful."[697] The British also had the support of the Gqunukhwebe, which was fortunate for them, because Gqunukhwebe territory lay across the crucial supply line from the port of East London to King Williams Town in the centre of the war zone.[698] Furthermore, the Ndlambe save for one minor chief remained neutral while some chiefs joined the colonial side.[699]

The initial Ngqika-coloured strategy was, with the Kat River valley, and particularly the Waterkloof (Mtontsi)[700], as the centre of their operations, to besiege and try to capture the principal British forts - Fort Cox, Fort White, Fort Beaufort, Fort Hare, all of which were more camps than 'forts' and were weakly fortified. It was essential for the British to hold these forts. If they lost them, it would probably sway the Ndlambe to enter the war against them, and even the Gqunukhwebe, as well as persuading wavering coloureds to join the rebellion. It would mean, for the British, retreat to Algoa Bay and Grahamstown, and fighting from there to reconquer the Xhosa, which would have led to a much longer war than the twenty-seven months which this war lasted. Smith commented early in it how the better fighting capacities of the Xhosa meant that a supply train had to be guarded by a column of 2200 rather than, as in 1836 "100 infantry and twenty Cape Mounted Rifles."[701] In the event the costs of the war and the unwillingness of the colonists to pay for it became major issues in British politics. A December 1851 editorial in the

London Times said that all the British empire required of South Africa was " 'a small territory round Cape Town.' If settlers chose to stay near the Xhosa, they should do so at their own risk." It conveyed the general mood in Britain. So the battle for the forts was decisive in the outcome of the war.[702]

Fort White was attacked first, under the leadership of Sandile, on 3 January. On 6 January Maqoma joined Hermanus' forces in an attack on Fort Beaufort. Both attacks failed, and Hermanus was killed at Fort Beaufort.[703] On 21 January about 5000-6000 Xhosa, as well a rebel Khoi, launched a determined assault on Fort Hare. The women, as usual, waited at the sides of the battle carrying the men's *knobkieries*. The battle lasted five hours, and was fought almost entirely against the 800 Mfengu defending the fort. Eventually the Xhosa retreated.[704] Mostert wonders why the Xhosa did not persist with the attack on the forts, or why they did not use a strategy of night attack, when their losses had not been that heavy, and when they knew the British were paralysed by lack of forces.[705] The Xhosa however seem to have wanted a limited war. Sandile made peace overtures between January and March, which Mostert does not mention.[706]

Fort Armstrong, at the Kat River, a solidly-constructed fort, which was garrisoned by coloureds, headed by the Field Cornet Christian Groepe with Andries Botha as his deputy. Groepe was regarded as "an old washer-woman" and a *smeerlap* (arse-wiper) by his rebel sons. On 22 January the garrison was confronted by 400 rebels led by William Uithaalder, successor to Matroos, who like numerous others, had served in the Cape Mounted Rifles and took over key skills to the rebels. The garrison surrendered, while the thirty-three English in the fort fled on horseback. The fort's isolation made the victory militarily unimportant. But its capture became a gaping sore for the settlers and for Smith, who were determined to rescue it.[707] The war now entered a period of stalemate with the British unable to act because of lack of reinforcements, and the Xhosa retreating to the fastnesses of the Waterkloof and the Amatolas. From here they emerged, not as in previous wars, to sweep across the frontier *en masse* and seize cattle from white farms. At first they moved in small bands, attacking white men, picking off farms one by one.[708] Meanwhile a number of chiefs took up positions in the Fish River bush from where they harassed the line between Graham's Town and Fort Beaufort, while the Ndlambe chief Siyolo threatened the supply lines between Graham's Town and King Williams' Town.[709]

First priority for Smith was the recapture of Fort Armstrong. On 23 January the first reinforcements for the frontier, 1500 coloured levies from the Western Cape, arrived at East London. These were augmented by British settler levies, and attacked Fort Armstrong on 22 February. As Read reported: "Some of the Commandoes marched out for Kat River as you will see from the papers with a red flag with the inscription written on it: Extermination."[710] The rebels resisted strongly, but gave up the fort when a cannon opened fire against them. Shops and houses through the fort and the Kat River settlement, whether of rebels or loyalists, were burnt in an orgy of settler revenge. Uithaalder escaped. When James Read and his son went to greet the British forces they were put under guard because of settler threats to kill them.

In March there was a big defection from the once 800-strong Cape Mounted Rifles (CMR). Four months later Smith was compelled to discharge the remaining conscripts . Throughout 1851 and 1852, moreover, there were fears among whites of the spread of the rebellion to the Western Cape.[711] The first small British reinforcements arrived only in April and May.[712] Thembu, Sarhili's Gcaleka, and rebel Khoi made 12 attacks on the settler village of Whittlesea in the open grasslands north of the Amatolas - land which had been annexed by Smith in 1847 as North Victoria. Sarhili lost hundreds of men at the battle of Imvane in April.[713] As time passed with Smith still without the forces to conduct a serious offensive, the Xhosa and their allies gained in confidence. In July and August they suddenly invaded and overran the whole colony up to Algoa Bay, isolating Grahamstown.[714] In July Read wrote that the Xhosa and coloureds were "committing great depredation in the whole district of Albany and Somerset, carrying everything before them."[715] Godlonton lamented that the "richest part of the Eastern Province...dotted with farm-houses and teeming a few weeks before with flocks of fine woolled sheep, troops of horses, and herds of cattle, was described as desolate."[716]

By September, however, Smith felt strong enough to send troops into the Waterkloof. Maqoma had been able to use this old haunt of his because the rebellion at the Kat River removed it as a buffer and turned it into a safe haven and retreat. The Waterkloof, with its thick jungle-like bush and steep ravines - brilliantly characterised by Mostert - was a far more difficult terrain for the British to fight the Xhosa in than even the Fish River bush or the Amatolas. The prolonged battle for the Waterkloof, where Maqoma was joined by Uithaalder and Brander[717] - a war within a war, in which the British troops experienced unrelieved hardship which eventually led to serious disquiet among them - began in September 1851 and lasted until March 1853. On the Ngqika side it was led by Maqoma, "the greatest military mind of his or any other Xhosa generation."[718] In it four thousand troops were tied down - against possibly few more than two hundred poorly-equipped men.[719] After the first two incursions, in September and October-November, while Smith claimed successes, the Port Elizabeth newspaper wrote that "Maqoma remains proud master of the field. He has outgeneraled the First Division. He has cut down its men and for the remainder he must entertain something very nearly approaching supreme contempt".[720] It was 'the greatest Xhosa military success over Europeans" and is remembered in many oral traditions.[721]

With the Xhosa still in occupation in the colony, and with the troops stymied against Maqoma, British forces were ordered in November across the Kei, as in 1835 and 1847, to invade Gcaleka territory. One officer called it 'the Great Cattle Patrol'. Sarhili offered little resistance, and some 30,000 head of cattle were seized.[722]

By the end of 1851, however, Grey and Prime Minister Russell in London had come to a decision - on the basis of the situation on the Xhosa frontier compounded by a new crisis in the Orange River Sovereignty - to abandon the Sovereignty. When war with the Xhosa had broken out in December 1850, Warden in the Sovereignty had been planning a military campaign against Moshoeshoe. Early the following July his force was soundly defeated in the battle of Viervoet. Warden urged on Smith the need to take revenge by putting down "the common enemy of the white man", but Smith, bogged down in fighting the Xhosa and Khoi rebels, demurred.[723] British settlers continued unavailingly to agitate for the crushing of the Basotho, while Boer discontent in the Sovereignty grew, with a faction colluding with Moshoeshoe, including supplying him with arms and ammunition. Pretorius at Potchefstroom saw the chance to negotiate formal independence for the Transvaal. This was achieved in January 1852 through the Sand River Convention, in which the British foreswore all alliances with black rulers, and granted the Transvaalers a monopoly of the arms and ammunition supply from colonial ports. The Boer elite of the south-western Transvaal were now equipped, in Keegan's phrase, to become "forward representatives of colonial capitalism." [724]

Meanwhile Grey sent out two assistant commissioners to organise the abandonment of the Sovereignty, leaving Smith to devote his full attention to the Xhosa war. One of the commissioners having died, the other, W. S. Hogge, wrote dispatches to Britain severely critical of Smith's conduct of the war: "we are beaten at all points, in the Fish River bush, in the Waterkloof, and across the Orange River."[725] As a result, Smith was recalled by the British government in January 1852 and left the country in April. Before his letter of recall reached Smith, the ministry of Lord John Russell, and with it, Earl Grey, had fallen - in February 1852, largely because of the costs of the war in the Cape. It was replaced by that of the Earl of Derby, with Sir John Pakington as colonial secretary.[726]

In January Sandile sued for peace on the basis that the Xhosa would keep the Amatolas, but - despite the war-weariness on both sides, Smith would not agree.[727] Since there were by December 8660 British regulars in South Africa (more than twice as many as ever before) it was now possible to penetrate the Amatolas for the first time. This was done on the basis of a 'famine strategy' proposed by Colonial Secretary Earl Grey - which amounted to the usual since 1812 scorched-earth destruction of crops and kraals. (In addition, Grey suggested that, to prevent cultivation, all Xhosa women should be captured and sent to the Cape as prisoners.) The fighting was organised by Lieutenant-

Colonel Eyre, who had become a specialist in countering the jungle-war tactics of the Xhosa. The effects were gruesome, and led to deaths from starvation among the Xhosa.[728]

Before he departed, Smith personally led, along with Eyre, one last campaign in the Waterkloof, "the most violently driven effort" of the war. Not only men, but also women and children were executed - often by the Mfengu after they had been taken prisoner.[729] Maqoma and the Khoi were temporarily driven from the Waterkloof by the thoroughness of the British assault, and Smith handed over amicably to his military colleague and successor, Sir George Cathcart - to return to Britain still, despite his utter failure in South Africa, regarded as a hero. But the Xhosa had been heartened by two developments: by Smith's recall, and by the sinking of the *Birkenhead*, which, carrying the last load of troop reinforcements, struck a rock off the southern Cape Coast on 26 February 1852. 445 of the 638 persons aboard died. The Xhosa imagined that they could secure better terms by fighting on and dealing with Smith's successor.[730]

Godlonton - Smith's closest confidante during the war - compiled a *Narrative* supporting Smith and the settler standpoint on the war from material in the *Journal*, painting the Xhosa as treacherous and cunning savages encouraged by unscrupulous philanthropists. The Kat River rebellion had particularly aroused the fury of the settlers, resulting in the unleashing in the *Journal* of an unprecedented "storm of vindictiveness...a campaign of vilification, innuendo and accusation."[731] Some of this material too was republished in Godlonton's pamphlet, *Review of the Condition of the Frontier Hottentots from 1799 to 1851*. In July 1851 Read could write: "The Frontier Colonists... have settled their minds as to every Hottentot being a rebel and seem determined that they shall be treated as such and every instrument will be employed to prevent even the best of our people settling in the Kat River again... They will also insist upon the breaking up of all the Institutions and doing away with Hottentots residing in groups anywhere - the feeling against the Hottentots and against our Society and Missionaries were never so high as now".[732]

It was a propaganda campaign to buttress the conservatives' case against the low franchise - and to discredit the Stockenstrom-Fairbairn mission to Britain on behalf of the 'popular party'. Read, who had pleaded with his flock not to rebel, was absurdly accused by Godlonton of fomenting the rebellion. As an LMS spokesman complained of Godlonton, he had "for years availed himself of his position as the editor of a public journal, to misrepresent facts to promote the circulation of falsehood.. [and] most pertinaciously to abuse the coloured races and all who have dared to appear as their friends."[733] Stockenstrom also came under unprecedentedly harsh attack. Not only had he been unpatriotic in preventing Boers fighting in the war against the

Xhosa.[734] He too had been instrumental in instigating the Kat River rebellion. The popular constitution was portrayed as seditious, and Stockenstrom with his coloured allies as the leader of 'discontented oppositionists". Godlonton wrote of Stockenstrom that "In my opinion his object is to stir up the colony to rebellion...He richly deserves prosecution... He knows he is backed by a good many disaffected Boers and by 2000 Kat River vagabonds."

The war was presented as the extension of the anti-British rebelliousness shown in the anti-convict campaign, instigated by treacherous Afrikaners to end British rule and drive out the British settlers. Their mission was "to secure for Cape Town the government of the rest of the colony, to augment the political power of the servile classes, so as that they may stand in successful antagonism to those who possess property." Smith lent his support to Godlonton against Stockenstrom, telling Grey that he had no doubt that the Xhosa "have been encouraged to revolt, by the disunion within the colony with which he has been so mixed up; and though I do not charge him with inciting the Kat River Hottentots to rebellion I have no doubt they believed they were promoting the views of their patron by taking up arms against a Government which he has constantly vituperated." Because Stockenstrom's farm near Bedford was the only one in the area not ransacked (because Sandile had posted a guard on it), anonymous settlers burnt the farmhouse to the ground while Stockenstrom was in London.[735] But the settler elite were fighting a rearguard action on the constitution.

Settler imperialism, assisted by the 'rogue governor' Smith, failed in its objectives of imperial expansion because it evoked massive resistance from both Boers and black people. Attempts to dispossess independent chiefdoms brought not support but intensified resistance from the Boers. British politicians in mid-century were not prepared to foot the bills for the wars which resulted, and wanted to shift financial and military responsibilities to the colonists. The settlers "ambitions for self-aggrandisement outstripped the economic potential that could be realised." Britain's interests should be secured through free trade and representative government to broaden the base of white rule rather than the 1840s and early 1850s militarisation of colonial society. This was what the new Governor Cathcart, arriving at the Cape on 30 March 1852, was sent to bring about.[736]

Chapter 13

The establishment of representative government

As Cathcart arrived, Montagu followed Smith into departure from office, harassed by numerous petitions for his dismissal.[737] Cathcart established himself on the frontier to end the war, with a lieutenant governor, Charles Darling, in Cape Town. Together they "dismantled the alliances [Smith and Montagu] had built. They broke the close circle of kinship and friendship, tracking back to the settlers, which had dominated official life... cleansing the civil service and exposing their financial malpractices... and they made possible the establishment of the Cape Parliament, with its low franchise, two years later."[738] It was a political revolution not incomparable to that of Bourke in 1827-1828, which consummated the breaking of the power of the eighteenth century Dutch elite.

First order of business, however, was settling accounts with the Khoi rebels. The land of all those considered as rebels was taken from them at the Kat River.[739] Andries Botha, with a long pro-British military, who had been "a reluctant rebel and then only for a short time", when he shot at "Englishmen and farmers", was made a scapegoat.[740] . Already, during 1851, a case of collusion had been prepared against Botha by Calderwood, and he had been arrested, released, and rearrested. In May 1852 he was put on trial for high treason, sentenced to death, and later reprieved. As Mostert remarks, it was the first treason trial to be heard by the Supreme Court - predecessor of the Rivonia trial just a hundred years later. John Philip had died almost a year before, on 27 August 1851, his death undoubtedly hastened by the Kat River rebellion and the settler backlash against it. James Read senior died aged 75 on 8 May 1852, just four days before Botha's trial began, broken-hearted also.[741]

Cathcart - though substantial reinforcements had come with him - temporarily suspended operations in the war. Thereafter, in June, colonial forces secured the wagon road from Grahamstown to King Williams' Town and established a fort (Fort Fordyce) in the Waterkloof. Patrols through the Waterkloof and Amatolas failing to remove Maqoma or Sandile, Cathcart launched a second invasion across the Kei in August 1852, seizing 10, 000 more Gcaleka cattle. Thereafter Eyre led an attack on the Waterkloof in

September, "by far the most vicious episode of the war". Maqoma fled to join Sandile in the Amatolas, where the Xhosa refused to surrender unconditionally or to cross the Kei. In October the one rebellious Ndlambe chief, Siyolo, was tricked into prison, court-martialled on a charge of sedition and sentenced to death. He was eventually reprieved and sent to Robben Island.[742] Through October and November crops and kraals were burnt in the Amatolas, until Cathcart set off across the Orange in November to seek revenge for Moshoeshoe's victory at Viervoet.[743] At the battle of Berea in December, the Basotho cavalry overwhelmed Cathcart's smaller force, but Mosweshwe tactfully allowed him to claim a victory and return to the colony. There, after negotiations with Sandile, his deposition was rescinded, and peace was concluded on 2 March 1853. Both in respect of Moshoeshoe and the Xhosa, settlers complained of Cathcart's lack of political will to finally 'subdue' the Xhosa.[744] The last rebels turned themselves in in 1856 and were given patches of land.[745]

At twenty-seven months, the colony-Xhosa war was to be the second-longest war in South African history. During it, some sixteen thousand Xhosa and 1,400 on the British side died, the highest in the history of the colonial wars with the Xhosa.[746] The Xhosa were able to deploy massive firepower, at times outgunning the colonial troops.[747] The war was brutal, with a "no prisoners policy" by the British and gruesome torture practiced by the Xhosa on prisoners.[748] When it broke out, a shaken Smith described it, correctly, as the "most important event that ever occurred in the Colony". The war put Smith's military reputation, as well as Earl Grey's career, on the line.[749] Mostert calls it a war of race, but it was directed by the Xhosa against the British and their black collaborators, not against the Boers.[750] In pitting the colonised proletariat against their colonial masters, it was also a war of class. As Smith remarked at the time, it had "arisen out of the direct relations to each other of the two Classes forming the great bulk of the Inhabitants of this Colony, the White and Black or in other words the Master and Servant."[751] Crais writes that "the poor rejected an entire system of settler capitalism."[752] Objectively, this was the case, though the methods of action and consciousness of the participants were more diverse.

Examples of Xhosa consciousness have already been given. Uithaalder's well known letter to Adam Kok, Griqua leader at Philippolis, expresses the idea of uniting all the 'brown' people on the basis of 'Hottentot nationalism'. "For as much as we the poor oppressed Hottentot race", it begins, have been "oppressed by the unrighteous British settlers", who constantly petition for laws "which tend to oppression and complete ruin of the coloured and poor of this land, a land which we, as natives, may justly claim as our mother land." It concludes, "Beloved, rise manfully and unanimously as a nation and children of one house to engage yourselves in this important work"[753] Particularly in the

Waterkloof with Maqoma, the coloured rebels brought with them their mission practices, of Bible reading and hymn-singing (before battle), in a fiercely millenarian form of Christianity passed down from van der Kemp. "Trust, therefore, in the Lord (whose character is known to be unfriendly to injustice), and undertake your work, and he will give us prosperity" as written in the rebel leader's letter quoted by Peires.[754]

Crais notes a general build up of resistance in the 1840s among the oppressed in the colony, with theft and desertion its main forms: by the end of the decade, "proletarian forms of opposition intersected with, and critically shaped, peasant and squatter movements and protest organised on the basis of ethnicity."[755] Keegan comments how, in the Xhosa-coloured alliance, "an element of class solidarity coexisted with the rhetoric of national liberation" - though there were also tensions in the alliance.[756] Rebel Khoi were related to have said to Xhosa: "Don't think that because we are with you against the settlers, we will submit to you; we are ready to fight you at any day if we see that you wish to domineer over us as you did before."[757] As if in reply, and to reintroduce notions of class oppression, Sandile before the battle for Fort Hare told Khoi rebels: "if you aid me, I shall re-establish the Kingdom of Chama" - an old Khoi dynasty - "I see that notwithstanding all the assistance you have given the government to fight against us in every war, and all your toil for the white man, you are still very poor...you have been... starved and oppressed... If you join me... you shall be completed with cattle and all that a man should have."[758] Of consciousness, Crais writes: "In Western Xhosaland, religious leadership resurfaced out of more traditional anti-witchcraft customs through which Xhosa, however fleetingly, constructed a unit beyond the *umzi* and beyond the chief's great place to challenge dispossession, proletarianization and the spread of empire. In some cases Xhosa fought alongside their chiefs, in other cases with rebel leaders such as Hermanus, Uithaalder or Brander. Rich peasants fought alongside squatters and rural proletarians and Xhosa chiefs and commoners. The growth of European domination in the Eastern Cape... produced a popular consciousness, which transcended the more localised identities rooted in the previous century... People defined themselves in a number of ways and one identity did not automatically exclude another. Africans could be, and typically were, Xhosa and workers and Christians and fathers all at the same time... Class entered the repertoire of people's definition of self and opened the possibilities for the rise of broader forms of resistance." And he emphasises how historical memory fuelled the resistance: "Chiefs and commoners discussed the long history of wars along the frontier and declared British rule alien and despotic. Ex-slaves and Khoikhoi recalled their days of servitude, remembered the 'taste of freedom' and proclaimed that they would never again become the slaves of the white man."[759]

But the war had been lost. For the Ngqika this meant, despite their bitter protests, the loss of the Amatolas. The Amatola district was renamed the Crown Reserve, and allocated for settler and Mfengu occupation. Thus Maqoma's and Sandile's lands fell finally into the hands of land speculators. From the Crown Reserve to the sea the border lands were handed out to loyalist chiefs with their people.[760] The Gqunukhwebe received, for example, a large territory along the Keiskamma and its tributaries: to their chief Kama, "a considerable proportion of the former inhabitants of these parts adhered, for the sake of being allowed to settle in the country to which they were attached."[761] The Ngqika were confined to a small and infertile reserve between the Amatolas and the Kei.[762] Britsih Kaffraria remained as a separate dependency, despite settler pressures for its incorporation into the colony. Colonel Maclean was appointed as its Lieutenant Governor. In 1859 more than 6000 Germans were settled along the supply-line between East London and King Williams Town.[763]

The Mfengu did very well in the settlement, with settlements from Tarkastad almost to the Indian Ocean near East London, in the Herschel district and at Whittlesea, as well as Maqoma's former land in the Kat River valley. "The land the chiefs received is approximately that which their descendants in the Ciskei govern today" wrote Moyer in the 1970s.[764] Moreover such was their effort in the war, that a permanent detachment of Mfengu troops was established.[765]

On 21 April 1853, little more than a month after the signing of peace with the Xhosa, the new representative government constitution for the Colony arrived in Cape Town. During the war the constitution had been deadlocked, with various proposals floated between London and the colony concerning forms of separatism, or moving the colonial capital to Grahamstown. 'Montagu's men', appointed to the Legislative Council conservatives had been quite content to use their positions to block and delay formal discussion.[766] Under the new regime of Cathcart, the British colonial secretary, the conservative Pakington, delayed the constitution once again. The 'popular party' furiously petitioned not only for its immediate introduction but the restoration of the £25 franchise which had been raised along the way.

However in January 1853 a coalition of Whigs and Peelites led by Aberdeen took over government in Britian, and the Duke of Newcastle, the new Colonial Secretary, advised Cathcart to stop all consideration of separatism or removal of the capital, and to ratify the constitution immediately. He also restored the £25 property franchise (or a £50 salary a year), but agreed with the conservatives to double the financial qualification for membership of the upper house. The upper house, however, was to be elected and not nominated. The franchise in the Cape Colony was in fact lower, i.e. more liberal, than in Britain at the time. Conservative settlers were mortified.[767] In a private letter Newcastle explained to Cathcart that the concessions were to prevent "the revival of political agitation at the close of the war", arguing the need to preserve the 'rising commercial classes' at the Cape as allies.[768] The aim, in other words, was the "empowering of local elites" - the development-oriented classes that supported the popular party: they wanted the stable conditions in which capital could be raised for infrastructure and company formation.[769]

Of the non-racialism of the franchise, Andrew Ross writes that it "owed not a little to John Philip's utter dedication to his vision of a Christian civilisation."[770] "The express reason for the £25 franchise" argues Ross, "was to give the vote to a substantial number of coloured men, particularly those resident on the mission stations."[771] Keegan disagrees. The Cape, he argues, was committed to non-racial legal forms because "liberal ideology had become embedded in British public discourse": it did not "imply any real intention to dilute racial hegemony in political or economic spheres" - rather its "major purpose was to maximize the political incorporation of white men."[772] In 1848 Fairbairn had declared in the *Commercial Advertiser* that it was clear that under representative government "both the electors and the elected would be of their [the whites] body" - and he was in fact elected to the assembly in 1854 as member for the rural Swellendam![773] What the low franchise did succeed in doing, however, was to consolidate the stress of Afrikaners on their status as subject of a British colony, rather than of Dutch descent. Thus in 1850 Christoffel Brand complained that the Attorney-General regarded Eastern Cape British as 'the only true British portion of the colony", whereas he too was an adopted British subject.[774]

Though the low franchise had initially been introduced into the constitution drafted by Porter, it is doubtful that it would have survived against the conservative onslaught without the 'Kat River rebellion' - the uprising of the oppressed in the colony, which placed a premium need on non-confrontational restabilisation, and virtually compelled the British government to underpin the popular party, for both economic and political reasons. Crais unfortunately deals barely at all with the intense struggle between conservatives and the 'popular party' over self-government, and thus completely de-emphasises the non-racial, or the relative lowness, of the franchise.[775] It was aimed in addition to the whites to recapture many of the small coloured property owners who had rebelled. A lot of small property owners went over to the Xhosa - hence the need for a low franchise. "I would rather meet the Hottentot at the hustings, voting for his representative" declared the Attorney-General, Porter, a defender of the low franchise, "than meet the Hottentot in the wolds with his gun on his shoulder."[776] But Porter had lost faith in the Khoi. He believed the rebellion had been inspired by a "foolish notion of nationality" based on their belief that they were ancient owners of lands of which whites had dispossessed them, and were now envious of the prosperity of whites which contrasted with their own poverty, "sloth and inactivity."[777] The low franchise was a conscious attempt to break the coloured-Xhosa alliance of unfree labour that was beginning to develop the uprising, and between philanthropy and humanitarianism had little part to play in the passage of the low and non-racial franchise. Equally, there was no humanitarianism remaining concerning the fate of the people of the chiefdoms - 'savages' as Fairbairn continued to call them. Only in 1865, when British Kaffraria was finally incorporated in the colony, could the black propertied become voters.[778]

Sir George Clerk arrived in Bloemfontein in August 1853 to carry through the disannexation of the Sovereignty, to the great anger of the land speculating settlers who had entrenched themselves there. Despite the strong anti-imperial sentiments of most Boers in the territory, argues Keegan, there was no "self-conscious republicanism or sense of national identity." The new state that emerged as the result of the Bloemfontein Convention of February 1854 as the Orange Free State continued the existing order, drawing in a wider range of the Boer elite to be sure, but continuing British domination at a local level. British withdrawal did not affect the value of land, the profitability of interior trade, or the prosperity of the wool farms. The temporary extension of formal sovereignty had been "a necessary step" in the creation of a state system through which British interests in the region could be secured. A white collaborating class had been strengthened, as a replacement for Moshoeshoe and the Griqua statelets with which the British had previously been allied. The creation of the Orange Free State was not a return to the *status quo ante*, but was made possible by the advance of settler capitalism, on the back of British imperialism. For the Orange Free State the new frontier of conquest was Lesotho, while the Philippolis Griqua trekked eastwards across the Drakensberg in 1861, and the Griquatown state was swallowed up in the land grab by Britain that followed the discovery of diamonds around Kimberley.[779]

Chapter 14

Conclusion

Had things been left to the Boers and indigenous people to negotiate and fight it out for themselves, South Africa might have become a different place. Instead, it was the British, at the height of their world power, who were in command in the first half of the 19th century. The first effect was to inflict, from the time of the war of 1812, serious damage upon the balance of Xhosa society with nature, rather than the desultory skirmishes which had been the 'first' and 'second' frontier wars.[780] By mid-century at least the Ciskeian Xhosa were under British rule, crowded onto insufficient land, and had become cheap labour for the colony.

Historians, writes Crais, have in the past "danced around the period, chanting praise for the enlightenment and exalting the arrival of liberalism, forgetting how the former was enormously paradoxical and the latter profoundly Janus-faced."[781] Together with the humanitarian anti-forced labour side (itself riddled with contradictions), there came the radically new idea that "African societies outside the immediate realm of the colonial household or enterprise should be subjugated and ruled in the interests of the colonial economy". This did not derive "from the era of slavery, nor did it derive from the Boer diaspora": it was a product of British rule, and of the growing integration of South Africa into the world economy of 19th century capitalism. British influence hardened the hierarchies of race, and strengthened the hegemony of white colonists.[782]

Militarily, there was a progressive displacement of the Boer commando, the classic colonial fighting instrument of the 18th century, until, by the 1846-1847 and 1850-1853 wars against the Xhosa, the boers were disinterested in fighting. Correspondingly the brunt of the front-line fighting came to be undertaken by Khoi or 'coloured' and later Mfengu soldiers, strengthened by the core of the British regulars and, sometimes, by British settler levies.

After the government authorities hostility to early Bethelsdorp, they came to see Christianity and 'respectability', as preached by the missionaries, as necessary to secure the fighting loyalty of the Khoi/coloured to the colony against the Xhosa. "The testimony of every senior military figure that served in the Cape Colony's frontier wars in the early 19th century had been that dependence upon the Khoikhoi was absolute."[783] (The same could later be said of the Mfengu). Contrary however to the hopes of Philip, in which coloureds acted as intermediaries for 'civilising' the Xhosa, their military force was used to clear land for white settlement, both on the eastern and (in a more complex way) on the northern borders of the colony. In 1870, no longer needed, the coloured Cape Mounted Rifles was disbanded, replaced by the white Frontier Armed and Mounted Police.[784]

The idea of 'civilising' in fact served to create 'the other', the barbarian. In this way Philip's adaptation of the early egalitarianism of van der Kemp - together with his actual support for British annexations - prepared the way for conquest.[785] At the same time many of the missionaries assisted in empowering the Khoisan, transforming them into "coloureds", and creating an independent elite. By mid-century, indeed, a self-conscious Christianised coloured community was in existence, formed from slaves and Khoisan with a certain infusion of European descent, as well as of Xhosa. Its fate was mostly to remain as labourers. The limits of evangelical humanitarianism, however, were that it required that "native peoples abandon not only their independence and their political systems, but all aspects of their social and cultural lives that did not accord with the liberals' definition of civilised standards and values, and that they submit to the tolerant paternalism of white patrons."[786]

The Wesleyans took the ideology of 'civilisation' in a conservative direction, adapting it to the needs of their part-settler flock. The idea of 'civilisation' was appropriated by the settlers - and their official champions, D'Urban, Smith, etc - and turned into one of civilisation through conquest and compulsion to labour. By the 1840s there was a virtually unified discourse of the majority of the missionaries and the settlers, which only the Reads actively stood outside, and were persecuted for this. From the earlier hostility between state and missionaries, there was now no longer simply co-operation, but the interchange of personnel between mission and state, as in the case of Calderwood.

Arriving in 1820, the British settlers came to be the motive force of colonial society during the 1830s. Crais believes that the racist ideology and unfree labour system of the settlers must be seen in the context of "a significant immigration of free people on top of a slave society on the verge of ... destruction".[787] Keegan writes, of the settler racist system, that "In the Dutch period, a hierarchy of legal status groups - free burghers, slaves and Khoi - laid the basis of a racial order which in its fundamentals was unaffected by the jettisoning of the legal foundation of inequality in the 1820s and 1830s".[788] It depends what one means by "the basis of", and "in its fundamentals." A new legal system took shape in the 1820s and 1830s, initially in the basis of formal equality. But it became turned by white colonist pressure into an instrument of racial subjugation - directed also against the Xhosa. This was a colonial post-slavery society in which the key point of coercion lay in the law rather than the personal authority of the master.

By mid-century a new concept had become popularised, that of 'extermination', which as we have seen, appeared on a banner carried by British settler levies in the 1850-3 war, after Smith had called for "extermination" of the Xhosa. Smith did not mean, in the 'polite' way in which the term has often been interpreted by historians, merely displacing people geographically - driving the Xhosa across the Kei. He meant the killing off of people. At the time Charles Stretch, former diplomatic agent to the Xhosa, wrote of Smith's 'extermination' policy that he "invited the colonists to come and shoot the Caffres without mercy."[789]

The term, as used by the settlers, was extrapolation from the past. In his famous dispatch of December 1835 Glenelg had written of the potential calamity of "adding Southern Africa to the list of the Regions which have seen their aboriginal Inhabitants disappear under the withering influence of European neighbourhoods."[790] Earl Grey, in the 1840s, wrote that it would "grieve" him if colonisation were to be accomplished by the gradual destruction of the native races.[791] Increasingly, however, the idea came to be translated into a law that indigenous peoples **would** disappear against the onward march of 'European civilisation' and then, as with the settlers, that they **should** disappear. The model for the expanding Cape Colony became, in other words, not India, but Australasia and North America.

Commenting on Bowker's notorious 'springbok' speech, the utilitarian liberal Attorney-General Porter said in the Legislative Council in 1845 that Bowker was not alone. "A member of the British House of Commons... has lately said that the brown man is destined every where to disappear before the white man, and that **such is the law of nature**. (my emphasis) It is true that... The history of colonisation is the record of the dark man's disappearance. But... while it is indisputable that the contact of civilisation.. with men uncivilised has been, and must always be, destruction to the latter, it is yet to be tried whether civilisation of a higher order is not destined to reverse the process." (At this stage Porter advocated this through treaties, though he was to turn to subjugation in 1846/7).[792] In an essay in 1851 on the causes of the 1846-7 war Stockenstrom wrote: "This much I predict with certainty: you must go on exterminating, or you must restore the powers of the chiefs. You must enact the Hottentot history over again, which with the Kaffirs and others will not be so easy a matter, or you must respect those for whom the natives have a natural and even a superstitious veneration."[793] Not only did he understand the resistance of the Xhosa, but he also believed that human action could transcend this 'law'.

The Special Commissioner Hogge sent by Grey to South Africa in 1852 however saw the same matter differently: "The history of the Cape is already written in that of America, and the gradual increase of the white race must eventually, though slowly, ensure the disappearance of the Black. Providence vindicates this its unalterable law by rendering all the philanthropic efforts that have been made to avert such a destiny subservient to its fulfillment."[794] These ideas were to be belied by the continued resistance of the Xhosa (despite the cattle-killing) and the failure ultimately to exterminate the blacks of South Africa (a prominent theme in the writings of De Kiewiet).[795] Maqoma set the precedent, his adaption of new tactics for dealing with the British later being compared by Stapleton with that of Samori Toure in West Africa.[706] But in the 19th century, buttressed by British power, the ideas of 'extermination' persisted among whites, dressed up no more as 'history' but as 'evolutionary science' in the ideas of Social Darwinism - of survival of the fittest, of British race pride, and of South Africa as a 'white man's country'.

From about 1844 a new era of imperial expansion began in Southern Africa. Its impetus was the rise of local rural capitalism - its needs for land and labour - and with it the rise of a racist discourse.[797] This grew into an expansionist drive - essentially of capital accumulation, in land, trade, wool, finance, that was partially curtailed in the 1850s, but in which the speculators would once again harness the imperial machine in the 1870s at Kimberley and later on the Witwatersrand.

As a result of, and together with this, the colony entered between 1846 and 1853 a more severe crisis than that of 1799-1803, beset by severe divisions at the top, rebellion inside and from the Boers outside, two bitterly-fought wars against the Xhosa both inside and outside, and the beginnings of military confrontation with Moshoeshoe.[798] Indeed, far from stabilising Southern Africa, Smith plunged it into its biggest conflicts up to that time, and put British rule at risk - while also militarising the region. The rescue for the British government was the institution of representative government - on a basis which involved the defeat of the Godlontonian elite by the 'popular party'.

Historians have variously characterised the kind of government which emerged under representativity on the basis of the low non-racial franchise. Bank terms it "racial conservatism", and Crais "conservative liberalism" and argues that the "the 1850s witnessed the consolidation of settler capitalism and white supremacy, not the defence of blacks" and that the "great bulk of the black population in the colony was effectively excluded from political participation in the new state." Keegan maintains that "'Cape liberalism' was a form of partial incorporation at the margins, arising as much out of colonial weakness as out of ideological commitment. Few white colonists could conceive of such rights ever being enjoyed by more than a small minority of Africans... "The exercise of racial domination within Cape colonial society took on a *laissez-faire* rather than a dogmatic character, allowing for some political participation and a degree of socioeconomic interaction and race mixing among the lower orders, without threatening racial hegemony... At the same time, labour relations were as exploitative, and the condition of the colony's labouring classes as impoverished and servile, as ever before."[799]

Throughout the period from 1800, in fact, "abstractions of freedom and equality existed in, served to reproduce, and were unable to explain, capitalist society as a class society."[800]

Conservatives defending white agrarian interests dominated representation of the Eastern Cape in parliament and in the local state. Already in the first session of parliament there was discussion of vagrancy and other coercive legislation. The 1856 Masters and Servants Act was a notoriously severe measure that, through 1857 amendments to pass laws, brought blacks as well as browns under it.[801] While coloureds at the Kat River voted overwhelmingly for Stockenstrom, in parliament he too was influenced by whites demanding repressive legislation. Coloureds, in fact, "were to be a marginal factor in the electoral politics of the colony."[802] Some Africans, at first particularly Mfengu succeeded in becoming, for a period, 'acculturated' and prosperous rich or middle peasants which with the incorporation of British Kaffraria in 1865 allowed them to vote.[803] By the time, in the 1880s, when the Afrikaner Bond challenged British domination of the legislature, the Eastern Cape was able to defeat Afrikaners with the assistance of the black vote.[804]

Though both coloureds and Africans were marginal, the extension of the 'non-racial' franchise at first differentially to coloured and Xhosa strengthened the differences between them, in particular between their elites. Crais, as we have seen, believes there were the elements of a cross-ethnic proletarian consciousness coming into being during the 1850-3 revolt. However these were a scattered rural proletariat, not yet a working class in factories producing collectively. The 1850-1853 revolt had far more in common with the methods of 'Captain Swing' - the rural revolt in Britain in 1830 - than with the German Social Democratic Party from the 1890s, for example - though it was far more organised, and sharpened by the military experience of the Khoi and the skilful military tactics of the Xhosa.

The coloured James Read junior, forlornly watching smoke rising over Fort Hare on 21 January 1851 wrote "who that was acquainted with the facts of history, could for a moment think otherwise than that the colony would at last conquer the Kaffirs? Though for a time the Kaffirs and Hottentots might triumph, that triumph would be ephemeral and short-lived, and soon would England reassert her supremacy as the mistress of Southern Africa... Insane must have been the man that could have thought otherwise."[805] Read's conclusion was correct. Incorporation for the indigenous was inevitable. The real question was the terms on which it would occur, with what history and what consciousness of that history. The destruction of the Khoisan social fabric already by 1900 gave them a susceptibility to the Christian culture of the missionaries, and this together with the role of the mission stations and the vote gave them an advantage in the colony over the Xhosa. Ironically, having been conquered, the Xhosa took up Christianity in a big way - though on their own, syncretic, often semi-millenarian, 'Zionist' terms.

Despite the mineral revolution and segregation, industrialisation, apartheid, and Bantustanisation which undermined it economically and politically, the efforts of colonialism to destroy the cultural roots of Xhosa society have not succeeded to this day.

Footnotes

1. T. Keegan, *Colonial South Africa and the origins of the racial order* (Cape Town: Philip, 1996), p. 45
2. G. McC Theal, *Compendium of South African History and Geography*, (Lovedale: Lovedale Press, 1877); *History of Souh Africa from 1795 to 1872*, 5 volumes, (5th edition, London: Allan and Unwin, 1915); *Documents relating to the Kaffir War of 1835* (London: Cowes, 1912); *Records of the Cape Colony* (RCC), 36 volumes (London: Clowes, 1897-1905); Sir G.E. Cory, *The rise of South Africa*, 6 vols, (1910-1939, reprint Cape Town: Struik, 1965). For the historiography see also C. Saunders, *The making of the South African past: major historians on race and class* (Cape Town: David Philip, 1988); K. Smith, *The changing past: trends in South African historical writing* (Johannesburg: Southern book publishers, 1988). For followers of Theal and Cory see for example I.E. Edwards, *The 1820 settlers in South Africa: a study in British colonial\policy* (London: Longmans Green, 1934); Harold E. Hockly, *The story of the British settlers of 1820 in South Africa*, (Cape Town: Juta, 1948); Guy Butler (ed) *The 1820 settlers: an illustrated commentary* (Cape Town: Human and Rousseau, 1974) Cory in particular is a work frequently cited by other historians, down to the 1960s and 1970s.
3. A. Bank, "The Great Debate and the origins of South African historiography", *Journal of African History,* 38, 1997, pp. 261-281. J. Philip, *Researches on South Africa: illustrating the civil, moral and religious condition of the native tribes*, 2 vols, (London: James Duncan, 1828). See also R. Ross, "Donald Moodie and the origins of South African historiography", in Ross, *Beyond the Pale: essays on the history of colonial South Africa* (Johannesburg: Wits, 1994), pp. 192-211; C. Crais, "The vacant land: the mythology of British expansion in the Eastern Cape, South Africa", *Journal of Social History,* xxv, 1991. Bank claims that earlier travel narratives are not 'histories'. However some of these, such as the works of John Barrow An account of travels into the interior of South Africa in the years 1797 and 1798, 2 vols, (London: T. Cadell, 1801, 1804) and Heinrich Lichtenstein, Travels into the Southern Africa in the years 1803, 1804, 1805 and 1806, 2 vols (London: Henry Colburn, 1810, 1815) champion, respectively, 'humanitarian' and 'settler' views of history.
4. Bank, "Great debate", pp. 265-277; Keegan, *Colonial South Africa*, p. 111. Donald Moodie, *The Record; or a series of official papers relative to the condition and treatment of the native tribes in South Africa* (Cape Town: 1838-1841)
5. See Bank, "Great debate", pp. 275-279. *Report from the Select Committee on Aborigines (British Settlements) with the Minutes of Evidence*: Part 1, 1836; Part 11, 1837 (London, 1836 7), referred to respectively as [538 of 1836] and [425 of 1837]; S. Bannister, *Humane Policy or Justice to the Aborigines of the New Settlements* (1830); T. Pringle, *Narrative of a residence in South Africa* (London: Moxon, 1835: reprint, Struik, 1966); 'Justus', *The Wrongs of the Caffre Nation* (1837) (not mentioned by Bank). Dr Ambrose George Campbell ('Justus') was one of three doctors in Grahamstown, who

edited a newspaper in the town in 1840 for four months: the Colonial Times (See B. Le Cordeur, *The politics of Eastern Cape separatism*, (Oxford University Press, 1981), pp.103-104; LG. Pretorius, "The humanitarians and the Cape eastern frontier, 1834-1836" (PhD, Wits, 1970). *Researches* is bland on colonial interaction with the Xhosa: he only took up the issue of the Xhosa in 1830, after its publication.

6. See Bank, "Great debate", pp. 278-279; Keegan, *Colonial South Africa*, pp. 72-74, 141-142. Also R. Godlonton, *A narrative of the irruption of the Kafir hordes into the eastern province of the Cape of Good Hope, 1834-1835, including parts I,II and III of the introductory remarks* (Grahamstown: Meurant and Godlonton, 1835; reprinted C. Struik 1965); *Case of the colonists of the eastern frontier of the Cape of Good Hope, in reference to the Kafir wars of 1835-1836 and 1846* (Grahamstown, Meurant and Godlonton, 1847); *Narrative of the Kafir war of 1850-1852* (Grahamstown: Meurant and Godlonton, 1851; reprinted Struik, 1962); *Review of the condition of the frontier Hottentots from 1799 to 1851, and of the incipient stages of the rebellion of the latter year* (Grahamstown: Meurant and Godlonton, 1851).

7. W.G. Boyce, *Notes on South African affairs from 1834 to 1838* (Grahamstown: Aldum and Harvey, 1838): For an analysis of Boyce's viewpoint in relation to that of other Wesleyan missionaries see B E. Seton, "Wesleyan missions and the sixth frontier war, 1834 to 1835" (Ph.D, UCT, 1962). Nor does Bank mention the humanitarian writings of the Afrikaner Andries Stockenstrom, for example, *Narrative of transactions connected with the Kaffir War of 1846 and 1847* (Grahamstown, 1848); *Light and Shade, as shown in the character of the Hottentots of the Kat River settlement*, being the substance of a speech by the Hon Sir Andries Stockenstrom in the Legislative Council of the Cape of Good Hope (Cape Town: 1854)

8. J. Peires, *The House of Phalo: a history of the Xhosa people in the days of their independence* (Braamfontein: Ravan, 1981), p. 180. For the stereotyping of coloureds see, eg G.J. Gerwel, *Literatuur en apartheid: Konsapsies van 'gekleurdes' in die Afrikaans roman tot 1948* (Kasselvlei: Kampen, 1983). Afrikaner nationalist writing on the Cape largely followed the lead of Theal and Cory, and was largely interested in the Cape as the seed-bed of the Great Trek.

9. W. M. Macmillan, *Cape Colour Question* (London: Faber and Gwyer, 1927); *Bantu, Boer and Briton* (London: Faber and Faber, 1929) The most recent sustained attack on Philip is by P.H. Kapp, "Dr John Philip se werksaamhede in Suid-Afrika, 1819-1828", *Archives Year Book for South African History*, 1985, II, pp. 1-310; J. S. Galbraith's de-emphasis of the influence of the humanitarians has never really caught on: *Reluctant Empire: British policy on the South African frontier, 1834-1854* (Berkeley: U Cal Press, 1963)

10. J. S. Marais, *The Cape Coloured People* (London: Longman, 1939)

11. T. Davenport, *South Africa: a modern history*, (London: Macmillan, 1st edition 1977); J. Butler, R. Elphick, D.Welsh, *Democratic Liberalism in South Africa: its history and prospect* (Middletown, Conn: 1987)

12. Zine Magubane, "Bringing the empire home" (Ph.D., Harvard, 2000)

13. E.A. Walker, *The frontier tradition in South Africa* (Oxford: University Press, 1930);*The Great Trek* (London: A and C. Black, 1934). M. Legassick, "The frontier

tradition in SA historiography" in S. Marks and A. Atmore (eds), *Economy and Society in pre-industrial South Africa* (London: Longmans, 1980); Keegan, *Colonial South Africa,* Chapter 1.

14. *Cambridge History of the British Empire, Vol VIII: South Africa* (Cambridge: University Press, 1938) (CHBE). Cory contributed one chapter to this volume, on the 1820 British settlers, while Macmillan contributed three.

15. Clinton, *The SA Melting Pit* (London: Longmans Green, 1937); D. Williams, *When Races meet: the life and times of William Ritchie Thomson, Glasgow Society Missionary, Government and Dutch Reformed Church Minister,* 1794-1891 (Johannesburg: APB Publishers, 1967); H. Gailey, "The LMS and the Cape Government, 1799-1828" (Ph.D., UCLA, 1957); Jane Sales, *Mission Stations and the Coloured Communities of the Eastern Cape, 1800-1852* (Cape Town, 1975)

16. Elphick and Giliomee, *The shaping of South African society, 1652-1820* (Cape Town: Longman, Penguin, 1979); *The shaping of South African society, 1652-1840* (Cape Town: Maskew Miller Longman, 1989). Giliomee's concept of a frontier zone for the eastern frontier was developed from M. Legassick, "The Grique, the Sotho-Tswana and the missionaries: the politics of a frontier zone, 1780-1840" (Ph.D., UCLA, 1969); The first edition had a chapter by W. Freund and the second edition chapters by Freund and Peires on the Cape Colony up to 1840. The work also takes up the history of Khoi and slaves more systematically. Another work in this vein is A. du Toit and H. Giliomee (eds), *Afrikaner Political Thought: analysis and documents I: 1780-1850* (Cape Town: David Philip, 1983)

17. For this period see particularly Nosipho Majeke [Dora Taylor], *The role of the missionaries in conquest* (Johannesburg, Society of Young Africa, 1953). Note its influence, for example, on C. Saunders "James Read: towards a reassessment", Collected Papers from the Societies of Southern Africa seminar, Institute of Commonwealth Studies, University of London, vol vii

18. B. Le Cordeur, "Robert Godlonton as architect of frontier opinion, 1850-1857", *Archives Yearbook for South African History,* 1959, II, (Pretoria, 1959); *The Politics of Eastern Cape Separatism* (Cape Town: Oxford University Press, 1981) T. Kirk, "Self-government and self-defence in South Africa: the interaction of British and Cape politics, 1846-1853" (D. Phil, Oxford, 1973). See also B. Le Cordeur and C. Saunders *The Kitchingman Papers* (Johannesburg: Brenthurst, 1976) and *War of the Axe* (Johannesburg: Brenthurst, 1981). Also D. Warren, "Class rivalry and Cape politics in the mid-nineteenth century: a reappraisal of the Kirk thesis", *South African Historical Journal,* 24, 1991

19. R. Derricourt and C. Saunders (eds) *Beyond the Cape Frontier: studies in the history of the Transkei and Ciskei* (London: Longmans, 1974). The book was preceded by two chapters by Monica Wilson on the Xhosa and the Eastern Cape in M. Wilson and L.M. Thompson (eds), *Oxford History of South Africa, Volume I,* (1969) and by L.M. Thompson (ed), *African Societies in Southern Africa* (1969). M. Legassick, "The Griqua," who also contributed a chapter to *Shaping;* R. Ross, *Adam Kok's Griquas* (1976); R. Moyer, "A history of the Mfengu" (Ph.D, University of London, 1976) wrote 'Afrocentric' versions of Griqua and Mfengu history respectively.

20. Peires, *The Dead will arise Nongqawuse and the great Xhosa cattle-killing movement of 1856-1857* (Braamfontein: Ravan Press, 1989). See also R. Beck, "The legalisation

and development of trade on the Cape frontier, 1817-1830" (Ph.D, Indiana, 1987).
21. Peires, *House of Phalo,* pp. 170-180
22. eg A.C. Jordan, *Towards an African Literature*, (University of California Press, 1973)
23. N. Mandela, *Long walk to freedom: the autobiography of Nelson Mandela* (London: Little, Brown, 1994), pp. 21-22. On Xhosa OT see also J. Opland, *Xhosa poets and poetry*; (Cape Town: David Philip, 1998) and on the interpenetration of written and oral versions of history see Opland and Isabel Hofmeyr, *We Spend our years as a tale that is told: oral historical narrative in a South African chiefdom*, (Johannesburg, x, 1993).
24. N.Worden and C. Crais (eds) *Breaking the Chains: Slavery and its legacy in the nineteenth century Cape Colony*, (Johannesburg, Witwatersrand University Press, 1994); N. Worden, *Slavery in Dutch South Africa* (Cambridge, 1985); R. Ross, *Cape of Torments* (London: Routledge and Kegan Paul, 1983); V. C. Malherbe, "Diversification and mobility of Khoikhoi labour in the eastern districts of the Cape Colony prior to the labour law of 1 November 1809" (UCT, M.A., 1978); S. Newton King and C. Malherbe, *The Khoikhoi rebellion in the Eastern Cape, 1799-1803* (Cape Town, 1981); E. Bradlow, "Emancipation and race perceptions at the Cape", *South African Historical Journal, XV,* 1981; E. Bradlow, "The Khoi and the proposed vagrancy legislation of 1834", *Quarterly Bulletin of the South African Library* XXXlX, 3, March 1985; E. Bradlow, "Capitalists and labourers in the post-emancipation rural Cape", *Historia, 30, 2,* (1985), pp. 49-62 and 31,1, (1986), pp. 57-58; N. Worden, "Rural slavery in the western districts of the Cape Colony during the 19th century", (Ph.D Cambridge, 1982); N. Worden, "Adjusting to emancipation" in W. James and M. Simons (eds), *The Angry Divide* (Cape Town: David Philip, 1989); D. Warren, "The early years of District Six: District Twelve in the 1840s", Cabo, (1985); D. Warren, "Property, profit and power: the rise of a landlord class in Cape Town in the 1840s", *Studies in the History of Cape Town*, Vol 6, Centre for African Studies, (Cape Town, 1988); J. Marincowitz, "Rural production and labour in the Western Cape, 1838-188, with special reference to the wheat growing districts" (Ph.D., University of London, 1985); Mary Rayner, "Wine and slaves: the failure of an export economy and the ending of slavery in the Cape Colony, South Africa, 1806-1834" (Ph.D., Duke University, 1986); K. D. Elks, "Crime, community and police in Cape Town 1825-1850" (M.A., UCT, 1986); K. Harris, "The slave 'rebellion' of 1808", Kleio, 20, 1988, pp. 54-65; M. Kinsman, "Populists and patriarchs: the transformation of the captaincy at Griqua Town, 1804-1822" in A. Mabin *Organisation and Economic Change*, (Johannesburg: 1989); B.J.I. Rutherford, "The Galant rebellion of 1825: a study of labour relations within the Worcester district, between the years 1820-1830" (BA Hons, UCT, 1990); A. Bank, The decline of urban slavery at the Cape, 1806-1834 (Communications No 22, Centre for African Studies, UCT, 1991); E. Host, "Capitalisation and proletarianisation on a Western Cape farm: Klaver Valley, 1812-1898" (MA, UCT, 1992); H. Ludlow, "Missions and emancipation in the South-Western Cape: a case stdy of Groenekloof (Mamre), 1838-1852" (MA, UCT, 1992); John Mason "Fit for Freedom: the slaves, slavery and emancipation in the Cape Colony, SA, 1806-1842" (Ph.D., Yale, 1992); W. Dooling, "Slavery and amelioration in the Graaff-Reinet District, 1823-1830", *South African*

Historical Journal, 27, (1992), pp. 75-94; W. Dooling, Law and Community in a slave society: Stellenbosch district, South Africa, c. 1760-1820 (Communications No 23, Centre for African Studies, UC, 1992); L. Whittaker, "In the shadow of slavery: masters and servants in the Worcester district, 1839-1845" (BA Hons, UCT, 1992); V. C. Malherbe, "The Cape Khoisan in the eastern districts of the colony before and after Ordinance 50 of 1828" (Ph.D, UCT, 1997)

25. S. Newton King, "The labour market of the Cape Colony, 1807-1828" in S. Marks and A. Atmore (eds), *Economy and Society in pre-industrial South Africa* (London: Longman, 1980)

26. B. Mclennan, *A proper degree of terror: John Graham and the Cape's eastern frontier* (Johannesburg: Ravan, 1986)

27. Jack Lewis, "An economic history of the Ciskei, 1848-1900", (Ph.D, UCT, 1984)

28. L. Meltzer, "The growth of Cape Town commerce and the role of John Fairbairn's *Advertiser*, 1835-1839" (MA., UCT, 1989)

29. S. Trapido, "The emergence of liberalism and the making of 'Hottentot nationalism', 1815-1834" (Paper, Societies of Southern Afric, ICS, 1990), pp. 34-60

30. J. Cobbing; "The case against the Mfecane" (Centre for African Studies, UCT, 1983); "Jettisoning the Mfecane (with perestroika)" (African Studies Institute, Wits, 1988); "Grasping the nettle: the slave trade and the early Zulu", in Edgecombe et al (comps), *The Debate on Zulu origins* (1992); "The mfecane as alibi: thoughts on Dithakong and Mbolompo", *Journal of African History*, 29, 3, (1988), pp. 487-519; A. Webster, "The mfecane paradigm overthrown", *South African Historical Journal*, 25, 1991 pp. 170-172; A. Webster, "Unmasking the Fingo: the war of 1835 revisited", in C. Hamilton, *The Mfecane Aftermath*, (Johannesburg; Wits University Press, 1995); T. Stapleton, *Maqoma: Xhosa resistance to colonial advance* (Johannesburg: Jonathan Ball, 1994); N. Etherington, *The Great Treks: the transformation of Southern Africa, 1816-1854* (London: Longmans, 2001)

31. C. Crais, *The Making of the colonial order: white supremacy and black resistance in the Eastern Cape, 1770-1865,* (Johannesburg: Wits University Press, 1992); N. Mostert, *Frontiers: the epic of South Africa's creation and the tragedy of the Xhosa people* (London: Cape, 1992); Keegan, *Colonial South Africa*

32. Compare with D. van Arkel, G.C. Quispel and Robert Ross, "Going Beyond the Pale: on the Roots of White Supremacy in South Africa", in Robert Ross, *Beyond the Pale: Essays in the History of Colonial South Africa,* (London and Hanover, Wesleyan University Press, 1992),

33. C. Crais, "Race, the state and the silence of history in the making of modern South Africa: preliminary departures" (Africa Seminar, Centre for African Studies, University of Cape Town, July 1992); see also N. Worden and C. Crais (eds) *Breaking the Chains*, p. 28; M Legassick, "The state, racism and the rise of capitalism in the 19th century Cape Colony", *South African Historical Journal*, 28, May 1993, pp. 329-368; Cooper and Stoler, Frederick Cooper and Ann Laura Stoler, Tensions of Empire: colonial cultures in a bourgeois world, (Berkeley: U Cal Press, 1997). See also the essay on "The Janus Face of Merchant Capital" in E.Fox-Genovese and E.D.. Genovese, *Fruits of Merchant Capital: slavery and bourgeois property in the rise and expansion of capitalism* (OUP, 1983), pp. 3-25

34. Noel Mostert's military history of the colonial wars against the Xhosa is masterly in its description and analysis. Keegan was the first to integrate my own evaluation of the state-building aspects of the program of John Philip into the history of the Cape, and he also has a particularly innovative interpretation of the role of the British settlers in distorting the grievances of Afrikaners of the Great Trek so as to incorporate their own complaints at the retrocession by Colonial Secretary Lord Glenelg of Queen Adelaide Province, annexed by Governor D'Urban in May 1835.
35. See Legassick, "The state, racism and the rise of capitalism", p. 349
36. E. Elbourne, "Early Khoisan uses of mission Christianity" in H. Bredekamp and R. Ross (eds), *Missions and Christianity in SA History* (Joburg: Wits U Press, 1995); E. Elbourne, " 'To colonize the mind': evangelical missionaries in Britain and the Eastern Cape, 1790 1837", D. Phil, U of Oxford, 1991; E. Elbourne, "A question of identity: evangelical culture and Khoisan politics in the early 19th century Eastern Cape", (Collected seminar papers on the societies of Southern Africa, Institute of Commonwealth Studies, University of London), Vol 18, October 1990 - June 1991, pp. 14-30; E. Elbourne, "Freedom at issue: vagrancy legislation and the meaning of freedom in Britain and the Cape Colony", *Slavery and Abolition*, 15, 2, 1994; E. Elbourne and R. Ross, "Combating spiritual and social bondage: early missions in the Cape Colony", in R. Elphick and R. Davenport, *Christianity in SA: a political, social and cultural history* (Cape Town: David Philip, 1997). The Comaroffs attempted the same for southern Tswana society, but a major defect of their analysis is its ignoring of the role of the Griqua as mediators of Christianity to the Tswana: J and J Comaroff, *Of revelation and revolution: Christianity, colonialism and consciousness in South Africa*, (Chicago: U of Chicago, 1991).
37. H. Bradford, "Women, gender and colonialism: rethinking the history of the British Cape Colony and its Frontier zones, c.1806-1870", *Journal of African History*, 37, 1996; H. Bradford, "The rise of the male peasantry: a South African 'case study', 1850-1886" *History and Theory,* 39, December 2000; H. Bradford, "Through gendered eyes: Nongqawuse and the great Xhosa cattle-killing", IHR, UWC, SA and contemporary history seminar, co-hosted with AGI, UCT, 9/10/2001. P van der Spuy, "A collection of discrete essays with the common theme of gender and slavery at the Cape of Good Hope with a focus on the 1820s" (MA, UCT, 1993); P. van der Spuy, "Gender and slavery: towards a feminist revision", *South African Historical Journal,* 25 (1991), pp. 184-195; P van der Spuy, "Slave women and the family in 19th century Cape Town", *South African Historical Journal*, 27, 1992, pp. 50-74. See also M. Kinsman, " 'Beasts of burden': the subordination of Southern Tswana women, ca 1800-1840", *Journal of Southern African Studies*, 10, 1, 1983, pp. 39-54; P. Scully, *"Liberating the Family?:* gender, labour and sexuality in the rural Western Cape, South Africa, 1823-1853" (Ph.D, University of Michigan, 1993).
38. Robert Ross, *Status and Respectability in the Cape Colony, 1750-1870: a tragedy of manners*, (Cambridge: University Press, 1999) K.E. McKenzie, "Gender and honour in middle-class Cape Town: the making of colonial identities 1828-1850" (Oxford, Ph.D. 1997). See also S Dubow, "An Empire of reason: Anglophone literary and scientific institutions in the 19th century Cape Province", (UWC Dept of History and IHR seminar, 4/5/1999)

39. Zakes Mda, *The heart of redness* (Oxford University Press, 2000); Premesh Lalu, "In the event of history", (Ph.D., University of Minnesota, 2003)
40. Compare Keegan, *Colonial South Africa*, p. 43; S Dubow, "Empire of Reason", p. 3. Until Cathcart in the 1850s, only Caledon (1807-1811) and Pottinger (1847) were not military men. Compare Bradford, "Through gendered eyes", pp. 3 and, on Grey, *Passim;* and Peires on Grey, *The dead will arise,* pp. 45-53
41. K. Marx, *Capital*, Vol I, (London: Lawrence and Wishart, 1970), p. 751
42. Crais, *Making*, p. 178; Walker, *History of South Africa* (London: Longmans Green, 1928) p. 148; Mostert, *Frontiers*, p. 979, 1129
43. Keegan, *Colonial South Africa,* p. 47
44. Keegan, *Colonial South Africa*, especially pp. 42-43, 47, 53 provides the best treatment. See also, more generally, Lonsdale and Berman, "Coping with the contradictions: the development of the colonial state in Kenya", *Journal of African History*, 20, 1970, pp. 487-506.
45. See Crais, *Making*, pp. 58-59
46. Table in S. Patterson, "Some speculations on the status and role of the free people of colour in the Western Cape" in M. Fortes and S. Patterson (eds), *Studies in African Social Anthropology* (London: Academic Press, (1975)
47. See particularly Wayne Dooling, " 'The Good Opinion of Others': Law, slavery and community in the Cape Colony, c1760-1830" in Worden and Crais, *Breaking the Chains*, pp. 25-44
48. See Keegan, *Colonial South Africa*, pp. 51-60; Adil Bradlow, "Imperialism, state-formation and the establishment of a Muslim community at the Cape of Good Hope", MA, UCT, 1988; Ross, Status, pp. 138-139; Achmat Davids, *The Mosques of Bo-kaap: a social history of Islam at the Cape* (Athlone, SA Institute of Arabic and Islamic Research, 1980). What is unclear is whether an Islamic tradition survived underground after Sheikh Yussuf, who was banned to Cape in 1694. The first clear evidence of Muslim worship is from the traveler Thunberg, at the Cape in 1772. The first mosques were established around the turn of the century.
49. S. Newton-King, *Masters and Servants on the Cape Eastern Frontier* (Cambridge: CUP, 1999). On forms of Khoi resistance in the late 18th century see Crais, *Making*, p 64
50. Peires, *House of Phalo*, p. 58; L. Switzer, *Power and Resistance in an African society: the Ciskei Xhosa and the making of South Africa* (Pietermaritzburg: University of Natal press, 1993), p49
51. For interpretations of the revolt see S. Newton-King and V. C. Malherbe, *The Khoikhoi rebellion in the Eastern Cape* (Centre for African Studies, UCT, Communications No 5, 1981) H.Giliomee, "The eastern frontier, 1770-1812" in Giliomee and Elphick (eds), *Shaping*, pp. 310-312; S. Newton-King, *Masters and Servants* pp. 210-231; Elbourne; For objectives see NK (May 1799); Elbourne, p. 139; Klaas Stuurman in Barrow, *Travels*, I, p. 402
52. See Newton-King, *Masters and Servants,* pp. 49-52, 63 for the reasons why the initial thrust of colonial settlement had moved inland, via Graaff-Reinet and then turned south rather than moved along the coast. Also Mostert, *Frontiers,* p. 334.
53. Rebel Klaas Stuurman received a small grant of land also, though after his death his brother was dispossessed of it by the British in 1808 and sent to Robben Island: see Maclennan, *Proper degree,* pp. 92-93 (Sales, *Mission Stations,* pp. 37-38) At

'Stuurman's kraal' there was at first preaching by native agents, but it was broken up in 1809 when David Stuurman was exiled to Botany Bay where he died about 1820. The land was then given to white farmers. Later the mission station of Hankey started in this area. See Mostert, *Frontiers*, pp. 350-351 and Pringle, *Narrative*

54. Newton-King and Malherbe, *Khoikhoi rebellion;* A. D. Martin, *Doctor van der Kemp* (London: Livingstone press, 1931); Clinton, *Melting Pot;* Mostert, *Frontiers;* Sales, *Mission stations*; Elbourne, "To colonize"
55. See, for summaries, Elbourne and Ross, "Combatting spiritual and social bondage"; Keegan, *Colonial South Africa*, pp. 75-83
56. See eg Elbourne, "To colonize", pp. 1-25; Elbourne and Ross, "Combatting spiritual and social bondage"; Crais, *Making*, pp. 60-61
57. Opland, *Xhosa Poets and Poetry* (Cape Town: David Philip, 1998), p. 29
58. Elbourne, "A question of identity", p. 26. She criticizes the Comaroffs for homogenizing missionary ideas; the same is to an extent true of for example Crais, *Making*, p. 101 etc, but see also *ibid*, p. 104.
59. Compare Keegan, *Colonial South Africa,* p. 83
60. Newton-King, *Masters and Servants*, p. 220. See also Newton-King and Malherbe, *Khoi rebellion*, p. 35.
61. On van der Kemp see Martin, *Van der Kemp*; Keegan, *Colonial South Africa*, pp.83-4; Elbourne, "To colonize" , chapter IV
62. Christopher Hill, *The world turned upside down* (Harmondsworth: Penguin, 1975); Elbourne, "A question of identity" pp. 15-18 etc; Crais, *Making*, p. 83. At the same time, of course, there were indigenous intellectual contributions to subsequent Khoi and Xhosa millenarianism.
63. See, especially, *Martin, Van der Kemp*, 158-166; Elbourne, "To colonize", pp 162-164
64. Maclennan, *Proper degree*, p. 55; Casalis, *My Life,* p. 104 from Ross, *Status,* p. 112
65. Quoted in Macmillan, *Bantu, Boer and Briton*, p. 97
66. Elbourne, "A question of identity" p. 22. See also F.A. Steytler, ed, Minutes of the First Conference held by African missionaries at Graaff-Reinet, 1814, Hertzog-Annale van die Suid-Afrikaanse Akademie vir Wetenskap en Kuns, 3, 1956
67. On early Bethelsdorp see Sales, *Mission stations*; Elbourne, "To colonize", chapter 4; Keegan, p. 84. There was ambiguity towards it by Khoi from the start: Elbourne, "To colonize", p. 151
68. Compare Legassick, "The Griqua"; Keegan, *Colonial South Africa,* pp. 170-172
69. See Elbourne, "To colonize", pp. 243-265
70. Sales, *Mission stations,* pp. 45-46
71. Elbourne, "A question of identity",. p. 19-20; "To colonize", p. 142, 209
72. Elbourne, "To colonize", , pp. 228-243
73. Elbourne, "To colonize", p. 160
74. Van der Kemp regarded the British reoccupation as caused by the providence of God, and immediately offered advice on treatment of the Khoi to the authorities: Elbourne, "To colonize", pp. 166-167
75. See eg Keegan, *Colonial South Africa*, pp. 84-85. Elbourne, "A question of identity", p. 20; V.C. Malherbe, "The life and times of Cupido Kakkerlak", *Journal of African History*, 20, 3, 1979, pp. 365-378

76. Elbourne, "A question of identity", p. 16
77. Mostert, *Frontiers*, p. 288
78. Elbourne, "A question of identity", p. 20
79. Elbourne, "A question of identity", p. 15 from Saxe Bannister, *Humane Policy*.
80. Read later claimed that their banishment from Bethelsdorp by the Batavians had been because of the complaints they had made: Elbourne, "To colonize", pp. 160-161
81. Elbourne, "To colonize", p. 167. In the 1790s Britain was responsible for 60% of the total slave trade: Keegan, *Colonial South Africa*, p. 78.
82. See, for example, Keegan, *Colonial South Africa*, pp. 107-109; Crais, *Making*, p. 61, 71
83. S. Newton-King, "The labour market of the Cape Colony, 1807-1828" in S. Marks and A. Atmore (eds), *Economy and society in pre-industrial South Africa* (London: Longmans, 1980), pp. 171-207; compare Elbourne, "To colonize", pp. 167-169; Keegan *Colonial South Africa*, pp. 52-53. See Crais, *Making*, pp. 65-70 for a description of the situation of the 'unfree' (slave, peon, etc) in the Eastern Cape at this time.
84. Compare Pringle, *Narrative;* John Philip as quoted in Keegan, *Colonial South Africa*, p. 332
85. Crais, *Making*, p. 96; Legassick, "Griqua", chapters 3-5
86. Elbourne, "To colonize", pp. 170-171; Keegan, *Colonial South Africa*, pp. 54, 86-92
87. W.W. Bird, *The state of the Cape of Good Hope in 1822*, p. 6, cited H. Giliomee, "Die administrasietydsperk van Lord Caledon 1807-1811", *Archiefjaarboek van Suid-Afrikaanse Geskiedenis*, II, 1966, p. 277
88. Elbourne, "To colonize", p. 171
89. Crais, *Making*, p. 60
90. Compare Philip, *Researches,* pp. 147-148, 176; Keegan, *Colonial South Africa*, pp. 54-56; Giliomee "Caledon", p. 171
91. Elbourne, "To colonize", p. 171
92. See London Missionary Society letters on microfilm, consulted in South African Library, Cape Town cited as MF LMS 3/5/B and also Transactions, III, 1803-1812, pp. 205-206 for Read to LMS, 30/8/08.
93. Giliomee, "Caledon", pp. 298-299 from Cory, *Rise of South Africa,* I, pp. 202-203 Giliomee refers to the letter from Wilberforce to Spencer Perceval [Colonial Minister] 5/8/1811 in Theal, *RCC*, VIII, p. 125. Also Giliomee in Elphick and Giliomee, *Shaping*, p. 454
94. Elbourne, "To colonize", pp. 178-179
95. Elbourne, "To colonize", p. 175; Giliomee, "Caledon", p. 299-300. Transactions; Evangelical Magazine and the Scottish Missionary Magazine published Van der Kemp's and Read's reports with little editing. Read to LMS 30/8/1808 [LMS 3/5/B]. Read to LMS 7/11/1809 [LMS 4/1/D] is a further unpublished letter on the difficulty for the Khoi in obtaining justice.
96. Giliomee, "Caledon", pp. 302-304. Cory, *Rise of South Africa,* I, p. 207 claims Read added oil to fire.
97. Van der Kemp to Caledon, 14 January 1811 in full in Bannister, *Humane Policy*, pp. ccxvi-ccxxi. See Elbourne, "To colonize", pp.17-27; Giliomee, "Caledon", p. 303
98. Elbourne, "To colonize", p. 177. Also *ibid*, p. 169
99. Theal, RCC, VIII, p. 112, Memorandum by Caledon 1/7/1811; Giliomee, "Caledon", p. 305

100. Read to LMS, 26/6/1811[LMS 4/4/D]
101. Giliomee, "Caledon", p. 304; Elbourne, "To colonize", pp. 177-178. Van der Kemp warned Caledon that if justice was not obtained, he would publicise the cases or communicate them to the Colonial Office.
102. Elbourne, "To colonize", pp. 176-177 Elbourne, *ibid*, p. 180 argues that Freund in *Shaping*, p. 341 and Sales, *Mission Stations*, pp. 52-53 are wrong in assuming that Colonial Office pressure on Cradock led him to institute the Circuit Court "as Caledon had adopted and adapted Van der Kemp's suggestion of a perambulatory commission by early 1811." (my emphasis). Keegan, *Colonial South Africa*, p. 55 however claims that the Fiscal van Ryneveld had already recommended circuit courts to Dundas in 1801: see Giliomee, "Caledon", p. 274 for Van Ryneveld's 1801 document. Giliomee, "Caledon", p. 310 [referring to CHBE, VIII, p. 200] identifies three factors leading to the decision to establish the circuit court: the unsatisfactory administration of justice in the outer districts, that the Council of Justice was overloaded with work, and the defects in the 1809 Caledon Code, in the sense that an impartial body to see that the proclamation was properly implemented, was lacking. "This fact was underlined by the missionary complaints" he adds, "and the circuit court was seen as an appropriate instrument to investigate and judge the missionary complaints of maltreatment of Hottentots."
103. Report of Commission of Circuit, 28/2/1812 in Theal, RCC, VIII pp. 288-344. Elbourne, p.184, says the commission appeared to Bethelsdorp on 12th December, the day Read retuned, interviewed him for a few minutes, and then disappeared
104. Elbourne, "To colonize", pp. 174, 179-180
105. Elbourne, "To colonize", pp. 180-182. See LMS (Home) 2/5/B Wilberforce to Burder, 3/8/1811; Wilberforce to Wellesley 5/8/1811 S and I Wilberforce, *The Correspondence of W. Wilberforce*, II, (London, 1840), pp. 213-216. See also Theal, RCC, VIII, p. 125, Wilberforce to Spencer-Perceval 5/8/1811
106. M. Borch, " 'Conciliating their affections': the development of official British attitudes and policy towards indigenous peoples in the colonies of settlement, 1763-1814", (Ph.D., University of Copenhagen, 1997), p. 143. In North America 50 years before the word justice occurred in British dispatches in relation to deprivation of land of indigenous Americans.
107. Theal, *RCC*, VII, p. 133. Elbourne, "To colonize", pp. 178-179, 182; Giliomee, "Caledon", p. 305. Van der Kemp immediately presented Cradock with a list of requests - including the prosecution of the cases
108. See Theal, *RCC*, VIII, 441, Truter to Cradock 1/6/1812; Giliomee, "Caledon", p. 305, who states that it was "first on 15 June 1812 that conditions on the frontier had sufficiently improved that the Fiscal could propose that the matter should be resumed."
109. Elbourne, "To colonize", pp. 184-187
110. "Proclamation by Sir John Cradock, 23/4/1812, Theal, *RCC*, VIII, pp. 385-387
111. Theal, RCC, IX, pp. 54-128, Report of Commission of Circuit [*circa* January 1813]; Elbourne, p. 170 comments that Macmillan, *Cape Colour Question,* saw the Black Circuit as the opening shot in the war between missionaries and government, though in fact it had begun much earlier. She also (p. 192) notes confusion among

historians over which cases were considered, and even over the date of the circuit.
112. Keegan, *Colonial South Africa*, p. 55
113. Elbourne, "To colonize", p.189 quoting LMS 5/2/B Read to LMS 3/2/1813. See also Campbell, Travels, pp. 344-345
114. Elbourne, "To colonize", p. 189. Reyburn, "Studies in Cape frontier history", *The Critic*, III (1934-1935), p. 55 however maintains the missionaries "came out of the ordeal with reasonable credit."
115. Elbourne, "Too colonize", pp 192-194; Elbourne, "A question of identity", pp. 21-22, 29; Keegan, *Colonial South Africa*, pp. 55-56. Compare with eg Giliomee, "Caledon", pp. 312-313. The first circuit court had also praised Genadendal and criticized Bethelsdorp though not so strongly: see Theal, *RCC*, VIII, pp. 303-304
116. Theal, *RCC*, IX, pp. 74-75
117. W.M. Freund, "The career of J.T. van der Kemp and his role in the history of South Africa", *Tijdschrift voor Geschiedenis*, 86, 1973. See also Elbourne, "To colonize", p. 174 quoting LMS 5/3/C Thom to Burder CT, 16/2/1814: Thom was jealous of the way that van der Kemp was presented. Philip had in fact a condescending attitude to van der Kemp. See for example Philip, *Researches*, I, 133-141 where he praises van der Kemp, but regrets his too easy intimacy with his charges and his marriage to a slave woman. See also Keegan, *Colonial South Africa*, pp. 317,392
118. Elbourne, "A question of identity", p. 21. She adds the result of the 1817 LMS 'synod' which inter alia censured Read: see below.
119. Peires, *House of Phalo*; *Switzer Power and Resistance*, pp. 34-35 See *Crais, Making*, p. 100 who emphasizes the role of reciprocity and redistribution in Xhosa economy/society.
120. Peires, *House of Phalo*, pp. 50-61; *Switzer Power and Resistance*, pp. 33-34, 39
121. Stapleton, *Maqomo*, p.21; Giliomee, *Shaping*, pp. 421-422, 462-463; Peires, *House of Phalo*, etc on lineage rels, power rels etc.
122. Peires, *House of Phalo*, p. 50
123. Peires, *House of Phalo*, pp. 51-52, 58
124. Peires, *House of Phalo*, p. 54
125. Giliomee in Elphick and Giliomee (eds), *Shaping*, p. 421. For causes of the wars see Peires, *House of Phalo*, pp. 55-56. Also Switzer, *Power and Resistance*, pp. 46-49
126. Peires, *House of Phalo*, pp. 57-58; Maclennan, *Proper degree of Terror*, p. 61 Switzer, *Power and Resistance*, p. 40
127. Peires, p. 59-60; Maclennan, *Proper degree of Terror*, p. 95. For Ngqika see Peires, "Ngqika, c.1779-1829" in C. Saunders (ed), *Black Leaders in southern Africa*, (London, 1979), pp. 15-30.
128. See *Oxford History*, I, pp. 254-256; Maclennan, *Proper degree of terror*, p. 228; Switzer, *Power and Resistance*, p. 41. In 1800 van der Kemp estimated 38,400 west of the Kei; in 1809 Colonel Collins estimated 40,000 Xhosa west and 10,000 (an underestimate?) east of the Kei. In 1826 Thompson estimated the total Xhosa population at 100,000.
129. R. Elphick and V.C. Malherbe, "The Khoisan to 1828", in Elphick and Giliomee, *Shaping*, pp. 55-56
130. Maclennan, *Proper degree*, pp. 30, 32
131. Maclennan, *Proper degree*, pp. 33, 119

132. Elbourne, *"To colonize"*, p. 169
133. For example Griquatown, where missionary Anderson, in accordance with the wishes of the Griqua, refused to send Griqua youth for enlistment in Cape Town: see eg Legassick, "Griqua", pp. 163-166; Keegan, *Colonial South Africa* p. 174.
134. See Maclennan, *Proper degree*, pp. 83-85
135. Elbourne, "To colonize", pp 183-184. Many of these were later to become the nucleus of the first LMS mission at Kat River run by Joseph Williams.
136. Different figures are given by Giliomee in *Shaping*, p. 448; Elbourne, "To colonize", p. 182; Maclennan, *Proper degree*, p. 89.
137. Maclennan, *Proper degree*, pp. 99-109. His son, Andries, was to become landrost in his place and thereafter an important figure on the frontier.
138. For the war see Peires in *Shaping*, pp. 65-66; Peires, *House of Phalo*, pp. 142-143; Maclennan, *Proper degree*; Switzer, *Power and Resisitance*, p. 51-52
139. Maclennan, *Proper degree*, p. 111
140. Maclennan, *Proper degree*, p. 125.
141. Maclennan *Proper degree*, p. 128 from Theal, *RCC*, VIII, pp. 160. See Borch, "Conciliating", pp. 147-151
142. Theal, RCC, viii, p. 160
143. Maclennan, *Proper degree of terror,* pp. 124-125; Theal, *RCC,* viii, p. 237; Cory, *Rise of South Africa*, I, p. 243
144. Campbell, *Travels*, p. 100
145. Maclennan, *Proper degree*, pp. 137-138, 143-144
146. Maclennan, *Proper degree*, p. 147.
147. Maclennan, *Proper degree,* pp. 132-133, 148
148. Maclennan, *Proper degree,* pp. 152-153
149. See for example, Peires, *House of Phalo*, pp. 59-60
150. See *Transactions*, III, 1803-1812, pp. 301-308 for Read's journey to Xhosaland in January 1810. In January 1811 he wrote to the LMS that "we are however concerned that the way to the neighbouring nations remains shut." [MF 47, 1811 LMS 4/4/A] Read to LMS, 7/1/1811
151. *Transactions*, IV, 1812-1817, Annual report for Bethelsdorp 1812, p. 18. Also in LMS 5/1/F. Compare Maclennan pp. 97-98 referring to Dec 1811 letter from Bethelsdorp.
152. Elbourne, "To colonize", p. 183
153. Compare for example MF 51 LMS 4/5/C, Bird to van der Kemp, 30/10/1811 refusing to permit the reopening of the Zak River or Tswana ('Briqua') mission.
154. Elphick and Giliomee, *Shaping*, p. 473
155. For the details see eg B. Holt, *Joseph Williams and the pioneer mission to the South-Eastern Bantu* (Lovedale: Lovedale Press, 1954), pp. 11-19; Williams, *When Races Meet*, p.16. See also Read's Journal of 1/4/1816 to 17/6/1816 in *Transactions of the London Missionary Society*, IV, 1812-1818, pp. 280-293. The station was established about 15 miles from Ngqika's Great Place
156. See Keegan, *Colonial South Africa*, pp. 86-87; Maclennan, *Proper degree*, pp. 169ff; Williams, *When Races Meet*, p. 16; Crais, *Making*, p. 60
157. Elbourne, "A question of identity", p. 22
158. Theal, RCC, XII, 199, and, generally, pp. 193-200: Somerset to Bathurst, 22/5/1819.

A. Lester, *Imperial networks: creating identities in nineteenth-century South Africa and Britain* (London, Routledge, 2001), pp. 19-20 quotes this but gives the wrong reference by two years, to Cape Archives (CA) Government House (GH) 23/5 Somerset to Bathurst 24/4/1817 [RCC reference].
159. Compare Holt, *Williams,* pp.36-37
160. Bird, Colonial Secretary, to J. Read 14/2/1816 CA, Colonial Office,[(CO)4832] cited in Holt, *Williams*, p. 19; Bird, Colonial Secretary, to Read 23/8/1816 [CA CO 4838, p. 475] quoted in Williams, *When Races Meet*, p. 16
161. Holt, *Williams*, pp. 40-111, 52-53 CA CO 2603 Frontier orders issued by Baird, Uitenhage, 11/6/1816. See also Philip, *Researches*, II, pp. 162-163
162. CA CO 2603 Williams to Fraser, Deputy Landrost, Grahamstown, 18/11/1816; Holt, *Williams*, pp. 53-55.
163. See eg, Saunders, "Read", pp. 3-4; Legassick, "Griqua", pp. 264-275, 285-289
164. For the conference, see Theal, RCC, XI, PP. 259-299; Somerset to Bathurst, 23/4/1817, Enclosure A: Bird 29/3/1817, Enclosure B: Minutes of conference 2/4/1817, Enclosure C: Bird 29/3/1817; Enclosure D: list of posts, pp. 303-321; Somerset to Bathurst 23/6/1817, pp. 357-359. See Holt, *Williams*, pp. 57-68; Philip, *Researches*, II, pp. 173-179; Peires, *House of Phalo*, p. 61; Stapleton, *Maqomo*, pp. 25-26.
165. See D. Stuart, "The 'wicked Christians' and the 'children of the mist': missionary and Khoi interactions at the Cape in the early 19th century"; CSPSSA, Vol 18, (U of London, Institute of Commonwealth Studies), pp. 1-13; Elbourne, "To colonize", pp. 201-217; D. Stuart, " 'Of savages and heroes': discourses of race and nation in the evangelical missions to southern Africa, 1790-1860"(Ph. D, U of London, 1994); Legassick, "Griqua", p. 288. See also the letter from Williams of 17/10/1817 quoted in Holt, *Williams*, pp. 69-71; Philip, *Researches*, II, p. 165; LMS 7/8/1817 Kat River, Williams to LMS; Holt, *Williams*, pp. 46-47. Shortly before his death, van der Kemp had drawn up regulations for missionaries.
166. Ross, *Status*; Mackenzie, "Gender and honour". Important discussions on the meaning of civilisation had previously been held by the LMS missionaries in 1814 in response to the Black Circuit's condemnation of Bethelsdorp. Read, appointed to succeed van der Kemp as superintendent, asked the first meeting of LMS missionaries in 1814 whether Bethelsdorp could have done better in 'civilising' its converts: as regards cleanliness, clothing, activity, housing, labour. This resulted in a three-day debate, in which, for example, van der Kemp was accused of discouraging washing: Elbourne, "A question of identity", p. 22. Also Steytler, ed, Minutes of the First Conference. (Sales, *Mission stations*, p. 69) Lichtenstein's *Travels* was published in English in 1812 - and its criticisms of Bethelsdorp were taken to be of contemporary Bethelsdorp rather than the Bethelsdorp he had visited in 1805. George Thom fuelled the critique among each newly arriving missionary group until his relationship with the LMS ended in 1818. Read wrote a lengthy answer to Thom's charges in 1814. (Compare Sales, *Mission stations,* pp. 69-71)
167. Elbourne, "To colonize", pp. 214-217
168. MF 304 LMS 21/2/B Cape Town 11/3/1845 Philip
169. CWM MF 92 LMS 7/4/C Kar River, Cafferland, 14/4/1818 J. Williams; compare Williams, *When Races Meet,* p.52; Holt, *Williams,* pp 79-84 quotes the letter in full. Nqgika

heard that a colonial commando had been sent against him and told Williams he was very angry with the mission, associating it with colonial injustice – "If adopt your law I must entirely overturn my own and that I shall not do." See also Sales, *Mission stations*, pp.63-64, who records that, four months before Williams' death, all the Bethelsdorp people left for Bethelsdorp, Including Jan Tshatshu. Ntinde, Tshatshu's people, were part of the Gcaleka Xhosa.

170. Stapleton, *Maqoma,* pp. 29-30; Switzer, *Power and Resistance*, p. 53. On Nxele, and Ngqika's prophet Ntsikane, see Peires in *Shaping*, p. 488; Peires "Nxele, Ntsikana, and the origins of Xhosa religious reaction", *Journal of African History*, 20, 1, 1979, pp. 51-61; Crais, *Making*, pp. 104. On Nxele, and Ngqika's prophet Ntsikane, see Peires in Elph/Gil p. 488; Peires "Nxele, Ntsikana, and the origins of Xhosa religious reaction", *Journal of African History*, 20, 1, 1979, pp. 51-61; Crais, *Making*, pp. 104-105; Bradford, "Through Gendered Eyes", p. 6

171. Stapleton, *Maqoma*, pp. 31-32; Peires, *House of Phalo*, pp. 62-63, 143-145.

172. Williams, *When Races Meet*, pp. 25-26; Holt,*Williams*, p.73; H.Reyburn, "Studies in frontier history", *The critic*, IV, 2, February 1936; Macmillan, *Bantu, Boer and Briton,* pp.81-84; Theal, RCC XII, 337-341: Somerset to Bathurst, 15/10/1819

173. Peires in *Shaping,* p 483. See also Switzer, *Power and Resistance*, p. 54. Already in May Somerset had recommended the frontier as "a spot of great resource" for some of "our [British] overflowing population" and referred to his dispatch of 18/12/1817 answering Bathurst's queries of 28/7/1817

174. Subsequently, in 1826, Boer slaveholders were prevented from acquiring lands in the 'ceded' territory: see Keegan, *Colonial South Africa,* p. 190, although before this Boers were allocated such farms: Peires in *Shaping*, p. 483. See also Theal, *RCC*, XIX, pp. 356-367 Bird to Commissioners of Enquiry, 27/12/1824.

175. Peires in *Shaping*, p. 483

176. Elbourne, "To colonize", p. 301 CA A50 Read to Philip, Kat River, 1/4/1833

177. Stapleton, *Maqoma*, pp. 33-34,38; Switzer, *Power and Resistance*, p. 56

178. Williams, *When Races Meet*, pp. 29-32. Philip's memorandum [CA CO 120/32 Philip to Donkin, nd, c. April/May 1820] dwelt on the conversion of Jager Afrikaner by Robert Moffat. Peires, in Elphick, *Shaping*, p. 483.

179. Stapleton, *Maqoma*, pp. 38

180. Bird to Brownlee 30/12/1818 [Theal, RCC, XII, p. 118ff; Williams, *When Races Meet*, p. 21-22, 29-32. Also Macmillan, *Cape Colour Question*, pp. 125-126 for Philip on government motivations re wating government missionaries (Williams, pp. 29-32)

181. See Williams, *When Races Meet*, pp. 36-38

182. Keegan, *Colonial South Africa*, pp. 81-82

183. For Fairbairn see Meltzer, "The growth of Cape Town commence", Keegan, *Colonial South Africa*, pp. 97-100

184. See, for example, Crais, *Making*, pp. 90-92. By 1823 only 600 out of the 5 000 who had arrived remained on farms.

185. Crais, *Making*, p. 87

186. Keegan, *Colonial South Africa*, pp.45-47,62-63,311. See, contrarily, Crais, *Making*, p. 87, who on the basis of Cape sources argues that frontier defence was more important than redundant population in Britain.

187. Keegan *Colonial South Africa*, p. 62 and Crais, *Making*, pp. 88-90
188. Keegan, *Colonial South Africa*, pp. 94-98
189. Keegan, *Colonial South Africa*, pp. 59-60
190. Keegan, Colonial South Africa, pp. 69-71, 95; Peires in *Shaping*, p. 488; Crais *Making*, p. 106 and generally pp. 106-112. Also Beck, "The legalization and development of trade".
191. Keegan, *Colonial South Africa*, p. 93; Saunders, "Read", p. 4; Legassick, "Griqua", pp. 442-443
192. See Lester, *Imperial networks*, p. 30; Elbourne, "To colonize", pp. 281-291; A. Ross, *John Philip (1775-1851): Missions, race and politics in South Africa* (Aberdeen: University press, 1986); Borch, "Conciliating", p. 270 etc
193. Elbourne, "A question of identity", p. 23; Elbourne, "To colonize", p. 266. On this question see also Keegan, *Colonial South Africa*, pp. 79-80
194. Keegan, *Colonial South Africa*, pp.102-103 Elbourne, "To colonize", p. 281 argues that Philip's coupling of missions to empire was a defensive reaction against the previous idea that they were a threat to empire, that only "later, in different hands" changed to an aggressive pro-empire stance. But Philip, too, came to that stance.
195. Elbourne, "To colonize", p. 288 gives examples, including James Read, of missionaries who rejected the idea that the Xhosa were savage or barbarous.
196. Lester, *Imperial networks*, p. 30; Elbourne, "To colonize", p. 266; Keegan, *Colonial South Africa*, p. 283; A. Bank, "Losing faith in the civilizing mission: the premature decline of humanitarian liberalism at the Cape, 1840-1860" in M. Daunton and R. Halpern, *Empire and others* (London: University College press, 1999), pp. 367-369
197. Elbourne, "To colonize", pp. 283-285
198. Philip, *Researches*, I, pp. 209-212 quoted in Borch, "Conciliating", p. 268
199. Memorial to Donkin, [May 1820?], quoted in Philip, *Researches*, II, pp. 72-75. See also Macmillan, *Bantu, Boer and Briton*, p. 450
200. Keegan, *Colonial South Africa*, p. 92
201. K. Crehan, "Khoi, Boer and missionary: an anthropological study of the role of missionaries on the Cape frontier, 1799-1850" (MA, University of Manchester, 1978), pp 134-140. Compare the comment of this in Elbourne, "Questions of identity", p. 25. Also Ross, *Status*, p. 120; Crais, *Making*, p. 82
202. Legassick, "Griqua", pp. 451-462
203. Philip to Moffat, 31/1/1822 in Macmillan, *Bantu Boer and Briton*, p. 456
204. Memorial of LMS January 22, 1827, Theal, RCC, 30, p. 121 quoted by Borch, "Conciliating", pp. 269-270
205. Compare Sales, *Mission stations*, Ross, *Status*, pp. 119, 124; Elphick and Malherbe in *Shaping*, pp. 43-49; Elbourne, "To colonize", *passim*.
206. See Keegan, *Colonial South Africa*, p. 85
207. Ross, *Status*, p. 124
208. Keegan, *Colonial South Africa*, p. 102; Elbourne, pp. 277-279 who was the first to make use of the papers of Sir Thomas Buxton.
209. In fact the commissioners were divided on the question of pass laws, with Bigge favouring them for non-whites under contracts of service and Colebrooke and Blair supporting colour-blind labour legislation: Elbourne, "To colonize", p, 277. See

Bigge to Huskisson 12/5/1828 and Colebrook to Huskisson 14/5/1828 in Theal, RCC XXXV, pp. 200-203ff.
210. Walker, *History*, p. 169
211. H. King, *Richard Bourke* (Melbourne: OUP, 1971), p. 87; Peires in *Shaping*, pp. 494-497; Keegan, *Colonial South Africa*, pp. 100-102; Ross, *Status*, p. 55; Crais, *Making* p. 55
212. Crais, *Making*, p. 61
213. King, *Bourke*, pp. 118-121; Newton-King, "Labour Market", pp. 171-207; le Cordeur and Saunders, *The Kitchingman Papers*, p. 135. See Stockenstrom, *Light and Shade*; LMS 10/1/C Foster to Burder, Bethelsdorp, 17/6/1826; LMS 10/3/C C van der Kemp to Hankey, Bethelsdorp, 28/12/1827; Elbourne, "A question of identity", p. 27.
214. For an assessment of the discussion, see Elbourne, "To colonize", pp. 292-296. Also King, *Bourke*, pp. 122,274; Keegan, *Colonial South Africa*, pp 103-104; Ross, *Status*, p. 117
215. For the memorandum see Stockenstrom, *Light and Shade*, pp. 41-44
216. du Toit and Giliomee, *Afrikaner Political Thought*, pp. 135, 160-161
217. Macmillan, *Cape Colour Question*, p. 129 footnote 1
218. Stockenstrom, *Autobiography*, I, 243-248.
219. Ross, *Beyond the Pale*, p. 44
220. Crais, *Making*, pp. 73-76
221. Keegan, *Colonial South Africa*, p. 104; Crais and Worden, *Breaking the Chains*, pp. 18-19, 271-288.
222. Keegan, *Colonial South Africa*, pp. 104-105; Newton-King, "Labour market". See also Stockenstrom in du Toit and Giliomee, *Afrikaner Political Thought*, pp. 69-71
223. MF 146 LMS 11/2/A Bethelsdorp, 28/8/1828 James Read
224. Crais, *Making*, p. 112
225. CO 165 Thomson to Scott 10/6/1822 quoted in Stapleton, *Maqoma*, p. 41
226. Stapleton, *Maqoma*, p. 25
227. Stapleton, *Maqoma*, p. 34
228. Peires in *Shaping*, p. 488
229. See Switzer, *Power and Resistance*, p. 121; Mostert, *Frontiers*, pp. 1007, 1023. Soga was baptized by Robert Niven of the United Presbyterian Church
230. Quoted by Seton, "Wesleyan missions" pp. 25-26 from W. Shaw journal 21/3/1821 [WMM 1821, p. 788]
231. See Williams, *When Races Meet*, pp. 54-57; Seton, "Wesleyan missions", pp. 30-143; Stapleton, *Maqoma*, pp. 51-54; etc.
232. See the characterization in Keegan, *Colonial South Africa*, pp. 65-57. For a view which regards William Shaw, at least, as more complex in his racial views see B. Seton, "Wesleyan missions", pp. 11-14 and *passim*.
233. Le Cordeur, "Eastern Cape separatism", p. 147 from CA A50 Read to Fairbairn, 12/4/1833 and Backhouse, *Narrative*, p. 303
234. Mostert, *Frontiers*, p. 595
235. Williams, *When Races Meet*, Chs 5-7
236. Williams, *When Races Meet*, pp. 103-107
237. Cobbing, "The mfecane as alibi"; Peires "Matiwane's road to Mbolompo" in C.

Hamilton, (ed), Mfecane, especially pp. 226-236); H. Fast, *The journal and selected letters of Rev W.J Shrewsbury, 1826-1835: first missionary to the Transkei* (Johannesburg: Witwatersrand University Press, 1994), pp. 53-90; Bannister, *Humane Policy*, pp. 152-159; Crais, *Making*, pp. 98-99. Also Le Cordeur, " Eastern Cape separatism", p. 47 who reports - from Stockenstrom, *Autobiography*, I, 281 - that "Stockenstrom was appalled not only at Somerset's ineptitude, but also at the atrocities committed by his forces; the expedition had been undertaken, he said, mockingly, in terms of the 'divine mission' of 'the go-ahead Anglo-Saxon race' - 'and it is to be presumed that these valiant deeds on the Umtata count among the 'distinguished or meritorious services' for which we are and have been receiving rewards, medals and promotions."

238. Stockenstrom, *Light and Shade*, p. 5; *Autobiography*, II, p. 358. His memorandum of 17/4/1829 on the subject is reprinted in *Light and Shade*, pp. 3-5. His "desire for a dense buffer settlement in the Ceded Territory preceded his concern for the Khoikhoi.", according to Peires, in *Shaping*, p. 484. See also Crais, *Making*, p. 79; Le Cordeur, *Eastern Cape separatism*, p. 47; J.D. Pitman, "The commissioner generalship of Andries Stockenstrom" (MA, UCT, 1939), p. 35

239. K. S. Hunt, *Sir Lowry Cole: a study in colonial administration* (Durban: Butterworth, 1974); Lester, *Imperial networks*, pp. 35-36; Elbourne, "To colonize", p. 285

240. Stapleton, *Maqoma*, pp. 57-58; Crais, *Making*, pp. 113-114. A moravian mission had recently been established among the Thembu; Le Cordeur, "Eastern Cape separatism", p. 147; J.D. Pitman, "The commissioner generalship of Andries Stockenstrom" (MA, UCT, 1939), p. 35

241. Stapleton, *Maqoma*, pp. 57-61. Also Elbourne, "To colonize", p. 302; Hunt, *Cole*, p. 100; Glasgow Missionary Society, *Quarterly Paper*, V, pp. 1-2; Stockenstrom, *Light and Shade*, p. 2. The indecisiveness of the home government at this point towards the Xhosa is indicated in a communication to Cole: that the area had been populated by Xhosa "is undoubtedly a great evil; for while, on the one hand, it is not to be expected that these people will ever voluntarily evacuate the colonial territory, I am not, on the other hand, prepared to authorize you to expel them by force of arms from the land of their birth. At the same time it is clear that, without entirely abandoning the policy which sought to set up a bar between the Caffres and the colonists, the former cannot be allowed to remain as owners of the soil in permanent occupation of the colonial territory." Borch, "Conciliating", pp. 160-161

242. Crais, *Making*, p. 114

243. From BPP 1835, xxxix (252), pp. 156-157 See Le Cordeur and Saunders, *Kitchingman Papers*, pp. 129-130. The idea was raised in November 1819 by Joseph Williams's widow to Philip, and in 1821 to Philip by Pringle. Brownlee also raised it with Philip in 1825 and it was probably discussed when Philip, Pringle, Read and Stockenstrom met in Graff Reinet in 1825. See also Pringle to Philip 15/1/1821 in Macmillan, *Bantu, Boer and Briton*, p. 83; Brownlee to Philip 28/3/1825 in *ibid*, p. 84

244. Philip in [538 of 1836, p. 605] quoted in Legassick, "Griqua", p. 475

245. Philip, *Researches*, II, 238-239 quoted in Legassick, "Griqua", pp. 458-459

246. Stockenstrom, *Light and Shade*, p. 2. Also Mostert, *Frontiers*, p. 617.

247. For the emergence of such in the Eastern Cape, elsewhere than Kat River, see Crais,

Making, pp. 77-79
248. Keegan, *Colonial South Africa*, p. 117
249. Elbourne, pp. 311-313; Keegan, *Colonial South Africa*, pp. 118-119
250. MF 631/2 LMS Philip 3/5 The Kat River Settlement. See also Keegan, *Colonial South Africa*, pp. 117, 323
251. Elbourne, pp. 308-310.
252. [Andries Stoffel, [538 of 1836], p. 588 q. 5062]; Mostert, *Frontiers*, pp. 355-356
253. Philip credited the GMS missionary at Balfour, John Ross, with persuading government to give the territory to Khoisan rather than colonists: see MF 631/2 LMS Philip 3/5 The Kat River Settlement.
254. MF 150 LMS 11/3/C Theopolis, 4/6/1829 Barker to Thomas
255. See for example Crais, *Making*, p. 79
256. MF 168 LMS 12/4/C Philipton, "No date but probably August 1831", James Read Sr to J. Campbell
257. MF 150 LMS 11/3/C Theopolis, 4/6/1829 Barker to Thomas
258. MF 151 LMS 11/3/D Bethelsdorp 30/7/1829 James Read [to Orme]
259. MF 150 LMS 11/3/C Theopolis, 4/6/1829 Barker to Thomas
260. MF 151 LMS 11/3/D Bethelsdorp 30/7/1829 James Read [to Orme]
261. Le Cordeur and Saunders, *Kitchingman Papers*, pp. 133-134 Read to Stockenstrom, 16/6/1829
262. Thomson to Cole, 1/7/1829 [CA CO 362/36]. See Seton, "Wesleyan missions", pp. 149-150; Williams, *When Races Meet*, pp. 113-114. Soon after the expulsion Thomson went to Cape Town where he saw governor Cole. See Hunt, Cole, pp. 100, 108 on the boundary.
263. CA CO 373/34 (enc) Stockenstrom to Read 5/7/1830 quoted in Williams, *When Races Meet*, pp. 116.
264. MF 631/2 LMS Philip 3/5 The Kat River Settlement
265. MF 158 LMS 12/1/D Cape Town, 18/12/30 John Philip
266. MF 158 LMS 12/1/D Cape Town, 18/12/30 John Philip
267. MF 631/2 LMS Philip 3/5 The Kat River Settlement
268. See CA CO 4900 Colonial Secretary to Stockenstrom 18/6/1830 quoted in Williams, *When Races Meet*, pp. 115. See CA Lieutenant Governor (LG), 6, Kat River, Read to Stockenstrom, 9/7/1830: he had heard something of Thomson's appointment but believed it to be abandoned.
269. CA LG 6 Kat River, Read to Stockenstrom, 14/6/1830: saying he had arrived from Bethelsdorp on 13/6 and would confine himself as much as possible to spiritual work.
270. MF 631/2 LMS Philip 3/5 The Kat River Settlement
271. MF 158 LMS 12/1/D Cape Town, 18/12/30 John Philip
272. See, eg Williams, *When Races Meet*, pp.113-119
273. Keegan, *Colonial South Africa*, p. 118
274. On Boyce's charge regarding the Kat River see MF 233 LMS 16/4/B, Philipton, 19/11/1839 James Read to LMS.
275. For Eastern Cape Basters see for example, Crais, *Making*,pp. 69-72
276. Though Kirk says 2114 in 1835 (p 416)
277. Stockenstrom, *Light and Shade*, p 15

278. Kirk, "Progress and decline in the Kat River settlement, 1829-1854", *Journal of African History,* XIV, 3, (1973), pp. 411-416; Elbourne, "To colonize", pp. 304-306; MF 168 LMS 12/4/C Philipton, "No date but probably August 1831", James Read Sr to J. Campbell; Stockenstrom, *Light and Shade,* pp. 44-54; Crais, *Making,* pp. 69-72. For the consciousness of the peasant inhabitants see e.g., Crais, *Making,* pp. 83-84; Keegan, *Colonial South Africa,* p. 118.
279. Stockenstrom, *Light and Shade*, p. 6; Crais, *Making*, pp. 85, 115
280. Legassick, "Griqua", pp. 459 and generally; Keegan, *Colonial South Africa*, pp. 180-182
281. Keegan, *Colonial South Afric,* pp. 179-180, etc; Legassick, "Griqua", pp. 461-465, Chs IX-XI
282. Mostert, *Frontiers*, p. 617
283. Le Cordeur, *Eastern Cape separatism*, pp. 51-4; Keegan, *Colonial South Africa*, p. 113; A. Ross, *Philip*, p. 210; Du Toit and Giliomee (eds), *Afrikaner Political Thought*, pp. 247-9, 275-282
284. Crais, *Making*, pp. 93-5
285. MF 151 LMS 11/3/D Bethelsdorp 30/7/1829 James Read [to Orme]
286. For Godlonton's early views see Keegan, *Colonial South Africa*, p. 119; Crais, *Making*, p. 139
287. Quoted Keegan, *Colonial South Africa*, p. 111
288. Crais, *Making*, pp. 128-129 Peires, , pp. 12-13 Legassick, "The State, racism and the rise of capitalism", p. 346. See also Lester, *Imperial networks* and A. Bank, "Liberals and their enemies: racial ideology at the Cape of Good Hope, 1820-1850" (Ph.D., U of Cambridge, 1996) base the transformation on the experience of the war of 1834-1835. But the I'ons cartoon dating from the early 1830s, discussed by the Crais on pp. 130-131, typifies the British settler anti-humanitarian attitude precisely.
289. Crais, *Making*, pp. 133, 138 and generally pp. 127-138
290. Ross, *Status*, pp. 43, 45-46
291. Le Cordeur, *Eastern Cape separatism*, p. 65 from Kirk, "Self-government", pp. 61-62
292. Elbourne, "To colonize", pp. 296-298; Crais, *Making,* pp. 139-140
293. Elbourne, "To colonize", p. 314; Keegan, *Colonial South Africa*, pp. 119-122; Stockenstrom, *Light and Shade,* pp. 71-72
294. Petition signed by 401 inhabitants of Kat River settlement.
295. S. Trapido, "The Emergence of Liberalism"; Crais, *Making*, pp. 74, 147; Ross, *Status*, pp. 117-119; Elbourne, "To colonize", pp. 315-317; Keegan, *Colonial South Africa*, pp. 120-121. Keegan points out that a similarly repressive New Poor Law was passed by the British parliament in 1834, supported by humanitarians: Keegan, *Colonial South Africa*, p. 323
296. Elbourne, "To colonize", pp. 317-318
297. Keegan, *Colonial South Africa*, pp. 110-112, 115
298. Crais, *Making*, pp. 62-63
299. Crais and Worden (eds), *Breaking the Chains*, p. 13
300. Keegan, *Colonial South Africa*, pp. 112-113, 122
301. MF 616/7 LMS Philip, Bethelsdorp, 22/2/1830; Rolland, *Journal des Missions*

Evangelique, 5, 1830 pp. 237-238; Rolland's journal 17/2/1830 forthcoming from the Van Riebeeck Society [Ross, *Status*, p. 118]

302. Quoted in Macmillan, *Bantu, Boer and Briton*, p. 97
303. *Missionary Herald*, XXIX, November 1833, p. 414, quoted in Lester, *Imperial networks*, p. 38
304. Macmillan, *Bantu, Boer and Briton*, pp. 98-100; Stapleton, *Maqoma*, p. 68. H. Ross to Parents 17/4/1830 describes Philip's visit with Maqoma. See also for the editorials, BPP 438 of 1836, p. 372, evidence of Colonel Wade 25/4/1836.
305. Macmillan, *Bantu, Boer and Briton*, pp. 99-100; Keegan, *Colonial South Africa*, pp. 138-139
306. See Bannister, *Humane Policy*, pp. 90-106; Pringle, *African Sketches*, (London: Moxon, 1834) *Narrative of a Residence in South Africa* (London: Moxon, 1835), pp. 309-311. Also Boyce, *Notes on South African Affairs*. See Seton, "Wesleyan missions", p. 152 for Shaw to Aborigines Committee See also Le Cordeur and Saunders (eds) *Kitchingman Papers*, pp. 136-137, Philipton, 27/5/1834, Read to Kitchingman, for Pringle etc.
307. Seton, "Wesleyan missions", pp. 152-154; BPP 503 of 1837, p. 78. Philip had written favourably of Wesleyans in his *Researches*, II, pp. 196-197. The same missionary also wrote at this time to the headquarters in London: "I do not wish you to understand that the fault is in our Government, even should Caffreland become a scene of war and bloodshed; for I believe there is no Government on earth that would have been so lenient with the Caffres as our own." Samuel Young, August 1830 WMM, 1831, pp. 55-56
308. Stapleton, *Maqoma*, p. 69
309. Stapleton, *Maqoma*, pp. 69-78. See also CA A50/4 Read to Fairbairn 7/12/1833: "There have been a number of the most aggravating circumstances possible, and every method contrived to agitate the Caffres with a view we think to have a pretext to take more land from them" [quoted by Webster, in Hamilton (ed), *Mfecane*, p.250]
310. MF 631/2 LMS Philip 3/5 The Kat River Settlement. See also Elbourne, "To colonize", pp. 319-320 for the role of Read; and for the tendency of historians to neglect Read see A. Ross, "John Philip: a reassessment" in H. Macmillan and S. Marks (eds), *Africa and Empire: W.M. Macmillan, historian and social critic* (London: Temple Smith, 1989)
311. Le Cordeur and Saunders (eds), *Kitchingman Papers*, 135-136, Philipton, Philip to Kitchingman, 2/10/1832; also Macmillan, *Bantu, Boer and Briton*, pp. 101-102
312. See Stapleton, *Maqoma*, pp. 75-76; C. Hummel (ed), *Reverend F.G. Kayser: journals and letters* (Cape Town: Maskew Miller, Longman, 1990), pp. 88-89,91, especially Kayser, Buffalo River, 3/12/1832. Stapleton makes no mention of the Maqoma-Philip meeting at Kat River in 1832 and thus fails to explain why the missionary came from the LMS rather than the GMS.
313. Stapleton, *Maqoma*, pp. 78-79, 235; Peires, *House of Phalo*, pp. 93, 227; Elbourne, "To colonize", p. 321. Compare Pringle, Narrative; also Grahamstown Journal, 17/10/1833; SA Commercial Advertiser, 4/12/1833; Le Cordeur and Saunders, Kitchingman Papers, pp. 138-145; MF 188 LMS 14/1/C Read to LMS, Philipton, Kat

River, 3/7/1834 The Wesleyans did not favour Maqoma, and the attitude of the Glasgow missionaries is less well researched
314. Quoted by Crais, *Making*, p. 115
315. My emphasis. Elbourne, "To colonize", p. 319 LMS 14/1/C Read to LMS, Philipton, Kat River, 3/7/1834. Le Cordeur and Saunders (eds) *Kitchingman Papers*, p. 139 quote from British Parliamentary Papers the evidence that "Macomo's heart was very sore about the land; the subject always set him on fire; he fought in hopes of getting it back" [BPP 503 of 1837, p. 77]
316. Elbourne, "To colonize", pp. 321-322; Stapleton, *Maqoma*, pp. 80-81. The letter is in *SA Commercial Advertiser*, 7/12/1833 and CA 1480 Macomo to J. Philip, Banks of the Keiskamma, 18/11/1833
317. Le Cordeur, *Eastern Cape separatism*, p. 49
318. See Macmillan, *Bantu, Boer and Briton*, pp. 104-105; Hunt, *Cole*, pp. 102, 106-7
319. Crais, *Making*, p. 116
320. Macmillan, *Bantu, Boer and Briton*, pp. 104-105
321. Stapleton, *Maqoma*, pp. 81-82; Seton, "Wesleyan missions", pp. 153-154
322. Elbourne, "To colonize", p. 320. CA 1480 Read to Philip, Philipton 12/4/1834, also, with James Read to Fairbairn, Philipton, 13/4/1834 enclosed in MF 198 LMS 14/3/D Philip 1/5/1835. In evidence to the Aborigines Commission in 1836, he claimed this was in June 1834: [538 of 1837], p. 697
323. Macmillan, *Bantu, Boer and Briton*, p. 109
324. Le Cordeur and Saunders (eds), *Kitchingman Papers*, pp. 138-145, MF 188 LMS 14/1/C Read to LMS, Philipton, Kat River, 3/7/1834
325. Macmillan, *Bantu, Boer and Briton*, pp. 119-120. See Seton, "Wesleyan missions", p. 158
326. Seton, "Wesleyan missions", pp. 157-158; Hummel, *Kayser*, p. 101; Stapleton, *Maqoma*, pp. 84-85; Keegan, *Colonial South Africa*, p. 140
327. When in 1830 Philip wrote "nine-tenths of the settlers are opposed to the civilisation of the Caffres.", he was referring only to the Boers: Macmillan, *Bantu, Boer and Briton*, p. 98.
328. Macmillan, *Bantu, Boer and Briton*, pp 120-121; Seton, "Wesleyan missions", pp. 156-157
329. Keegan, *Colonial South Africa*, p. 182; Legassick, "Griqua", pp. 480-497.
330. Keegan, *Colonial South Africa*, pp. 182-184; Legassick, "Griqua", pp. 524-531; 619-623
331. Keegan, *Colonial South Africa*, p. 143
332. Peires, *House of Phalo*, p. 145
333. See the analysis in Legassick, "The state, racism and the rise of capitalism", pp. 342-344
334. Mostert, *Frontiers*, pp. 655, 664. Stapleton, *Maqoma*, p. 86 however claims that in December only "small parties of Rharabe warriors infiltrated the Ceded Territory and the colony" and "very few Europeans were killed" (*Maqoma*, p. 86)
335. Hummel, *Kayser*, pp. 102-106; Stapleton, *Maqoma*, pp. 86-87; Mostert, *Frontiers*, pp. 650-653, 665
336. MF 198 LMS 14/3/D Cape Town, 1/5/1835 J. Philip [Very long letter]

337. Keegan, *Colonial South Africa*, pp. 74, 140-141
338. Peires, *House of Phalo*, pp. 94, 109
339. Stapleton, *Maqoma*, p. 92; Peires, *House of Phalo*, p. 160
340. Peires, *House of Phalo*, p. 146; Mostert, *Frontiers*, pp. 667, 675-676, 700, 736; Crais, *Making*, pp. 85-86. Also Stapleton, *Maqoma*, pp.94-95 for British insistence in peace negotiations that "Khoi allies" be given up by the Xhosa, suggesting that there were some. Also Le Cordeur and Saunders (eds) Kitchingman Papers, pp. 146-147: Philipton, 31/12/1834 Read jr to Kitchingman. "It is strange that no Hottentots have in any part of the colony fallen victims to their fury. I cannot consider this a favourable omen either way. They (the Xhosa) either wish to bribe the Hottentots, or lull them into a state of security and then fall on them on their way homewards." He added: "I am extremely sorry that the Caffres have at last come to this. I think that the abettors of the rotten system will rejoice at the present state of things, in as much as it will weigh heavy in keeping up a strong military force on the frontier. We on the contrary maintain that the old system has bought things to so painful an issue."
341. See for example MF 203 LMS 14/5/A Cape Town, 9/12/1835 John Philip
342. Le Cordeur and Saunders, *Kitchingman Papers*, pp. 156-159; MF 203 LMS 14/5/A Bethelsdorp, 16/11/35 James Read Jr to Philip; also quoted by Williams, *When Races Meet*, pp. 131-133
343. Stockenstrom, *Light and Shade*, pp. 12-13
344. Kirk, "Progress and decline", pp. 414-415; Crais, *Making,* p. 85
345. Stapleton, *Maqoma*, p. 88. Compare Crais, *Making*, pp. 115-116
346. See the condensed biography of Smith in Mostert, *Frontiers*, pp. 658-664
347. Peires, *House of Phalo*, pp. 146-148; Mostert, *Frontiers,* pp. 684-685, 688, 690-694, 702-709; Maclennan, *Proper degree of terror*, p. 224
348. Mostert, *Frontiers*, 709-718, 724-728; Crais, *Making,* p. 116; Keegan, *Colonial South Africa*, p. 143
349. See for example Keegan, *Colonial South Africa*, p. 44
350. Keegan, *Colonial South Africa*, pp. 141-142; Le Cordeur, *Eastern Cape separatism,* p. 69.
351. Keegan, *Colonial South Africa*, pp. 141-329; Le Cordeur, *Eastern Cape separatism*, pp. 126-127. For the Fairbairn-Godlonton conflict see J. Frye, "The SA Commercial Advertiser and the eastern frontier" (MA, Rhodes, 1968). Also R.A. McKend, " 'A Journal Among Them': Colonial Discourse and the Creation of an Imaginary Community in the *Graham's Town Journal*, 1831-1836", (MA, UCT, 1997)
352. Keegan, *Colonial South Africa*, p. 141.
353. Macmillan, *Bantu, Boer and Briton*, p. 130
354. Quoted Keegan, *Colonial South Africa*, p. 144
355. Stapleton, *Maqoma*, p.90-91; Mostert, *Frontiers,* pp. 720, 722-723, 727; Macmillan, *Bantu Boer and Briton*, pp. 131-132
356. Elbourne, "A question of identity", p. 25
357. Stapleton, *Maqoma*, pp.92-97; Mostert, *Frontiers*, p. 749; Macmillan, *Bantu, Boer and Briton*, pp. 149-150; Le Cordeur, "Eastern Cape separatism", pp. 75-76
358. Seton, "Wesleyan missions", pp. 308-317

359. Stapleton, *Maqoma*, **pp. 97-98**
360. Stapleton, *Maqoma*, p. 93
361. Crais, *Making,* p. 152
362. Stapleton, *Maqoma*, p. 98
363. Peires, *House of Phalo*, pp. 110-111; Crais, *Making*, p. 117; Keegan, *Colonial South Africa*, pp. 145-147; Mostert, *Frontiers*, pp. 697-698, 714-715, 719-720, 722; Switzer, *Power and Resistance*, p. 60
364. See Webster in Hamilton (ed), Mfecane aftermath; A.C. Webster, "Land expropriation and labour extraction under Cape colonial rule: the war of 1835 and the 'emancipation' of the Fingo" (MA, Rhodes University, 1991); Stapleton, Maqoma, pp. 50, 90-91; Crais, *Making*, p. 99 and, for critique, Keegan, Colonial South Africa, pp. 330-331; Switzer, Power and Resistance, pp. 58-60 See also, for example, MF 224 LMS 16/2/C Kat River report for 1838 where Read recalls his travels in Xhosa territory with Richard Miles in 1826: the "late chief Hintza had given the Fingoes twenty cattle kraals, many other chiefs did the same… D'Urban brought them to the colony….many have returned to the caffres…. We have about 1500 of them in this settlement."
365. Crais, *Making*, p. 118
366. D'Urban to Col Hare, 17/9/1835, D'Urban papers, quoted Seton, "Wesleyan missions", p. 319
367. Quoted Peires, *House of Phalo*, p. 113
368. From an 1835-1836 census, cited by Seton, "Wesleyan missions", p.322
369. Quoted Crais, *Making,* p. 118
370. Peires in *Shaping*, pp. 489-490; Peires, *House of Phalo*, pp. 113-115; Mostert, *Frontiers*, pp. 762ff, 784; Stapleton, *Maqoma*, p. 101; Seton, "Wesleyan missions", p. 323; Keegan, *Colonial South Africa*, p. 148.
371. Seton, "Wesleyan missions", pp. 329-333. Only three missionaries who were asked refused to serve as commissioners, one of them Brownlee of the LMS
372. Smith, 4/6/1836 in Theal, Records of the Province of Queen Adelaide, (RPQA), II, p. 625 [Cory Library, Rhodes University] quoted in Seton, "Wesleyan missions", p. 324. See also Peires, p. 114
373. Keegan, *Colonial South Africa*, p. 148
374. See Stapleton, *Maqoma,* p. 101-102, 103,104; Crais, *Making*, p. 121. In 1835-1836 *Maqoma* was looking unsuccessfully for a way out through moving his people northward across the Orange.
375. Peries, *House of Phalo*, pp. 105, 159
376. Lester, *Imperial networks*, p. 63
377. Le Cordeur, *Eastern Cape separatism* p. 71 from I. Mitford-Barberton, *Commandant Holden Bowker* (Cape Town, 1970), pp. 115-116; Peires, *House of Phalo*, p. 123.
378. Quoted Le Cordeur, *Eastern Cape separatism*, pp. 75-76. See also Seton, "Wesleyan missions", p. 319
379. Crais, *Making*, p. 118; Crais, "The vacant land"; Keegan, *Colonial South Africa*, pp. 141-142, 144; Le Cordeur*, Eastern Cape separatism,* pp. 71-72
380. Keegan, *Colonial South Africa*, p. 145
381. Keegan, *Colonial South Africa*, p. 148 For some of the letters see MF 199 LMS

14/4/A Cape Town 4/6/1835 John Philip; MF 200 LMS 14/4/B Cape Town, 29/6/1835 John Philip on the death of Hintsa; Mostert, *Frontiers*, pp. 740-741. See also J.G. Pretorius, "The British humanitarians and the Cape eastern frontier, 1834-1836" (PhD, Wits, 1970); P. Lalu, "In the event of history".
382. MF 204 LMS 14/5/A Cape Town, 19/12/1835 Philip
383. Keegan, *Colonial South Africa*, pp. 148ff; Elbourne, "To colonize", p. 322ff
384. Le Cordeur and Saunders, *Kitchingman Papers*, pp. 163-164: Hackney, 22/6/1836, Read sr to Kitchingman
385. For the interaction between humanitarians and Glenelg see for example Mostert, *Frontiers*, pp. 754-755
386. Mostert, *Frontiers*, p. 756
387. Borch, "Conciliating", p. 162; Seton, "Wesleyan missions", pp. 351-353; Keegan, *Colonial South Africa*, pp. 149-150 Crais, *Making*, pp. 119-120; Mostert, *Frontiers*, pp. 759-760. The Glenelg dispatch may be found in BPP 39 of 1836,279, pp.59-73
388. Galbraith, *Reluctant Empire* argues that the decision was motivated by economic and not humanitarian factors but recent research restresses the humanitarian drive.
389. Le Cordeur and Saunders, *Kitchingman Papers*, pp. 163-164:Hackney, 22/6/1836, Read sr to Kitchingman; pp. 167-170: Hackney, 4/9/1836, Read sr to Kitchingman
390. Macmillan, *Bantu, Boer and Briton*, p. 146. However he also told the Aborigines Committee that "Had I been consulted before the Caffre War on the propriety of annexing the country between the Keiskamma and the Kye to the Colony, I should have said, let the Caffres alone, the work of civilization is going forward among them, and in a little time what you wish for will come about by itself": quoted by Keegan, *Colonial South Africa*, p. 331.
391. Keegan, *Colonial South Africa*, p.149. Mostert seems incorrect to believe that Philip changed his views: See Mostert, *Frontiers*, pp. 738, 755-756, 797-801
392. Quoted in Legassick, "Griqua", pp. 478-479
393. Compare Seton, "Wesleyan missions", pp. 214-215, 298-299; Boyce, *Notes*, Appendix 1; Mostert, *Frontiers*, p. 738.
394. MF 201 LMS 14/4/C Cape Town, 11/7/1835 John Philip
395. J.V.B. Shrewsbury, *Memorial of the Reverend William J. Shrewsbury*, (London: Hamilton Adams, 1869), p. 409
396. Seton, "Wesleyan missions", pp. 209-212; Shrewsbury, *Memorial*, pp. 407-419 Shrewsbury's letter of 16/1/1835 is in BPP 39 of 1836, 279, p. 44. It was enclosed in D'Urban to Sec of State 19/6/1835. See also Seton, "Wesleyan missions", p. 213 for Shrewsbury, Young and Haddy to WMS London 31/1/1835, with a pro-colonist view of the cause of the war; Seton, pp.222-225, Boyce to D'Urban 31/3/1835. See also Le Cordeur and Saudners (eds), *Kitchingman Papers*, pp. 163-165: Hackney, 22/6/1836, Read sr to Kitchingman, "Lord Glenelg has exposed poor Shrewsbury, and 'tis said his Society are obliged to disown him. Shaw is sent out to save the rest."; Hackney, 2/8/1836, Read sr to Kitchingman, "The poor Wesleyans are done for; their committee passed a resolution disapproving of all their proceedings and censuring poor Shrewsbury strongly…. What will Godlonton and Sir Benjamin now say?… We have not trusted the Lord in vain. He surely is our rock whose work is perfect." See also BPP 39 of 1836, p. 120

397. (London: John Mason, 1839)
398. (London: John Mason, 1839). On 12/10/1836 Boyce sent to D'Urban "Skeleton of a Plan for the arrangement of Facts calculated to exhibit the true state of Colonial Affairs to uninformed and prejudices persons in England", undoubtedly the seeds of his Notes: Seton, "Wesleyan missions", pp. 338-339; Theal, *Records PQA*, I, pp. 62-69
399. Le Cordeur and Saunders, *Kitchingman Papers*, p. 212: Philipton, 9/12/1839 Read sr to Kitchingman
400. Opland, *Xhosa Poets*, pp.230-234
401. William Govan, *Memorials of the missionary career of the Rev James Laing*, (Glasgow: David Bryce, 1875), p. 49; journal 19/9/35
402. He particularly tries to distinguish Shaw's views from those such as Shrewsbury and Boyce on the one hand and Kay on the other: Seton, "Wesleyan missions", pp. 225-226, 278-280. Thus Shaw in August in Britain said of D'Urban's May proclamation: 'I certainly regret that he should have been induced to make the Kye river the boundary of the Colony ... I cannot easily bring my mind to the total disinheriting 80,000 people of the lands which belong to them... without lifting up my voice against so sweeping a measure ... the death of Hintsa is a most calamitous event." On Kay see Le Cordeur and Saunders (eds), *Kitchingman Papers*, pp.173-176:Hackney,26/1/1837 Read sr to Kitchingman, who writes of "Kay, the Wesleyan missionary, who boldly came forward and reprobated the conduct of the Governor, Sir Benjamin, and that of the colonists towards the Caffres...[and] made strong allusions of dissatisfaction of his Brethren."
403. Seton, "Wesleyan missionaries", pp. 302, 326
404. Lester, *Imperial networks*, p. 64; Le Cordeur, *Eastern Cape separatism*, pp.66-67
405. Peires, p. 131-132
406. Le Cordeur, *Eastern Cape separatism*, p. 86; Keegan, *Colonial South Africa*, pp. 150-151; du Toit and Giliomee (eds), *Afrikaner Political Thought*, pp. 139-140, 166-170, 176. Switzer argued that the treaty system froze Africans into locations: *Power and Resistance*, pp. 60-61.
407. Du Toit and Giliomee (eds), *Afrikaner Political Thought*, p. 175; Le Cordeur, *Eastern Cape separatism*, p. 97; Le Cordeur and Saunders (eds), *The Kitchingman Papers*, pp. 194-195: Philipton, 4/6/1837 Read jr to Kitchingman
408. Peires in *Shaping*, p. 490
409. Le Cordeur, *Eastern Cape separatism*, p. 89: Napier to Stanley 21/12/1841 GH 23/13. Compare M. West to Fairbairn, 9/10/1840 BC312 (Mears collection), UCT.
410. Keegan, Colonial South Africa, pp. 115-116, 151-152, 181-182; Crais, Making, pp. 134-136. See also Meltzer in Worden and Crais (eds), Breaking the Chains, pp. 15-16, 169-200
411. Crais, *Making*, p. 153. See also Peires, *House of Phalo*, p. 120.
412. Le Cordeur, *Eastern Cape separatism*, pp. 78, 85, 88; Keegan, *Colonial South Africa*, p. 151; Peires, *House of Phalo*, pp. 124-126. However by the latter 1830s Godlonton's claims to speak for all eastern opinion was being challenged even within Grahamstown, among others by Dr Ambrose George Campbell, one of the town's three doctors, for four moths in 1840 he published the *Colonial Times*, after which it was taken over and became the *Cape Frontier Times*: Le Cordeur, *Eastern Cape separatism*, pp. 103-104

413. MF 223 LMS 16/2/A Philipton, 10/9/1838, Read to LMS
414. Le Cordeur and Saunders, *Kitchingman Papers*, pp. 200-201: Cape Town, 25/5/1838 Philip to Kitchingman
415. MF 229 LMS 16/3/B Cape Town 22/3/1839 John Philip.
416. Mostert, *Frontiers*, pp. 796-797, 803; Le Cordeur, *Eastern Cape separatism*, pp. 88, 92-93, 95-96, 100-102, 104-109; Keegan, *Colonial South Africa*, pp. 151-153; Macmillan, *Bantu, Boer and Briton*, p. 266; Peires, *House of Phalo*, p. 126.
417. Keegan, *Colonial South Africa*, pp. 197, 200
418. Keegan, *Colonial South Africa*, pp. 200-201; Stockenstrom, *Autobiography*, II, pp. 50-64. See also Le Cordeur, *Eastern Cape separatism*, p. 146. From the time of the 1835 war, frontier farmers were not inclined to accept the lead of Grahamstown commerce. Also du Toit and Giliomee, *Afrikaner Political Thought*, p. 137 for the lack of involvement of other Afrikaners in frontier policy or frontier affairs.
419. Le Cordeur, *Eastern Cape separatism*, p. 88
420. Keegan, *Colonial South Africa*, pp.192-194
421. Keegan, *Colonial South Africa*, pp. 186-197; Le Cordeur, *Eastern Cape separatism*, p. 90.
422. Worden and Crais (eds), *Breaking the Chains*, pp. 14-15
423. Keegan, *Colonial South Africa*, pp.123-124 Marincowitz, "Rural production", p. 38; Crais, *Making*, pp. 154-158
424. Crais, *Making*, pp. 148-149, 157, 163-164, 184
425. Legassick, "Griqua", pp. 491-493
426. Quoted Legassick, "Griqua", p. 557
427. Legassick, "Griqua", p. 559
428. Le Cordeur and Saunders, *Kitchingman Papers*, pp. 217-218 Philipton, 2/12/1840, Read sr to Kitchingman
429. Keegan, *Colonial South Africa*, pp. 88-9; Legassick, "Griqua", p. 441
430. Le Cordeur and Saunders, *Kitchingman Papers*, pp. 217-218: Philipton, 2/12/1840, Read sr to Kitchingman
431. Le Cordeur and Saunders, *Kitchingman Papers* pp. 225-226: Graaff-Reinet, 13/6/1842, Read sr to Kitchingman
432. Keegan, *Colonial South Africa*, pp. 249, 350
433. Keegan, *Colonial South Africa*, pp. 249-250
434. Keegan, *Colonial South Africa*, pp. 204ff
435. Moyer, "History of the Mfengu", pp. 209-211
436. Keegan, *Colonial South Africa*, pp. 207-208
437. Stapleton, *Maqoma*, pp. 106-116, 121; Hummel, *Kayser*, pp. 140-151; Le Cordeur and Saunders (eds), *Kitchingman Papers*, pp. 201-203
438. Le Cordeur and Saunders (eds), *Kitchingman Papers*, pp.196-197: Cape Town, 15/2/1838, Read sr to Kitchingman
439. Le Cordeur and Saunders (eds), *Kitchingman Papers*, pp.207-208: Philipton, 15/4/1839, Read sr to Kitchingman, Also, *ibid*, pp. 208-209: Philipton, 20/5/1839 Read sr to Kitchingman
440. Stapleton, *Maqoma*, p. 117;
441. For the start of these stations see MF 233 16/4/B Philipton, 19/11/1839 James Read

to LMS; MF 243 17/2/A Philipton, 15/6/1840 Read to Philip; Le Cordeur and Saunders (eds), *Kitchingman Papers,* pp. 190-193, 231-232: Philipton, 4/5/4[3] Read sr to Kitchingman; Saunders, "Read", p. 5. [In conflict with Wesleyans who move into

442. The incident is also related in Henry Calderwood, *Caffres and Caffre Missions*, (London: Nisbet, 1858), pp. 65-72
443. MF 234 LMS 16/4/B: Blinkwater, 30/12/1839 Calderwood. See also Stapleton, *Maqoma*, p. 117 for Calderwood's initial favourable impression of Maqoma.
444. Stapleton, *Maqoma*, p. 120
445. MF 254 LMS 18/1/C Blinkwater 13/5/1841 Calderwood. See also MF 249 LMS 17/3/B Calderwood to Sec 28 August 1840 Annual report for 1840
446. Stapleton, *Maqoma,* pp. 77, 111, 113, 118, 121-122, 127, 131, 138-140, 223-224, Hummel, Kayser, pp. 100, 137, 155; Calderwood, *Caffres and Caffre Missions*, p. 86; Peiries, p. 129.
447. Le Cordeur and Saunders (eds), *Kitchingman Papers*, pp. 222-223: Blinkwater, 5/12/1841, Read Jr to Kitchingman
448. Le Cordeur and Saunders (eds), *Kitchingman Papers*, p. 224: Blinkwater, 23/1/1842, Read jr to Kitchingman. Also MF 234 LMS 16/4/B Blinkwater, 30/12/1839 Calderwood; MF 263 LMS 5/4/1842: Philipton, James Read Jr; MF 267 LMS 18/4/B Zuurbraak, 10/10/1842 Calderwood; Stapleton, Maqoma, p. 122
449. Peires, *House of Phalo*, p. 129; Stapleton, *Maqoma*, pp. 120-6; MF 263 LMS 5/4/1842 Philipton, James Read Jr
450. MF 274 LMS 19/1/C Blinkwater 20/3/1843 Calderwood. Also MF 267 LMS 18/4/C Philipton, 19/11/1842, J Read sr. In an allusion to the Reads, Calderwood wrote, "Some very disagreeable circumstances in reference to him and this station have occasioned before our return and since which have grieved and tried us… but to these circumstances I shall now no further allude"
451. Le Cordeur and Saunders (eds), *Kitchingman Papers*, pp.230-231: Philipton, 26/3/1843, Read sr to Kitchingman
452. Le Cordeur and Saunders (eds), *Kitchingman Papers*, pp. 210-211: Philipton, 24/6/1839 Read sr to Kitchingman; See also *ibid*, p. 211: Philipton, 29/8/1839 Read sr to Kitchingman.
453. MF 277 LMS 19/2/C Blinkwater 10/7/1843 Calderwood. He continued "If Natives and Europeans are to be united the reciprocal influence of the one upon the other is a question of much importance ‑ I certainly think we are not yet prepared for such a union in South Africa - this opinion has no reference to colonial prejudice or colour."
454. Le Cordeur and Saunders (eds), *Kitchingman Papers*, pp. 214-217, 220-201:Philipton, 11/7/1840, Read sr to Kitchingman; Philipton, 24/9/1840, Read sr to Kitchingman; Philipton, 22/3/1841, Read sr to Kitchingman
455. Le Cordeur and Saunders (eds), *Kitchingman Papers*, pp.233-234: Philipton, 12/6/1843, Read sr to Kitchingman; *ibid*, pp. 192, 194, 235: Cape Town, 26 June 1843 - Philip; *ibid,* pp. 234-235: Philipton, 3/7/1843, Read sr to Kitchingman; *ibid,* pp. 234-235: Philipton, 3/7/1843, Read sr to Kitchingman MF 277 LMS 19/2/B Minutes of meeting, Grahamstown 21-2/6/1843; Blinkwater 28/6/1843;
456. Le Cordeur and Saunders (eds), *Kitchingman Papers,* pp. 236-237, 239-240, 242-244:

Philipton, 17/7/43, Read sr to Kitchingman; Philipton, 11/12/1843, Read sr to Kitchingman; Philipton, 22/1/1844, Read sr to Kitchingman
457. Crais, *Making*, pp. 152-153
458. Sales, *Mission stations*, pp. 121-134
459. Crais, *Making*, pp. 148, 159
460. Stockenstrom, *Light and shade*, p. 72 [James Read Jr, 27/3/1851]; Crais, *Making*, p. 159; Le Cordeur and Saunders, *Kitchingman Papers*, p. 191: CA LG 592 p. 93 Borcherds report on Kat River Settlement 10/2/1842; Kirk, "Progress and decline", pp. 415-418
461. Crais, *Making*, pp. 159-163, 166; Stapleton, *Maqoma*, p. 110; Peires, *House of Phalo*, pp. 129-130. On Matroos see Stockenstrom, *Light and Shade*, pp. 13-14; Keegan, *Colonial South Africa*, p. 238; Mostert, *Frontiers*, p 990; Kirk, "Progress and decline", p. 415; Stapleton, *Maqoma*, p.154
462. Calderwood, *Caffre and Caffre missions*, p. 38
463. MF 224 LMS 16/2/C Kat River report for 1838, Read
464. Crais, *Making*, p. 153
465. Le Cordeur, *Eastern Cape separatism*, p. 129 from BPP 635 of 1851, p. 72.
466. Crais, *Making*, p. 173
467. Crais, *Making*, p. 121. Also *ibid*, pp. 126-127
468. Crais, *Making*, pp. 136, 138
469. Crais, *Making*, p. 141
470. J.M. Bowker, *Speeches, letters and selections from important papers* (Grahamstown: 1864; Cape Town, Struik reprint, 1964), p. 125. See also Crais, *Making*, p. 140; A. Ross, *Philip*, p. 191 on Bowker and Carlyle.
471. By M.J. McGinn quoted in Lester, *Imperial networks*, p. 70
472. Le Cordeur, *Eastern Cape separatism*, pp. 128-129; Ross, *Status*, pp. 65-66
473. Lester, *Imperial networks*, pp. 75-80
474. Keegan, *Colonial South Africa*, pp.108,126-127;Crais and Worden (eds), *Breaking the Chains*. p. 14; Scully in Crais and Worden (eds), *Breaking the Chains*, pp. 17.
475. Crais, *Making*, pp. 149-150
476. Crais, *Making*, pp. 164, 166; Also Peires, *House of Phalo*, p. 121 on the increase in Xhosa labour in the colony in this period.
477. For Afrikaner positions on representative government at this time see Du Toit and Giliomee, (eds), *Afrikaner Political Thought*, pp. 249-250, 288-291.
478. Mostert, *Frontiers*, p. 872; Keegan, *Colonial South Africa*, pp. 214, 216-217. Also *ibid* p. 106; Lester, *Imperial networks*, pp. 147-148; Le Cordeur, *Eastern Cape separatism*, pp. 135, 138; Ross, *Status*, p. 166; Bank, "Losing faith", pp. 369-370
479. Keegan, *Colonial South Africa*, pp. 106-107. Also *Ibid*, pp. 99, 357 citing K. Mackenzie and Meltzer.
480. Ross, *Status*, p. 167; Le Cordeur, *Eastern Cape separatism*, pp. 136-137; Keegan, *Colonial South Africa*, pp. 108-109
481. Keegan, *Colonial South Africa*, p. 211. Le Cordeur, *Eastern Cape separatism*, pp. 130-132
482. MF 374 LMS 26/2/A, Glen Anan, 11/6/51, Stretch to Freeman
483. Stapleton, *Maqoma*, p. 126; Peires, *House of Phalo*, p. 129; Mostert, *Frontiers*, p. 861.

CA LG 401. Stretch to Hudson 17/10/1843
484. Le Cordeur, *Eastern Cape separatism*, p. 110; Peires, *House of Phalo*, p. 133; Stapleton, *Maqoma*, pp. 128-129; Mostert, *Frontiers,* pp. 842-844; Switzer, *Power and Resistance*, p. 61; Crais, *Making*, P. 143; A. Ross, *Philip*, pp. 196-197
485. Le Cordeur, *Eastern Cape separatism*, pp. 110, 113, 155
486. Stapleton, *Maqoma*, pp. 140-141. For a different assessment of Sandile at this time see Peires, *House of Phalo*, p. 130
487. Mostert, *Frontiers*, p. 856
488. Stapleton, *Maqoma*, pp. 129-130. See also Crais, *Making*, pp. 103, 239; MF 276 LMS 19/2/B Blinkwater 12/6/1843 Calderwood
489. MF 304 LMS 21/2/B Cape Town 11/3/1845 Philip
490. Le Cordeur and Saunders, *Kitchingman Papers,* p. 194
491. Bank, "Losing Faith", p. 373
492. Mostert, *Frontiers*, p. 835
493. Le Cordeur and Saunders, *Kitchingman Papers*, pp. 246-7: Philipton, 6/4/1844, Read sr to Kitchingman. See also Read sr, 29/4/1844 enclosed in MF 293/4 LMS 20/2/D Calderwood 26/9/1844. Also Ross, *Status*; Hummel, Kayser, pp. 164-177; Mostert, *Frontiers*, p. 836ff; Sales, "Mission stations", p. 119; Lester, *Imperial networks*, pp. 141-2, Ross, "John Philip" in Macmillan and Marks (eds), *Africa and Empire*, pp. 127-8
494. J. Bennie et al, 1/5/1844 enclosed in MF 293/4 LMS 20/2/D Calderwood 26/9/1844
495. Le Cordeur and Saunders, *Kitchingman Papers*, pp. 246-247: Philipton, 6/4/1844, Read sr to Kitchingman; Summary of Read to Kayser, 17/5/1844 enclosed in MF 293/4 LMS 20/2/D Calderwood, 26/9/1844; *ibid* pp. 249-251: Philipton, Read sr to Kitchingman 1/7/1844
496. MF 293/4 LMS 20/2/D Umxelo, Cafferland, 26/9/1844 H. Calderwood (Chairman) Richard Birt (secretary) to LMS directors
497. MF 295 LMS 20/3/A Umxelo, 10/10/1844 Brownlee et al to LMS directors
498. Calderwood to Col Johnstone of the 27th regiment, Blinkwater 27/10/1844 enclosed in MF 304 LMS 21/2/B Cape Town, Philip, 11/3/1845
499. Chalmers et al, 20/9/1844 enclosed in MF 293/4 LMS 20/2/D Calderwood 26/9/1844
500. Le Cordeur and Saunders, *Kitchingman Papers*, pp. 246-8: Philipton, 6/4/1844, Read sr to Kitchingman; Philipton, 13/5/1844, Read to Kitchingman
501. Le Cordeur and Saunders, *Kitchingman Papers*, pp. 249-251: Philipton, 1/7/1844, Read sr to Kitchingman. Philip wrote that missionaries Niven and Campbell, as well as the agent Stretch, supported Read: MF 295 LMS 20/3/A Cape Town 10/10/1844 John Philip. Interestingly enough, this is the same Niven who in 1840 published a racist work, *Impartial analysis of the Kafir character*: see Crais, *Making*, p. 132
502. Le Cordeur and Saunders, *Kitchingman Papers,* pp. 251-252: Philipton, 30/9/1844 Read sr to Kitchingman
503. 'Notes' enclosed in Calderwood and Birt to directors LMS, 26/9/1844 in Hummel, Kayser, p. 172; Ross, *status*, pp. 154-5
504. Sales, *Mission stations*, p. 120
505. Le Cordeur and Saunders, *Kitchingman Papers*, p. 194
506. MF 314 LMS 22/1/D Cape Town, 17/4/1846, Philip to Foreign Secretary

507. MF 295 LMS 20/3/A Cape Town 10/10/1844 John Philip
508. Le Cordeur and Saunders, *Kitchingman Papers,* pp. 252-254: Philipton, 17/2/1845, Read sr to Kitchingman
509. MF 304 LMS 21/2/B Cape Town 11/3/1845 Philip
510. Le Cordeur and Saunders, *Kitchingman Papers* pp. 251-252: Philipton, 30/9/1844 Read sr to Kithingman; Mostert, *Frontiers,* p. 856
511. Mostert, *Frontiers,* p. 832
512. MF 314 LMS 22/1/D Cape Town, 17/4/1846, Philip to Foreign Secretary; Williams, *When Races Meet,* p. 145
513. In an early paper, Saunders criticizes Kaplan for arguing this was what the missionaries believed, but refutes it only in the case of Philip. Saunders, "Read", p. 6 referring to M. Kaplan, "Aspects concerning British administration on the Cape Eastern Frontier with special reference to the origins of the war of 1846" (UCT, Honours essay, 1975). Kaplan is undoubtedly right. However Calderwood, undoubtedly under the influence of Maqoma, did write an extraordinary letter in January 1846, shortly before the outbreak of the war, making it clear that the principal grievance of the Xhosa was the loss of their land: Block Drift, 18/1/1846, Calderwood to Philip quoted in Macmillan, *Bantu, Boer and Briton,* pp. 287-289 and discussed by Mostert, *Frontiers,* pp. 862-863.
514. Keegan, *Colonial South Africa,* pp. 77, 284
515. MF 314 LMS 22/1/D Philip to LMS, 13/5/1846, Macmillan, *Bantu, Boer and Briton,* p. 291
516. Calderwood, *Caffres and Caffre Missions,* pp. 55-56
517. Bank, "Losing Faith", p. 366. See also Crais, *Making,* p. 141; Keegan, *Colonial South Africa,* pp. 282-283; A. Ross, *Philip,* pp. 191-192
518. Thus missionary William Elliott wrote complainingly that slaves and Khoisan on missions "prefer abundant leisure and unrestrained freedom to those habits of industry and those salutary restraints, which must be sustained and submitted to in ordinary social life" (quoted in Bank, "Losing faith", p. 374)
519. Keegan, *Colonial South Africa,* p. 216; Mostert, *Frontiers,* pp. 871-873, 907, 955-956; Lester, *Imperial networks,* p. 148; A. Ross, *Philip,* pp. 136, 178, 198; Macmillan, *Bantu, Boer and Briton,* pp. 290-291
520. Called by Xhosa "the war of the whites" or "the war of the boundary".
521. Le Cordeur, *Eastern Cape separatism,* pp. 216-217; Mostert, *Frontiers,* pp. 857-860
522. Le Cordeur, *Eastern Cape separatism,* p. 145; Keegan, *Colonial South Africa,* p. 215
523. Peires, *House of Phalo,* pp. 133-134; Stapleton, *Maqoma,* pp. 131-132
524. Stapleton, *Maqoma,* p. 141
525. Crais, *Making,* p. 143
526. Le Cordeur, *Eastern Cape separatism,* p. 152; Crais, *Making,* p. 143
527. Keegan, *Colonial South Africa,* p. 215
528. Mostert, *Frontiers,* pp. 868-871; Stapleton, *Maqoma,* pp. 133-134. For the Dange tribe see footnote 120.
529. MF 312 LMS 22/1/C Fort Beaufort, 2/3/1846, Calderwood makes clear the missionaries were ordered out: compare with Mostert, *Frontiers,* p. 869; Stapleton, *Maqoma,* p. 133; Macmillan, *Bantu, Boer and Briton,* p. 290

530. Mostert, *Frontiers*, pp. 876-877; Stapleton, *Maqoma*, p. 134; Peires, *House of Phalo*, pp. 153, 156-157
531. Mostert, *Frontiers*, pp. 875-878, 881ff, 900
532. MF 314 LMS 22/1/D Fort Beaufort, 5/5/46 Calderwood; Mostert, *Frontiers*, p. 877
533. Stapleton, *Maqoma*, p.134; Switzer, *Power and Resistance*, pp. 61-62. See Peires, *House of Phalo*, pp. 148, 150 for why the Gqunukhwebe joined the war and for their tactics.
534. Mostert, *Frontiers*, pp. 873-874
535. Peires, *House of Phalo*, p. 117
536. Moyer in Derricourt and Saunders (eds), *Beyond the Frontier*, pp. 114-115; Peires, *House of Phalo*, p. 150. The Mpondo also tried to join the colonial side: *ibid*, p. 117
537. James Read Jr, Kat River, 27/3/1851 in Stockenstrom, *Light and Shade*, pp. 72-74
538. Stockenstrom, *Light and Shade*, p. 16
539. MF 325 LMS 23/2/B Hankey 4/8/1847 Philip
540. Le Cordeur and Saunders, *Kitchingman Papers*, p. 259
541. MF 322/3 LMS 23/1/C Eilands River Post, Kat River, 23/3/47, Read
542. Le Cordeur and Saunders (eds), *Kitchingman Papers*, pp. 262-267: Elands Post, 30/12/1846, James Read sr to Kitchingman; Eland's Post, 23/1/1847 James Read sr to Kitchingman.
543. Le Cordeur and Saunders (eds), *Kitchingman Papers*, pp.266-267: Eland's Post, 23/1/1847 James Read sr to Kitchingman. Read's critique of Fairbairn was however purely on the basis that the colony did not have the necessary forces. See also Read to Fairbairn, 4/2/1847 [Philip transcripts, UCT]; MF 322/3 LMS 23/1/C Eilands River Post, Kat River, 23/3/47, Read
544. Peires, *House of Phalo*, p. 150; Mostert, *Frontiers*, pp. 884-886
545. Mostert, *Frontiers*, pp.887-888; Le Cordeur, Eastern Cape separatism, p. 154. Stockenstrom's appointment was also supported by Calderwood and Read: MF 314 LMS 22/1/D Fort Beaufort, 5/5/46 Calderwood; MF 315 LMS 22/1/A Eilands River, post Kat River, 31/8/46 Read. Keegan, *Colonial South Africa*, p. 216 is wrong that the British settlers disliked the appointment of Stockenstrom
546. Mostert, *Frontiers*, p. 890; Stapleton, *Maqoma*, pp. 135-136
547. Stapleton, *Maqoma*, p. 135; Peires, *House of Phalo*, p. 153
548. MF 315 LMS 22/1/A Eilands River, post Kat River, 31/8/46 Read
549. MF 315 LMS 22/1/A Eilands River, post Kat River, 31/8/46 Read
550. Mostert, *Frontiers*, pp. 899-900
551. Crais, *Making*, p. 146
552. Mostert, *Frontiers*, pp. 901-902
553. Peires, *House of Phalo*, pp. 117, 150-151; Mostert, *Frontiers*, 902-903; Keegan, *Colonial South Africa*, p. 216
554. Stapleton, *Maqoma*, pp. 134-135
555. Peires, *House of Phalo*, p. 151
556. Peires, *House of Phalo*, pp, 151-152; Mostert, *Frontiers*, pp. 896, 904-905; Le Cordeur and Saunders, *Kitchingman Papers*, pp. 260-262; Stapleton, *Maqoma*, pp. 136-137
557. MF 315 LMS 22/2/A Fort Beaufort, 13/8/1846, Calderwood. For slightly different versions of his understanding of the causes of the war, compare MF 314 LMS 22/1/D Fort Beaufort, 5/5/46 Calderwood with MF 315 LMS 22/2/A Fort Beaufort, 13/8/1846, Calderwood

558. MF 316 LMS 22/1/B Grahamstown, 26/9/46 Calderwood. At about the same time Read was speculating on forms of settlement: "in fact no one knows what terms Govt demands, nor how the Caffres are to be managed in future, some are for annihilation, some to drive them all over the Kei river, and make that river the boundary, others to add Caffraria to the colony and thus the Caffers governed by our laws – the first is out of the question – to accomplish the second will be a mark of time, and then by having… Gaikas and Hintsa's people united they would be more formidable on the new boundary – and require a very strong force to protect – and to add them to the Colony and govern them by or laws and institutions would be an expence [sic] the Colony would not bear, and it is to be questioned whether England will do it. I believe Sir Andries Stockenstrom would hazard and other [sic] treaty if he was at the head of Government and could see it carried out himself" MF 315 LMS 22/1/A Eilands River, post Kat River, 31/8/46 Read

559. MF 316 LMS 22/1/B Grahamstown, 8/10/1846 Calderwood. He added "Maqoma was much more subdued than the others and seems much inclined to break off from the Caffers and join the government but how far he would like to submit is yet uncertain. He said to me privately 'I am willing to put myself in the hands of the government but let me lie at my old place.' "

560. Quotes by Peires, *House of Phalo*, p. 152

561. Stapleton, *Maqoma*, pp. 136-137; Le Cordeur, *Eastern Cape separatism*, pp. 260-262; Mostert, *Frontiers*, p. 913; MF 318 LMS 22/2/D Kingwilliamstown, 23/12/46, Calderwood

562. MF 316 LMS 22/1/B Read, Elands Post, 6/10/1846

563. Mostert, *Frontiers*, pp. 905-906

564. MF 318 LMS 22/2/D Kingwilliamstown, 23/12/46, Calderwood. Mostert, *Frontiers*, p. 907 gives a slightly different perception of the settlement "The borders of the Cape Colony would continue to be the Fish River, extending along the Kat river, and the old Ceded Territory would be occupied by Khoikhoi and Mfengu to form a military barrier against the Xhosa. The country between the Keiskamma and Kei was to be firmly policed."

565. Mostert, *Frontiers*, p. 907

566. Mostert, *Frontiers*, p. 907 quoting LMS Philip letters, Box 22, Philip to one of Maitland's sons, 5/11/1846

567. Keegan, *Colonial South Africa*, pp. 209-210; Crais, *Making*, pp. 144, 149, 192

568. Shaw to Philip, 3/12/1847 quoted in MF 622 LMS Philip 2/6/B Hankey, 22/12/1847, Philip; A. Ross, *Philip*, p. 206. The letter was written in response to the attack on the Kat River settlement by Governor Pottinger (see below).

569. Keegan, *Colonial South Africa*, p. 217

570. Mostert, *Frontiers*, p. 909

571. Mostert, *Frontiers*, p. 909

572. Lester, *Imperial networks*, pp. 148-149

573. Keegan, *Colonial South Africa*, p. 27; Le Cordeur, *Eastern Cape separatism*, p. 168; Mostert, *Frontiers*, p. 912; A. Ross, *Philip*, p. 211. On the 'protectorate' see Mostert, *Frontiers*, pp. 910-911

574. Mostert, *Frontiers*, p. 924

575. Keegan, *Colonial South Africa*, p. 215
576. Le Cordeur, *Eastern Cape separatism*, p. 186; *Documents relative to the question of a separate government for the Eastern District of the Cape Colony* (Grahamstown, 1847), p. 97. Until the 1870s this book, *Documents*, was the settlers official bible of separatism: Le Cordeur, *Eastern Cape separatism*, p. 197.
577. Le Cordeur, *Eastern Cape separatism*, p.186: *Documents*, p. 150; Keegan, *Colonial South Africa*, p. 218
578. Le Cordeur, *Eastern Cape separatism*, p. 281 explains separatism as a combination of a drive for expansion(Kirk) and frontier fears (Cory)
579. Le Cordeur, *Eastern Cape separatism*, pp. 171, 178, 179-180, 185, 191, 209.
580. Peires, *House of Phalo*, p. 155
581. Le Cordeur, *Eastern Cape separatism*, p. 168 Proclamation of 3 March 1847 enclosed in Pottinger to Grey 14/4/1847 PP 1847-8, xliii [912] pp. 37-42. See also, for Godlonton's "very strong" influence on government, Read to Fairbairn, 10/6/1847 BC 312 Mears collection, UCT.
582. MF 324 LMS 23/2/A Hankey, 21/7/1847 Philip to Tidman; MF 325 LMS 23/2/B Hankey 4/8/1847Philip
583. Philip, however, seemed unaware that Pottinger did not wish to abolish the chiefs: MF 324 LMS 23/2/A Hankey, 21/7/1847 Philip to Tidman
584. Peires, *House of Phalo*, p. 155
585. Keegan, *Colonial South Africa*, pp. 217-218; Mostert, *Frontiers*, pp. 915-921, 956; Lester, *Imperial networks*, p. 149
586. Mostert, *Frontiers*, 917-918, 922-925; Keegan, *Colonial South Africa,* p. 218
587. Mostert, *Frontiers*, pp. 925-926
588. Mostert, *Frontiers*, pp. 926-928; Stapleton, *Maqoma*, pp. 138-139, 144-145
589. Mostert, *Frontiers*, p. 919
590. A. Ross, *Philip*, pp. 199-200; James Read Jr, 27/3/1851 in Stockenstrom*, Light and Shade,* pp. 74-75
591. Keegan, *Colonial South Africa*, p. 237; Le Cordeur, *Eastern Cape separatism*, p. 188; Crais, *Making*, p. 165; Mostert, *Frontiers*, pp. 919-920; A.Ross, *Philip*, pp. 201-202
592. Le Cordeur and Saunders (eds), *Kitchingman Papers*, p. 271: Biddulph's report was in the *Grahamstown Journal,* 6/11/1847; Kirk, "Progress and decline", pp. 419-420
593. Mostert, *Frontiers*, p. 919. Also Crais, *Making*, p. 164
594. MF 331 LMS 23/3/C Philipton, 21/1/1848 Read sr to Tidman. See also MF 329 LMS 23/3/B Philipton, 1/12/1847 Read
595. Le Cordeur and Saunders (eds), *Kitchingman Papers*, p. 271
596. A. Ross, *Philip*, pp. 203-205; Le Cordeur and Saunders (eds), *Kitchingman Papers*, pp. 244-245; Mostert, *Frontiers*, p. 987. However, as Le Cordeur and Saunders point out. Read made the same proposal privately to his Betheksdorp colleague and friend James Kitchingman in 1844: *Ibid*, pp. 244-245: Philipton, 25/3/1844 Read sr to Kitchingman; Bank, "Losing Faith", p. 605.
597. A. Ross, *Philip*, pp. 205-6
598. Peires, p. 165. See also Keegan, *Colonial South Africa*, p. 219
599. Mostert*, Frontiers*, pp. 910, 928-929;
600. Le Cordeur, *Eastern Cape separatis*m, p. 198, 205; Mostert, *Frontiers,* pp. 930ff;

Keegan, *Colonial South Africa*, p. 219
601. *Grahamstown Journal*, 17/12/1847 quoted by Le Cordeur, *Eastern Cape separatism*, p. 216
602. Stapleton, *Maqoma*, p. 145; Peires, *The Dead will arise*, pp. 4-6
603. Keegan, *Colonial South Africa*, p. 220
604. Mostert, *Frontiers*, p. 932; Peires, *The Dead will arise*, p. 6
605. Stapleton, *Maqoma*, p. 147; Mostert, *Frontiers*, pp 933-934; Peiries, *The Dead will arise*, pp. 6-7 Not long after, Smith was persuaded by land speculators to extend the boundary of the district of Albert, incorporating part of Thembuland in the colony: Le Cordeur, Eastern *Cape separatism,*, pp. 208, 217; Keegan, *Colonial South Africa*, pp. 221-222
606. Mostert, *Frontiers*, p. 934
607. Mostert, *Frontiers*, pp. 936-937; Keegan, *Colonial South Africa*, p. 220; Peires, *House of Phalo*, p. 165; Crais, *Making*, p. 145
608. MF 331 LMS 23/3/C Philipton, 21/1/1848 Read sr to Tidman
609. Switzer, *Power and Resistance*, p. 62-63
610. Crais, *Making*, pp. 144, 174; Keegan, *Colonial South Africa*, 221-222
611. Moyer, "History of the Mfengu", p. 217; Moyer in Derricourt and Saunders (eds), *Beyond the Frontier*, p. 116
612. Stapleton, *Maqoma*, p. 147
613. Stapleton, *Maqoma*, p. 147; Mostert, *Frontiers*, pp. 910-911, 952; Peires, *House of Phalo*, p. 167. See Kirk, "Self-government", pp. 169, 288
614. Mostert, *Frontiers*, pp. 943, 980-983; Stapleton, *Maqoma*, p. 148
615. Lewis, "Census", p. 5; Stapleton, *Maqoma*, p. 148; Keegan, *Colonial South Africa*, p. 221; Mostert, *Frontiers*, pp. 939, 979-980
616. Mostert, *Frontiers*, pp. 949-950
617. Opland, *Xhosa poets and Xhosa poetry*, pp. 236-237
618. Mostert, *Frontiers*, pp. 956-964
619. Mostert, *Frontiers*, pp. 950-951
620. See Lewis, "Class and gender", p.4; Peires, *House of Phalo*, pp. 160, 167; Stapleton, *Maqoma*, p. 148
621. Mostert, *Frontiers*, pp. 948, 1009-1110. For Calderwood in this period see also MF 566 LMS Freeman 1/3/D Mission House, 21/5/49 Philip to Freeman; MF 570 LMS Freeman 1/5/A Philipton, 3/8/49 Read sr; MF 570 LMS Freeman 1/5/A Philipton, 6/8/49, Read sr; MF 574 LMS Freeman 1/6/B Philpton, 18/10/1849 Read sr; MF 575 LMS Freeman 1/6/B Alice, 24/10/1849, Calderwood [to Freeman]; MF 354 LMS 25/2/A Philipton, 29/1/50, Read sr
622. Bradford, "Through Gendered Eyes", p. 8
623. Peires, *House of Phalo* p. 167; Mostert, *Frontiers,* pp. 948-949; Switzer, *Power and Resistance*, p. 63. In 1849 Calderwood instituted an agricultural system for the Xhosa which was the prelude to the Glen Grey system of the 1890s; see *Brownlee J.Ross: his ancestry and some writings*, (Lovedale, Lovedale Press, 1948), pp. 28-29. See also MF 365 LMS 25/4/C Alice, 2/7/1850 H. Calderwood to Freeman, a self-righteous letter defending his conservative 'native policy'.
624. Peires, *House of Phalo*, p. 168; Crais, *Making*, pp. 142, 174

625. Keegan, *Colonial South Africa*, pp. 252-255; A. Ross, Philip, pp. 179-184
626. Keegan, *Colonial South Africa*, p. 255
627. Keegan, *Colonial South Africa*, pp. 219, 222, 256
628. Keegan, *Colonial South Africa*, pp. 206, 256-257
629. Significantly the money raised for it was in fact diverted to the Anti-Convict Association, an anti-government vehicle which was the forerunner of a move for settler self-government (see below); Mostert, *Frontiers*, pp. 967, 977; Keegan, *Colonial South Africa*, p.223
630. Keegan, *Colonial South Africa*, pp. 257-259, 350
631. Keegan, *Colonial South Africa*, 259-271, 353; Crais, *Making*, pp. 143-144
632. Crais, *Making*, p. 142; Keegan, *Colonial South Africa*, pp. 221, 237-238
633. Stockenstrom, *Light and Shade*, p. 19
634. Crais, *Making,* pp. 165-169, 180; A. Ross, *Philip*, p. 208; Kirk, "Progress and decline", pp. 420-422
635. Keegan, *Colonial South Africa*, p. 238; Crais, *Making*, p. 178; Mostert, *Frontiers*, pp. 989-992
636. A. Ross, *Philip*, p. 207
637. Keegan, *Colonial South Africa*, p. 244; Ross, *Status*, p. 167; Mostert, *Frontiers*, p. 973
638. Mostert, *Frontiers*, p. 973; Le Cordeur, *Eastern Cape separatism*, pp. 212-3; Keegan, *Colonial South Africa*, pp. 225-226
639. A. Ross, *Philip*, p. 211
640. Keegan, Colonial South Africa, pp. 214-215, 223-224, 227-229; Mostert, Frontiers, pp. 971-975
641. Le Cordeur, *Eastern Cape separatism*, p. 214; Keegan, *Colonial South Africa*, pp. 222-224. 235-236, 245, 282, 348, 350; Mostert, *Frontiers*, pp. 947, 975-976, 988-999 Legassick, "The state, racism and the rise of capitalism", p. 357. On Stockenstrom's views at this time see Du Toit and Giliomee, *Afrikaner Political Thought*, pp. 140, 180-181, on Afrikaner thinking on representative government see *ibid,* pp. 250-251, 291-299, and on frontier policy see *ibid,* pp. 183-188; Du Toit "The Cape Afrikaner's failed liberal moment" in J. Butler, R. Elphick, and D. Welsh (eds), *Democratic Liberalism in South Africa,* (Cape Town: David Philip, 1987) pp. 35-63. Also Stockenstrom, *Light and Shade,* p. 1
642. Keegan, *Colonial South Africa*, p. 229; Le Cordeur, *Eastern Cape separatism*, pp. 219, 220, 223, 282
643. Keegan, *Colonial South Africa,* pp. 230-231; Le Cordeur, *Eastern Cape separatism,* p. 225; A. Ross, *Philip,* pp. 211-212; Ross, *Status,* p. 170
644. Keegan, *Colonial South Africa*, pp. 224, 232; Le Cordeur, *Eastern Cape separatism*, p. 220
645. Ross, *Status*, p. 170; Le Cordeur, *Eastern Cape separatism*, p. 228
646. Mostert, *Frontiers*, pp. 1102-1103. Also, for Southey, *ibid,* p. 1101
647. Ross, *Status*, p. 169
648. Le Cordeur, *Eastern Cape separatism*, pp. 268-269
649. Trapido, "Origins", p. 53; Bank, "Losing Faith", p. 375;
650. Du Toit and Giliomee, *Afrikaner Political Thought*, p. 251

651. Keegan, *Colonial South Africa,* p. 282; Crais, *Making,* pp. 192-194 Bank, "Losing Faith ", pp. 375-378
652. Ross, Status, pp. 168,170; Crais, *Making,* p. 185; Williams, *When Races Meet,* p. 132
653. Keegan, *Colonial South Africa,* p. 232; Le Cordeur, *Eastern Cape separatism,* p. 235
654. Le Cordeur, *Eastern Cape separatism,* p. 245; Mostert, *Frontiers,* pp. 1100-1102
655. Le Cordeur, *Eastern Cape separatism,* p. 217
656. A. Ross, *Philip,* p. 208; Switzer, *Power and Resistance,* pp. 63-64; Mostert, *Frontiers,* pp 1014-1023; Peires, *The dead will arise,* pp. 8-12; Crais, *Making,* pp. 175-177
657. Crais, *Making,* pp. 144-145; Stapleton, *Maqoma,* pp. 149, 172-174. See also Mostert, *Frontiers,* p. 952, 1073-1075 on the position of the chiefs and the consequences for administration of law at this point
658. Bradford, "Through Gendered Eyes", p. 7
659. Stapleton, *Maqoma,* p. 150
660. Bradford, "Through Gendered Eyes", p. 7. Also Peires, *The Dead will arise,* pp. 1-4; Crais, *Making,* pp. 175-176
661. Crais, *Making,* pp. 176-177
662. Mostert, *Frontiers,* pp. 1005, 1046
663. Crais, *Making,* p. 176
664. Stapleton, Maqoma, pp. 150-151
665. Mostert, *Frontiers,* pp. 1015-1016; Stapleton, *Maqoma,* p. 153; Peires, *The Dead will arise,* pp. 28-30
666. MF 373 LMS 26/1/C, Philipton, Read to Freeman 13 (15?)/4/1851
667. Mostert, *Frontiers,* pp. 1040
668. MF 373 LMS 26/1/C, Philipton, Read to Freeman 13 (15?)/4/1851
669. Peires, *The Dead will arise,* pp. 8-11; Keegan, *Colonial South Africa,* p. 233; Stapleton, *Maqoma,* pp. 151-3; Mostert, *Frontiers,* pp. 1014-1040, 1060-1064, 1069; Crais, *Making,* p. 178
670. Crais, *Making,* p. 176
671. Mostert, *Frontiers,* p. 1031
672. Mostert, *Frontiers,* p. 1010
673. Mostert, *Frontiers,* p. 1051
674. Mostert, *Frontiers,* pp. 1085-1086
675. Mostert, *Frontiers,* p. 1087
676. Mostert, *Frontiers,* p. 1076
677. Crais, *Making,* p. 181. See also Peires, pp. 129-130. See also R. Ross, "Hermanus Matroos aka Ngxukumeshe: a life on the border" (Working paper no 12, The Eastern Cape: historical legacies and new challenges. Fort Hare Institute of Social and Economic Research, 27-30 August 2003).
678. MF 373 LMS 26/1/C, Philipton, Read to Freeman 13 (15?)/4/1851
679. Quoted Mostert, *Frontiers,* p. 1081
680. Mostert, *Frontiers,* p. 1082
681. Stapleton, *Maqoma,* p. 153. Also Crais, *Making,* pp. 177-180, 183-184; Sales, pp. 135-155; Williams, *When Races Meet,* pp. 154-195; Keegan, *Colonial South Africa,* pp. 238-239
682. MF 374 LMS 26/2/B Alice, 9/7/1851, Read to Freeman

683. Mostert, *Frontiers*, p. 1083
684. MF 373 LMS 26/1/C, Philipton, Read to Freeman 13 (15?)/4/1851
685. Quoted by Mostert, *Frontiers*, p. 1081
686. Keegan, *Colonial South Africa*, p. 239; Crais, *Making*, pp. 179, 182; Ross, *Status*, pp. 156-157 who refers to a memorandum by Montague in BPP 1636 of 1852-1853; Stockenstrom, *Light and Shade*
687. Elbourne, "To colonize", p. 318. Also Keegan, *Colonial South Africa*, pp. 348-349
688. MF 374 LMS 26/2/B Alice, 9/7/1851, Read to Freeman
689. Crais, *Making*, pp. 185-186
690. Kirk, "Progress and Decline", p. 426
691. Mostert, *Frontiers*, p. 1071
692. Mostert, *Frontiers*, pp. 1000, 1005-1006, 1046; Keegan, *Colonial South Africa*, p. 234
693. MF 374 LMS 26/2/B Alice, 9/7/1851, Read to Freeman; Mostert, *Frontiers*, p. 1100
694. Calderwood to Godlonton, 8/1/1851 A43 Godlonton Papers, Wits quoted in Le Cordeur, *Eastern Cape separatism*, p. 245
695. Southey to Godlonton, 17/5/1851 A43 Godlonton Papers quoted in Le Cordeur, *Eastern Cape separatism*, p. 270; Keegan, *Colonial South Africa*, p. 234.
696. Moyer in Derricourt and Saunders (eds), *Beyond the frontier*, pp. 116-117; Mostert, *Frontiers*, p. 1046
697. MF 374 LMS 26/2/B Alice, 9/7/1851, Read to Freeman
698. Stapleton, *Maqoma*, pp. 151-152; Mostert, *Frontiers*, pp. 980, 1004
699. Mostert, *Frontiers*, pp. 1071-1072; Peires, *The Dead will arise*, p. 16
700. Stapleton, *Maqoma*, p. 157
701. Mostert, *Frontiers*, p. 1098
702. Mostert, *Frontiers*, pp. 1077-1079, 1085, 1091-1092, 1133
703. Stapleton, *Maqoma*, p. 154; Mostert, *Frontiers*, pp. 1079-1080; Crais, *Making*, p. 182. Ross, "Hermanus", p. 21 states that James Read sr sent a letter to his old adversary Henry Calderwood informing him of the planned attack on Fort Beaufort, which forewarned the British forces: this betrayal, sources told the historian Elizabeth Elbourne, was that the Xhosa today most remember about Read.
704. Mostert, *Frontiers*, pp. 1090-1091. Also Moyer in Derricourt and Saunders (eds), *Beyond the Frontier*, pp. 117-118
705. Mostert, *Frontiers*, pp. 1092-1093
706. See Peires, *The Dead will arise*, p. 12; Bradford, "Through Gendered Eyes", p. 5 compared with Mostert, *Frontiers*, pp. 1092-1096
707. Mostert, *Frontiers*, pp. 1083, 1094-1095. On Uithaalder see Crais, *Making*, pp. 182-183
708. Mostert, *Frontiers*, pp. 1096-1098
709. Peires, *The Dead will arise*, pp. 15-16; Stapleton, *Maqoma*, p. 155
710. MF 374 LMS 26/2/B Alice, 9/7/1851, Read to Freeman. Also MF 373 LMS 26/1/D Philipton 12/5/51, Read sr; MF 374 LMS 26/2/A, Glen Anan, 11/6/51, Stretch to Freeman; Crais, *Making*, p. 191; Mostert, *Frontiers*, p. 1093
711. Mostert, *Frontiers*, p. 1105; Peires, *The Dead will arise*, p. 19; Keegan, *Colonial South Africa*, pp. 238-239, 241; Ross, *Status*, pp. 162-165; Crais, *Making*, p. 177; Stapleton, *Maqoma*, p. 155; E. Bradlow, " 'The Great Fear' at the Cape of Good Hope, 1851-1852", *International Journal of African Historical Studies*, 22, 2, 1989;

712. Mostert, *Frontiers*, p. 1107
713. Mostert, *Frontiers*, pp. 1077, 1109; Peires, *The Dead will arise*, p. 17; Switzer, *Power and Resistance*, p. 64
714. Mostert, *Frontiers*, pp. 1109-1110
715. MF 374 LMS 26/2/B Alice, 9/7/1851, Read to Freeman
716. Quoted by Crais, *Making*, p. 182
717. Crais, *Making*, p. 183; MF 374 LMS 26/2/B Alice, 9/7/1851, Read to Freeman
718. Peires, *The Dead will arise*, p. 15. Also Stapleton, *Maqoma*, pp. 166-167, 219-221
719. Peires, *The Dead will arise*, pp. 12-13, 15, 19; Mostert, *Frontiers*, pp. 1114-1127, 1130, 1141-1143; Stapleton, *Maqoma*, pp. 157-160; Switzer, *Power and Resistance*, p. 64. Read, however, writes of an incursion by Somerset with 12-1400 men as early as July: MF 374 LMS 26/2/B Alice, 9/7/1851, Read to Freeman
720. Quoted by Stapleton, *Maqoma*, p. 160; Mostert, *Frontiers*, p. 1127
721. Stapleton, *Maqoma*, p. 160
722. Mostert, *Frontiers*, pp 1127-1128; Peires, *The Dead will arise*, p. 17; Stapleton, *Maqoma*, p. 161
723. Keegan, *Colonial South Africa*, pp. 269-270; Mostert, *Frontiers*, pp. 1131-1132
724. Keegan, *Colonial South Africa*, pp. 271-275
725. Mostert, *Frontiers*, 1132-1133; Keegan, *Colonial South Africa*, p. 244
726. Le Cordeur, *Eastern Cape separatism*, pp. 261, 263, 265-267; Peires, *The Dead will arise*, p. 15; Mostert, *Frontiers*, pp. 1134-1137. Peires mentions the death of Colonel Fordyce in connection with Smith's recall.
727. Mostert, *Frontiers*, pp. 1129-1131; Peires, *The Dead will arise*, p. 22
728. Mostert, *Frontiers*, pp 1128-1130; Stapleton, *Maqoma*, p. 161. See Peires, *The Dead will arise*, pp. 19-22. who attributes the strategy to Eyre not Grey.
729. Mostert, *Frontiers*, pp 1111-1112, 1141-1143; Stapleton, *Maqoma*, p. 162 (who mentions also Smith's final campaign in the Amatolas in late March).
730. Mostert, *Frontiers*, pp. 1137-1141, 1143-1145. Compare, however, Peires, *The Dead will arise*, p. 15
731. Mostert, *Frontiers*, p. 1095, 1099; 1102-1103
732. MF 374 LMS 26/2/B Alice, 9/7/1851, Read to Freeman
733. Mostert, *Frontiers*, pp. 1095, 1103-1105
734. Mostert, *Frontiers*, pp. 1100-1102
735. Keegan, *Colonial South Africa*, p. 235; Le Cordeur, *Eastern Cape separatism*, p. 246; Mostert, *Frontiers*, pp.1100-1102, 1159
736. Keegan, *Colonial South Africa*, pp. 244, 278, 285-286
737. Le Cordeur, *Eastern Cape separatism*, p. 263
738. Ross, *Status*, pp. 67, 171-172; Kirk, "Self-government", pp. 447-486; Keegan, *Colonial South Africa*, p. 242
739. Kirk, "Progress and decline", p. 427
740. Crais, *Making*, p. 180
741. Mostert, *Frontiers*, pp. 1095, 1104, 1145-1148; Keegan, *Colonial South Africa*, pp. 239-240; Anon, *The trial of Andries Botha, field cornet of the Upper Blinkwater in the Kat River settlement, for High Treason in the Supreme Court of the Colony of the Cape of Good Hope* (Cape Town,1852)

742. Mostert, *Frontiers*, pp. 1149-1154; Peires, *The Dead will arise*, pp. 26-27; Stapleton, *Maqoma*, pp. 162-165
743. Mostert, *Frontiers*, p. 1154; Keegan, *Colonial South Africa*, pp. 275-276
744. Peires, *The Dead will arise*, pp. 27-28; Mostert, *Frontiers*, pp. 1154-1155; Keegan *Colonial South Africa*, p. 243. Also Crais, *Making* pp. 186-187; Stapleton, *Maqoma*, pp. 165-167
745. Crais, *Making*, p. 187
746. Mostert, *Frontiers*, p. 1158; Switzer, *Power and Resistance*, p. 64
747. Mostert, *Frontiers*, p. 1113; Crais, *Making*, p. 178. For a somewhat different view see Peires, *The Dead will arise*, pp. 17-18
748. Peires, *The Dead will arise*, pp. 23-25; Mostert, *Frontiers*, pp. 1096, 1117, 1142
749. Mostert, *Frontiers*, pp. 1098, 1108-1109
750. Mostert, *Frontiers*, p. 1077
751. Crais, *Making*, pp. 178, 181
752. Crais, *Making*, p. 184
753. Crais, *Making*, p. 186
754. Peires, *The Dead will arise*, p. 135. See also Elbourne, "A question of identity", p. 18; Mostert, *Frontiers*, p. 1120
755. Crais, *Making*, p. 175. Also *ibid*, p. 184-185
756. Keegan, *Colonial South Africa*, p. 239
757. Mostert, *Frontiers*, p. 1085
758. Mostert, *Frontiers*, p. 1088
759. Crais, *Making*, pp. 174, 186-188
760. Peires, *The Dead will arise*, p. 28; Mostert, *Frontiers*, p. 1155; Le Cordeur, *Eastern Cape separatism*, p. 270; Crais, *Making*, p. 197; Stapleton, *Maqoma*, pp. 174-176
761. Govan, *Memorials of Laing*, book, pp. 129, 137-138
762. Peires, *The Dead will arise*, p. 28; Mostert, *Frontiers*, p. 1155; Le Cordeur, *Eastern Cape separatism*, p. 270
763. Le Cordeur, *Eastern Cape separatism* p. 217; Mostert, *Frontiers*, pp. 1156-1157; Crais, *Making*, p. 197. A Kaffrarian Charter was sent in March 1854: GH 1/49 Newcastle to Cathcart 14/3/1854.
764. Moyer, "History of the Mfengu", pp. 223-226
765. Moyer in Derricourt and Saunders (eds), *Beyond the frontier*, p. 120
766. Le Cordeur, *Eastern Cape separatism*, pp. 249-262; Mostert, *Frontiers*, pp. 1159-1160
767. Keegan, *Colonial South Africa*, p. 243; Le Cordeur, *Eastern Cape separatism*, pp. 265-267. Compare with Ross, Status, pp. 171-172 who gives more of the initiative to Cathcart and Darling.
768. Le Cordeur, *Eastern Cape separatism*, p. 267
769. Keegan, *Colonial South Africa*, pp. 245, 247
770. A. Ross, *Philip*, p. 228. See also Fairbairn's tribute to Philip, in November 1850: Mostert, *Frontiers*, pp. 1104-1105
771. Ross, *Status*, p. 170
772. Keegan, *Colonial South Africa*, pp. 245, 282, 287
773. Keegan, *Colonial South Africa*, pp. 246-247

774. Ross, *Status*, pp. 50-51. See also du Toit and Giliomee, *Afrikaner Political Thought*, pp. 250-251
775. Crais, *Making*, pp. 192-193
776. Quoted by Ross, *Status*, p. 171
777. Bank, "Losing faith", pp. 371-372
778. Keegan, *Colonial South Africa*, pp. 245, 289, 357; Legassick, "The state, racism and the rise of capitalism", p. 358
779. Keegan, *Colonial South Africa*, pp. 276-278, 286-287
780. For these, see Giliomee in *Shaping*, pp. 434-435; 439-440; Newton-King, *Masters and Servants*, p. 144; Peires, *House of Phalo*, pp. 53-58. In Graaff-Reniet the main attention from the 1770s was being paid to wars against the San: Newton-King, *Masters and Servants*, p. 73ff
781. C. Crais, "Race, the State", pp. 3, 7-8
782. Keegan, *Colonial South Africa*, p. 292
783. Mostert, *Frontiers*, p. 984
784. Maclennan, *Proper degree*, p. 224
785. See Keegan, *Colonial South Africa*, p. 284
786. Keegan, *Colonial South Africa*, pp. 284-285
787. Crais, *Making*, p. 87
788. Keegan, *Colonial South Africa*, p. 231
789. Mostert, *Frontiers*, p. 1096. See also Peires, *House of Phalo*, p. 113 for Smith's use of the term in August 1835
790. Quoted by Keegan, *Colonial South Africa*, p. 50
791. Mostert, *Frontiers*, p. 1136
792. Mostert, *Frontiers*, p. 847; J. L. McCracken, *New light at the Cape of Good Hope: William Porter the father of Cape liberalism*, Belfast: Ulster Historical Association, 1993, p. 108-109; Bank, "Losing Faith", pp. 370-371
793. Du Toit and Giliomee (eds) *Afrikaner Political Thought*, pp. 140, 181-182
794. Quoted by Ross, "John Philip" in Macmillan and Marks (eds), *Africa and Empire*, p. 138
795. De Kiewiet, *A history of South Africa: social and economic* (Oxford University Press, 1941), pp. 78-87
796. Stapleton, *Maqoma*, p. 221. See Martin Legassick, "Firearms, Horses, and Samorian Army Organisation 1870-1898", *Journal of African History,* VII, 1, (1966), pp. 95-115. Also Peires, *House of Phalo*, p. 160
797. See Crais, *Making*, p. 145
798. Keegan p. 215. Crais, *Making, passim* argues there was an equivalent crisis in the early 1830s. Mostert identifies the peak of the later crisis in 1851: *Frontiers,* p. 1099
799. Keegan, *Colonial South Africa*, pp. 287, 290; Crais, *Making*, p. 192
800. Legassick, "The state, racism and the rise of capitalism", p. 338. See Ross, *Status*, p. 175
801. Crais, *Making*, pp. 193-194
802. Keegan, *Colonial South Africa*, p. 247
803. Keegan, *Colonial South Africa,* pp. 289-290; Bundy, *The Rise and Fall of the South African Peasantry* (London: Heinemann, 1979); Bradford, "The rise of the male

peasantry"; Switzer, *Power and Resistance*, pp. 80-96
804. S. Trapido, " 'The Friends of the Natives': Merchants, peasants and the political and ideological structure of liberalism at the Cape, 1854-1910", in S. Marks and A. Atmore, (eds), *Economy and Society in Pre-Industrial South Africa* (London: Longmans , 1980), pp. 247-274
805. Mostert, *Frontiers*, p. 1089

Glossary

Xhosa Chiefs
Bhotomane of the Dange
Chunga of the Gqunukhwebe
Hintsa of the Gcaleka
Kama of the Gqunukhwebe
Pato of the Gqunukhwebe
Maqoma of the Ngqika
Ngqika of the Rharabe
Ndlambe of the Rharabe
Rharabe of the Rharabe
Sandile of the Ngqika
Sarhili of the Gcaleka
Siyolo of the Ndlambe

Xhosa war-prophets
Nxeli (Makana)
Mlanjeni

British Governors
Earl Alexander of Caledon, May 1807-July 1811
Sir Francis Cradock, September 1811-April 1814
Lord Charles Somerset, April 1814-March 1826
Sir Rufane Donkin (Acting), January 1820-November 1821
Sir Richard Bourke (Acting), March 1826-September 1828
Sir Lowry Cole, September 1828-August 1833
Colonel Thomas Francis Wade (Acting), August 1833- January 1834
Sir Benjamin D'Urban, January 1834-January 1838
Sir George Napier, January 1838-March 1844
Sir Peregrine Maitland, March 1844-January 1847
Sir Henry Pottinger, January 1847-December 1847
Sir Harry Smith, December 1847-March 1852
Sir George Cathcart, March 1852-May 1854
Charles Henry Darling (Acting), May-December 1854

Missionaries
John Ayliff, Wesleyan MS
George Barker, London MS
John Bennie, Glasgow MS
William Boyce, Wesleyan MS
John Brownlee, London MS
Henry Calderwood, Wesleyan MS
William Elliott, London MS
Stephen Kay, Wesleyan MS
Friedrich Kayser, London MS
James Laing, Glasgow MS
Robert Moffat, London MS
John Philip, London MS
James Read, London MS
John Ross, Glasgow MS
Theophilus Shepstone, Wesleyan MS
William Shaw, Wesleyan MS
William Shrewsbury, Wesleyan MS
George Thom, London MS
William Thomson, Glasgow MS
Johannes van der Kemp, London MS
Joseph Williams, London MS
Peter Wright, London MS

Abbreviations
CA	Cape Archives (GH Government House; LG Lieutenant Governor, etc)
DEIC	Dutch East India Company
MF LMS	Microfilm London Missionary Society records,
SANL	South African National Library
RCC	G. McCall Theal (ed) Records of the Cape Colony
RPQA	G. McCall Theal (ed) Records of the Province of Queen Adelaide
GMS	Glasgow Missionary Society
LMS	London Missionary Society
WMS	Wesleyan Missionary Society